ETHICS AND THE PROBLI

INDIANA SERIES IN THE PHILOSOPHY OF RELIGION

Merold Westphal, *editor*

ETHICS AND THE PROBLEM OF EVIL

Edited by James P. Sterba

Indiana University Press

Bloomington and Indianapolis

This book is a publication of

Indiana University Press
Office of Scholarly Publishing
Herman B Wells Library 350
1320 East 10th Street
Bloomington, Indiana 47405 USA

iupress.indiana.edu

© 2017 by Indiana University Press

⊗ The paper used in this publication meets the minimum
requirements of the American National Standard for Information
Sciences—Permanence of Paper for Printed Library Materials,
ANSI Z39.48-1992.

Manufactured in the United States of America

Cataloging information is available from the Library of Congress.

ISBN 978-0-253-02425-1 (cloth)
ISBN 978-0-253-02431-2 (paperback)
ISBN 978-0-253-02438-1 (ebook)

1 2 3 4 5 22 21 20 19 18 17

Contents

Acknowledgments

THIS COLLECTION WOULD not have been possible without the generous support of the John Templeton Foundation and the University of Notre Dame, especially the Institute for Scholarship in the Liberal Arts. I would also like to thank my colleagues and students who contributed in various ways to making this collection possible, in particular, Karl Ameriks, Robert Audi, Rebecca Chan, Ting Cho Lau, Nevin Climenhaga, Richard Cross, Dustin Crummett, Richard DeGeorge, Michael DePaul, Paul Draper, Alfred Freddoso, Gary Gutting, Liz Jackson, Janet Kourany, John Lachs, Samuel Newlands, Caleb Ontiveros, Michael Rea, Margaret Schmitt, David Solomon, Meghan Sullivan, Michael Tooley, Louise Williams, and Peter van Inwagen.

ETHICS AND THE PROBLEM OF EVIL

Introduction

IN RECENT YEARS, discussion of the problem of evil has been advanced by using resources of contemporary metaphysics and epistemology such as Alvin Plantinga's application of modal logic to logical problem of evil and William Rowe and Stephen Wykstra's application of probabilistic epistemology to the evidential problem of evil. The results have been impressive. What is a bit surprising, however, is that philosophers currently working on the problem of evil have yet to avail themselves of relevant resources from ethical theory that could similarly advance the discussion of the problem.[1]

For example, there is no discussion of the doctrine of double effect,[2] or whether the ends justify the means, or how to resolve hypothetical trolley cases that have become the grist for moral philosophers ever since they were introduced by Judith Thompson and Philippa Foot. Even though cognitive psychologists now regularly employ hypothetical trolley cases to determine what parts of the brain are involved in making ethical judgments, philosophers of religion have yet to recognize the relevance of such cases to the problem of evil.

What is particularly surprising, given that most of the defenders of theism in this debate are self-identified Christian philosophers, is that the central underlying element in the doctrine of double effect, what has been called the Pauline principle—never do evil that good may come of it—has been virtually ignored by contemporary philosophers of religion despite its relevance to the problem of evil.

Thus, while the principle has been a mainstay of natural law ethics at least since the time of Aquinas (notice, for example, the fundamental role it plays in the natural law ethics of John Finnis), contemporary philosophers of religion have simply ignored it when evaluating the goods and evils that are at stake with regard to the argument from evil. Rather, they have focused on the total amount of good or evil in the world or on particularly horrendous evils and whether those evils can be compensated for.

The Pauline Principle

Now it is true that the Pauline principle has been rejected as an absolute principle. This is because there clearly are exceptions to it. Surely doing evil that good may come of it is justified when the resulting evil or harm is

1. trivial (as in the case of stepping on someone's foot to get out of a crowded subway),
2. easily reparable (as in the case of lying to a temporarily depressed friend to keep her from committing suicide).

There is also disagreement over whether a further exception to the principle obtains when the resulting evil or harm is:

3. the only way to prevent far greater harm to innocent people (as in the case of shooting one of twenty civilian hostages to prevent, in the only way possible, the execution of all twenty).

Yet despite the recognition that there are exceptions to the principle, and despite the disagreement over the extent of those exceptions, the Pauline principle still plays an important role in contemporary ethical theory.

Trolley Cases

Moreover, the widespread discussion of hypothetical trolley cases in contemporary ethical theory is frequently just another way of determining the range of application of the Pauline principle. To see this, consider the following trolley case, first put forward by Philippa Foot:

A runaway trolley is headed toward five innocent people who are on the track and who will be killed unless something is done. You can redirect the trolley on to a second track, saving the five. However, on this second track is an innocent bystander who will be killed if the trolley is turned onto this track.

Is it permissible to redirect the trolley? Would that be doing evil? Clearly your redirecting the trolley would not be intentionally doing evil. What you would intentionally be doing is trying to save the five people on the track. You would not be intentionally trying to kill one to save the five, although you would foresee that one person's death would definitely result from your action of saving five. So given that the Pauline principle, properly understood, only requires that we never intentionally do evil that good may come of it, the principle does not prohibit redirecting the trolley in this case. Moreover, not only is redirecting the trolley in this case not prohibited by the Pauline principle, it also satisfies the additional requirements for being permitted by the doctrine of double effect.

But consider another trolley case:

Again, there is a runaway trolley headed toward five innocent people who are on the track and who will be killed unless something is done. This time the only way for you to stop the trolley and save the five is to push a big guy from a bridge onto the track.

In this case, by contrast, what you are doing, pushing the big guy onto the tracks, is intentionally doing evil. You are intentionally killing this large innocent person in order to save five other innocent people. Nor arguably would your action count as an exception to the Pauline principle here, even in virtue of its contested third class of exceptions, because in this case killing one to save five would presumably be judged insufficiently beneficial to justifying the killing. Thus, pushing the big guy onto the tracks in this case would be seen to be a violation of the Pauline principle.

However, consider a widely discussed trolley case put forward by Bernard Williams.[3] In Williams's case, Jim, an explorer, arrives in a South American village just as Pedro, an army officer, is about have his soldiers kill a random group of twenty Indians in retaliation for protests against the local government. In honor of Jim's arrival, Pedro offers to spare nineteen of the twenty Indians, provided that Jim will shoot one of them. Surely this looks like a case where the explorer should shoot one of the Indians in order to save the other nineteen. If you need to be further convinced that this type of irreparable harm to innocents can be justified for the sake of achieving greater benefit for others, then just imagine that larger and larger numbers of innocents (e.g., one hundred, one thousand, one million, whatever number you want) would be lost unless one particular (innocent) individual is killed. Surely, at some point, any defensible moral theory would justify such sacrifices for agents like ourselves.

There is then an intertwining discussion of trolley cases with the Pauline principle which underlies the doctrine of double effect that is ignored by contemporary philosophers of religion when they seek to morally evaluate the problem of evil.[4]

Today no one working on the problem of evil ever imagines backing away from the advances that Alvin Plantinga made by applying modal logic to the logical problem of evil or to the advances that William Rowe and Stephen Wykstra made by applying probabilistic epistemology to the evidential problem of evil. All now can agree that our understanding of the problem of the evil has undeniably been improved by these advances. Could it be, then, that by bringing to bear the untapped resources of ethics on the problem of evil, there would be a similar advance in our understanding of the problem?

I think that we can expect a similar advance once we do bring to bear the yet untapped resources of ethics on our understanding of the problem of evil. But I also think that this advance will be even more important than the other advances that have come from modal logic and probabilistic epistemology. This is because these other advances have really helped us more to restate the problem of evil rather than to solve it. Bringing untapped resources of ethics to bear on the problem, however, should actually help us advance toward a solution to the problem of evil. This is because the problem of evil is fundamentally an ethical, not a logical or epistemological problem. Accordingly, once the relevant resources of ethical theory have been incorporated into our discussion of the problem of evil, it should be difficult to comprehend how we ever previously attempted to address the problem of evil without them.

Pursuing the goal of bringing untapped resources from ethical theory to bear on the problem of evil, two conferences where held at the University of Notre that were generously supported by the John Templeton Foundation. The contributors to this volume all accepted invitations to address the thesis that there are yet untapped resources in ethical theory for affecting a more adequate solution to the problem of evil. Those who participated in the second conference had access to the papers presented at the first conference and the videoed discussion of those papers, so they would be able to use that material as a resource for their own papers. The papers and videoed discussion from both conferences were available to all the contributors to this volume as they revised their papers for publication. I commented on each paper. The contributors then revised their papers in light of my comments and the lively discussion of the papers we had at the conferences. In the remainder of this introduction, I will say a few words about what each has contributed to the volume.

Marilyn McCord Adams

In applying moral theory to the problem of evil, Marilyn Adams cautions us to focus on how horrendous moral evils can be, as, she points out, much of contemporary moral theory has failed to do so. She also cautions us to attend to the fragility and gross imperfections in human agency, frequently caused by in-group cultures that again, she points out, much of contemporary and even medieval moral theory, has failed to address. Then Adams takes from theology the idea that our relationship with God should be one of a developing friendship, in order to frame the problem of evil as how a trustworthy friend could allow the inflicting of horrendous evil on us for our own good. This is especially problematic in light of the Pauline principle's requirement never to do evil that good may come of it.

However, Adam's focus is on what God has to do to make up for allowing the infliction of horrendous evils on its victims. She argues that what is required is that the horrendous evil in the victim's life be organically related to the victim's overall good. This is the main conclusion that Adams arrives at in her chapter from applying ethical theory to the problem of evil.

John Hare

In order to consider how ethical theory might be applied to the problem of evil, John Hare discusses Immanuel Kant's fairly radical solution concerning how this might be done. Kant's solution is fairly radical because it rejects every known attempt to deal with God and the problem of evil in favor of Kant's own unique form of theodicy, which moves from an understanding of morality to postulates of God and an afterlife, where happiness is in proportion to virtue. Now if morality does in fact practically support these two postulates, we would really have just the kind of useful contribution of moral theory to the problem of evil that my Templeton project was hoping to undercover. However, in my comments on Hare's original conference paper, I expressed skepticism about whether Kant's two postulates were needed to either justify morality itself or secure the proper motivation for people to abide by it. I even suggested that believing these postulates might serve to undermine the moral motivation people would otherwise have, possibly putting in its place a less desirable self-interested justification and motivation for being moral. In his now revised paper, Hare has partly responded to my concern, claiming that for Kant there was also an other-regarding motivation for wanting the postulates to be true, namely, that their being true would secure that happiness was in proportion to virtue not just for ourselves but for others as well. Admittedly, this does improve Kant's case for our believing the two postulates.

Linda Zagzebski

Linda Zagzebski brings ethical theory to bear on the problem of evil by providing a novel critique of proponents of the argument from evil, such as Mackie, Tooley, and Rowe. They all, she claims, implicitly endorse the idea that a good person aims at producing good and preventing evil, where the morality of the consequences is understood as primary. Zagzebski notes that many theistic critics of the argument from evil, like skeptical theists, endorse this as well. Zagzebski claims that we have a problem here because the goodness of an agent or the goodness of an agent's action may be understood to be independent of the production of good or bad consequences. In fact, according to the Pauline principle, it would be wrong even to maximize good consequences if that required doing an evil action to produce those consequences. Clearly, Zagzebski does raise a problem for both the proponents and opponents of the argument who rely exclusively on consequential justifications.

Laura Garcia

In her paper, Laura Garcia deals mainly with a debate among moral theologians as to how expansively to understand the action of cooperating with evil. Some theologians understand cooperating with evil very broadly, such that to avoid all cooperation with evil "would require that we abandon almost all arenas of human activity."[5] Hoping to avoid the "creeping consequentialism" which she thinks such a view entails, Garcia favors a more restricted notion of cooperating with evil such that to be cooperative in the evil act of another is "to endorse, assist, or further that act either formally or materially." She is then able to distinguish cooperating with evil from just permitting it. Permitting evil can just involve failing to prevent an evil when one is in a position to do so. Using these definitions, Garcia reaches her desired moral conclusion that God does not cooperate with evil.

On the question of whether God could be charged with intentionally permitting evil when it is morally objectionable to do so, Garcia has much less to say. At the end of her chapter, she claims not to be in a good position to weigh the good reasons God might have for permitting evil. In so doing, Garcia allies herself with theists who hold that we should be skeptical about our ability to know the reasons that God would have permitting evil, at least in particular cases. In the two chapters that follow, Bruce Russell seeks to undermine skeptical theism while Stephen Wykstra seeks to further defend it.

Bruce Russell

Bruce Russell begins his chapter with an argument from evil:

> 1. If God exists he would not allow excessive, unnecessary suffering.
> 2. But there is excessive unnecessary suffering
> 3. So God does not exist.

He then considers whether the first premises could be supported by a Kantian moral prohibition not do to or allow harm, as he once thought was possible. He now argues that it cannot be done. To show this, Russell uses another trolley case put forward by Foot of a big guy stuck in the mouth of a cave blocking others from getting out while flood waters are rising. As Russell sees it, allowing the others to dynamite the big guy out of the mouth of the cave "opens the door" for the theist to claim that God could have a comparable justification for all the evil we observe in the world.

Accordingly, most of Russell's paper is directed at critiquing skeptical theism's defense of theism, particularly the version of skeptical theism defended by Stephen Wykstra and Timothy Perrine. Russell raises two basic criticisms to Wykstra and Perrine's attempt to add auxiliary hypotheses to core theism to produce an expanded theism that they claim can then provide a defensible solution to the problem of evil. First, Russell claims that their expanded theism hypothesis is no different in form from that of Young Earthism which holds that the world is just a hundred years old. Second, Russell claims that the skeptical theism hypothesis is also like that of the person in Anthony Flew's parable who believes that a particular garden is being cared for by an unvisible gardener. Russell maintains that both views are unfalsifiable. In this way, Russell thinks he has provided an epistemological but not an ethical critique of skeptical theism and thereby provided the support needed for his argument from evil.

Stephen Wykstra

In his chapter, Stephen Wykstra seeks to achieve two goals, first to properly interpret the Pauline principle, particularly as it applies to God, and second to improve on Michael Bergmann's defense of skeptical theism.

To properly interpret the Pauline principle (that one should never do evil that good may come of it), Wykstra looks to Augustine. In the passage Wykstra cites, Augustine distinguishes between doing evil and the evil that people suffer, which he labels Evil-1 and Evil-2, respectively. Taking then the evil prohibited by the Pauline principle to be Evil-1, Wykstra suggests that we should initially view this evil to be just prima facie morally prohibited by the principle. Only when the prima facie moral prohibition is weighed against other moral considerations, including morally relevant good consequences, and an all-things-considered moral evaluation is thereby arrived at, could we could end up with an all-things-considered moral prohibition of doing evil. Wykstra further speculates that it will be the rarest of cases when prima facie evils cannot be justifiable, outweighed by good consequences that at least God could derive from allowing them. In fact, he can only think of only two sorts of cases where this would not hold. The first would be allowing all sentient life in all possible worlds to be subject to endless hellish suffering (imposed by whom it is not clear), so as to make each sentient life on the whole a bad thing. For Wykstra, the Evil-1 would have to be of this magnitude before he thinks God could not permit it for the sake of the morally good consequences that God could derive therefrom. The second is the evil of hating God, which he thinks that we (or God?) should not permit irrespective of the moral consequences that could be achieved thereby. The first sort of case would presumably allow God to permit worlds having tens, hundreds, even thousands of holocausts as long as some sentient creatures in them had lives worth living.

In the second half of his chapter, Wykstra takes on the task of coming up with a way of understanding skeptical theism that does not lead to a "paralyzing moral skepticism." Here drawing on the work of Richard Brandt and Derek Parfit, Wykstra seeks to improve on Bergmann's account of what consequences we have to take into account when determining what we ought to do. Bergmann wants to specify those consequences as ones we could reasonably expect. Wykstra thinks that Bergmann's specification is too narrow and that it should include all those consequences that we would be aware of, assuming that our "moral horizons" were not blocked in some way or other due to our own fault. Despite this disagreement, Wykstra still agrees with Bergmann that God's knowledge of consequences, especially future good consequences, so far outstrips our own reasonable expectations or moral horizons as to undercut any argument from evil.

Stephen Maitzen

In his attempt to apply ethics to the problem of evil, Stephen Maitzen makes a strong case against Marilyn Adams's view that God does not have moral obligations. Maitzen goes on to challenge William Hasker and Daniel Howard-Snyder's view that God does not intervene to prevent evil in order to give us the opportunity to do so ourselves. Yet, even assuming there were no transfer of obligation here, Maitzen still objects to seeing ourselves as having the obligation to act first to prevent evil in the world when God is almost always in a better position to do so himself. Maitzen suggests that God should, in fact, prevent all the evil in this life that theists claim God prevents in the next.

Hopefully, this brief account of the contributions to this volume will lead you to now give them your careful study, thereby advancing your own understanding of how the untapped resources of ethics can be brought to bear on the problem of evil.

Notes

1. I do not intend the make any distinction between moral theory and ethical theory but instead treat them as synonymous.

2. According to the doctrine of double effect, an action with two effects, one good and the other bad or evil, can be justified provided that the good effect is intended and the bad or evil effect is not intended but merely foreseen, and also provided that the bad or evil effect is not disproportionate to the good effect.

3. Thompson calls all such life and death hypothetical cases "trolley" cases. For the case more fully set out, see Bernard Williams and J. J. C. Smart, *Utilitarianism: For and Against* (Cambridge: Cambridge University Press, 1973), 98–99.

4. We can also give an account of why the Pauline principle is morally justified with its focus on prohibiting intentional harm (or evil) and its more permissive stance toward foreseen harm (or evil). It is because those who suffer harm have more reason to protest when the harm is done to them by agents who are intentionally engaged in causing harm to them than when the harm done to them is merely the foreseen consequences of actions of agents whose ends and means are good. It is also because those who cause harm have more reason to protest a restriction against foreseen harm than they do to protest a comparable restriction against intended harm. This is because a restriction against foreseen harm limits our actions when our ends and means are good, whereas a restriction against intended harm only limits our actions when our ends or means are evil or harmful, and it would seem that we have stronger grounds for acting when both our ends and means are good than when they are not. In brief, the Pauline principle can be morally supported because we have more reason to protest when we are being used by others than when we are being affected simply by the foreseen consequences of their actions, and because we have more reason to act when both our ends and means are good than when they are not.

5. Anthony Fisher, "Cooperation in Evil: Understanding the Issues," in *Cooperation, Complicity, and Conscience: Problems in Healthcare, Science, Law and Public Policy,* ed. Helen Watt (London: Linacre Center, 2005), 29.

1   A Modest Proposal?

Caveat Emptor! Moral Theory and Problems of Evil

Marilyn McCord Adams

Catching Up on Moral Theory?

James Sterba has challenged philosophers of religion, not only those who work on the problem of evil, to take moral theory more seriously, for multiple reasons. Most obviously, good and evil, right and wrong, motivation in voluntary action, make up a large part of the subject matter of ethics. At least since positivism began to lose its grip, at least for the last sixty years, there has been a lot of fine-grained thinking on the subject (by Philippa Foot, Alan Gibbard, Christine Korsgaard, Alasdair McIntyre, Robert Nozick, John Rawls, and Tim Scanlon, among others). A variety of contrasting positions has been debated and worked out in detail.

By contrast, many treatments of the problem of evil have seemed ethically under nuanced. Back in the 1960s, but also later, there were appeals to ordinary moral sensibilities (e.g., by Nelson Pike). Others have commended as obviously acceptable principles ripped out of context: that an agent who did not produce the best (even where "best" is metaphysically impossible) would be morally defective (e.g., Rowe). Others have merely taken for granted principles or their applications, such as that God would be justified in making the best world that God could (Plantinga). Still others—some skeptical theists, including Justin McBrayer—confidently assume a thoroughgoing consequentialism. Recently, John Bishop and Ken Perszyk have reemphasized how responses to problems of evil are norm relative and noted how participants in the discussion often presuppose different moral norms.[1] Overall, the state of debate in analytic philosophy of religion lends credence to the idea that wider and more nuanced acquaintance with moral theory would be a very good thing.

A Medieval Analogy

Because I am a medievalist, the idea of applying moral theory to philosophy of religion brings to mind Western scholastic appropriations of Aristotle and his Arab commentators, especially Avicenna and Averroes. Aristotle was dubbed "the Philosopher," Averroes "the Commentator." Together with others, they formed a philosophical canon to which would-be philosophers and philosophical theologians put themselves to school. Medieval Latin scholastics had a lot to gain from this. Aristotle had fenced off, and Aristotle and his commentators had ploughed and cultivated many fields and subfields. They had set important questions and pursued them with analytical skill and technical precision. They had developed conceptuality, categories and distinctions for managing issues in metaphysics, epistemology, psychology, and morals. They had offered systematic theories in each. What medievals stood to gain by engaging these was philosophical training and a leg up on wide-ranging issues. They simply didn't have to reinvent the wheel. They had a place to start, research programs to participate in and continue, questions to pursue, theories to refine.

Nevertheless, putting themselves to school did not mean uncritical appropriation. They read, marked, learned, and inwardly digested the texts of the philosophers, the better to be in a position to question and dispute them. Small-scale refinements, applying them to shifting and new questions—that is what is always involved in carrying on a field. But absorbing as it was to understand Aristotle's ideas and extend his research programs, Christian philosophers soon recognized that the philosophical systems of Aristotle and the Arab commentators needed more than minor tweaking. Christian theology widened the data base of phenomena to be preserved and accounted for: creation ex nihilo, the Trinity, the Incarnation, Eucharistic presence. This meant that Aristotle's metaphysical categories and taxonomy of causation and understandings of corporeal placement required substantial conceptual revision and innovation. Christian theology implied that there were points on which Aristotle was clearly wrong, for example about whether the unmoved mover was an efficient cause of the existence of the world, about whether motion and time were without beginning or end, about whether the world here below is necessary, about whether future contingents could be knowable determinately and with certainty. The condemnations of 1270 and 1277 issue emphatic caveats. In effect, they warned, "Impressive as they are, you have to use what Aristotle, Avicenna, and Averroes say with caution. By all means, get inside and understand their theories. But then question and dispute them. Don't lose sight of important points that you need to accommodate."

Overall, it was a very fruitful engagement, arguably one which has given both Aristotle and Christian worldviews a longer academic run. Twentieth century theological critics to the contrary, notwithstanding, theology had a lot to learn from Aristotelian philosophy. What is less often noticed is that Aristotelian philosophy had things to learn from theology: the possibility of something incorruptible being the form of some matter, the possibility of an individual substance nature being alien-supposited and/or multiply supposited, the possibilities of multiple locations for bodies, efficient causality as an explanation of being and not just of locomotion and/or material transformation.

Evil and Problems with Morality

So also and all the more so if philosophers of religion get more nearly up to speed with what contemporary moral theories have to offer.

To this, my honest response has to be: "Caveat emptor." Certainly, it will not do for us simply to pick one of the ethical theories on offer, let it tell us what counts as evil and what it would take for an agent to be perfectly good, and grind out the results. Claudia Card points to one reason: many prominent ethical theorists skirt the topic of evil. W. D. Ross does not even mention it in *The Right and the Good*. Nor does the term "evil" appear in the index to Henry Sidgwick's *The Methods of Ethics*. John Rawls's *A Theory of Justice* contains only one mention of "the evil man." Even more telling, Rawls's concern with the distribution of primary goods that any person may be presumed to desire is not matched with any balancing consideration of basic harms to be avoided in the ideal society.[2] How can such theories help us wrestle with problems of evil, when they seem to sweep problems with evil under the rug?

Indeed, in my past work on problems of evil, I have argued for de-emphasizing the role of moral theory. Shifting attention from abstract to concrete problems of evil—from the issue of whether the existence of God is compatible with some evil or other to the question of whether an omniscient, omnipotent, and perfectly good God could have produced human beings in a world with evils in the amounts and of the kinds and with the distributions found in the actual world—I have often spoken of the poverty of morality, and rubbed readers' noses in its difficulty in conceiving, much less managing the difficulties raised by the worst evils. I have put forward the idea that other systems of evaluation—namely, the purity and defilement calculus and the honor code—outstrip contemporary moral theory when it comes to capturing what is at stake with the worst evils and to identifying the obstacles to harmonious Divine-human relationships.[3]

Mostly, my suggestions have been met with incomprehension and mockery. Do I seriously think that we should replace modern morality (note the hint that the term is univocal and its referent obvious) with the holiness code, evaluations of morally right and morally wrong with the verdicts "tainted" and "undefiled"? Do I really believe that the challenge and riposte of the honor code would be a good substitute for talk of virtue and vice? Do I really want to go back to evaluating social behavior like the Dinkas, or is the feudal world of Don Quixote (I am a medievalist after all) my all-things-considered choice?[4]

My response to such rhetorical questions is that I was not simply being silly. I meant to make three serious points. First, I wanted to warn colleagues against anachronistic eisegesis. Many biblical passages, like many traditional theological teachings, are framed by the holiness and/or honor codes. It is unfaithful to the (in this case, authoritative) texts and so misleading to read modern moral theories into them.

Second, I wanted to call attention to the fact that—however much they may have gone underground—the holiness and honor codes have not disappeared from our evaluative practices. Sexual sins still defile and certain kinds of graft blot the politician's copybook. Philosophical colloquia provide ready evidence that competition for honor, the need to show how much there is to us philosophically is alive and well.

Third, and most important for present purposes, I wanted to show how these frameworks do a better job of getting at what's so bad about the worst evils and of suggesting what might be done to remedy them. My thought was and is that putting ourselves to school to these neglected value frameworks might refocus our attention and sensitize us to factors that moral categories blindside. My thought was and is that getting inside these evaluative frameworks enough to understand how they work might put us in touch with neglected resources for both formulating and resolving problems of evil.

A More Modest Proposal

If there is anything to my medieval analogy, however, Sterba and other conference-organizers were not aiming for Christian philosophers to "read, mark, learn" and "swallow whole" what contemporary ethical theory has to offer. Rather, they are urging that we "read, mark, learn, and inwardly digest" them, the better to question and dispute them, the better to assess how they need to be "transmogrified" in the face of Christian theological commitments.

For the sake of argument, let me back off a bit from my most negative verdicts about moral theory. Let me take a page from Claudia Card, who does not want to abandon moral theory but to supplement and rejig theories of moral wrongness that fail to grapple with the worst evils. Instead of writing off ethical theories in advance, let me try once again to rivet attention on five factors that—in my judgment—any theologically adequate ethical theory will have to address seriously.

Facing the Worst

Honest wrestling with problems of evil requires us to face up to the worst that we can suffer, be, or do. Several rubrics have been proposed for picking out the worst.

For my own part, I have proposed the category of horrendous evils (for short, horrors), which I have defined as "evils participation in which constitutes prima facie reason to believe that the participant's life cannot be a great good to him/her on the whole" or "prima facie life-ruinous evils." As dramatic examples, I have instanced the rape of a woman and axing off of her arms, psycho-physical torture whose ultimate goal is the disintegration of personality, cannibalizing one's own offspring, child abuse of the sort described by Ivan Karamazov, participation in the Nazi death camps, the explosion of nuclear bombs over populated areas, avoidable death by starvation of populations driven off their land by hostile forces or natural disasters, being the accidental and/or unwitting agent in the disfigurement or death of one loves best. Domestic examples include corporate cultures of dishonesty that coopt workers into betraying their deepest values, schoolyard bullying, parental incest, clinical depression, schizophrenia, degenerative diseases such as multiple sclerosis or Alzheimer's that imprison and/or unravel the person we once knew.

Claudia Card advances her atrocity paradigm, which she defines as "foreseen intolerable harms produced by culpable wrong-doing."[5] Alternatively, she speaks of harms that deprive or seriously risk "depriving others of the basics that are necessary to make a life possible or tolerable or decent," where a "'tolerable' life is at least minimally worth living for its own sake and from the standpoint of the being whose life it is, not just as a means to the ends of others."[6] Her list of examples overlaps mine: "genocide, slavery, torture, rape as a weapon of war, saturation bombing of cities, biological and chemical warfare, unleashing lethal viruses and gases, domestic terrorism of prolonged battering, stalking, and child abuse."[7]

Still others propose the rubric "unjustifiable." Ivan Karamazov declares that his ghastly cases of child abuse cannot be swallowed up in the higher harmony. John Roth identifies the Nazi holocaust in particular, the "slaughterbench of history" of which it is characteristic in general, as "waste" beyond justification.[8] Likewise, D. Z. Phillips finds obscene any suggestion that the Nazi holocaust could be justified by "consequentialist" reasoning—as a means, consequence, or side effect to obtaining some great good or avoiding an equally bad or worse evil.[9] In the same spirit, Stewart Sutherland charges that anyone who thinks the worst evils can be justified, does not take them with full moral seriousness.[10]

Perhaps all of these attempted rubrics need refinement. Even so, they combine with the examples to point us in the right direction.[11] My contention has been and is that—where the worst evils are concerned—we cannot appreciate how bad they are or what's so bad about them without engaging them face to face. By "face to face," I mean either experiencing them in one's own person (first-person experience) or through firsthand empathetic engagement. Moreover, once is not enough. Repeated or at least periodic confrontations are necessary to keep alive one's sense of how ghastly they are.

Repeated face-to-face engagement is important, not only for apt conceptualization, but for accurate moral reasoning. The worst evils mess with our theories and demand that our theories become messier, because the worst evils cannot be subsumed under attractive generalizations that work well enough for the small, medium, and large evils of ordinary time. Job's ruin explodes the act consequence principle ("good for good; evil for evil"). Terrorists' torturing and beheading of journalists cannot be set right by *lex talionis*, by the state's torturing and beheading terrorists. Ivan Karamazov insists that—unlike broken arms, skinned knees, and the common cold—bouncing babies on bayonets before their mothers' eyes cannot be justified as constitutive means to the higher harmony. D. Z. Phillips is appalled at the suggestion that Sophie should consider her hands washed by the fact that she did what she had to do in the circumstances, that it was better to save one of her children than to let both be killed. Maternal betrayal of one child is not a morally acceptable means to saving the other.[12]

Horrors are difficult to domesticate theoretically. They require separate consideration. Not only that. Their prevention and (if possible) remedy deserves priority in deliberation and action.[13] Not keeping the sense of ghastliness fresh makes it much easier to do the opposite. Consider the child sex abuse scandal in the Roman Catholic Church. Priests senior enough to become bishops and high-level archdiocesan officials did not lack an abstract conceptual grasp of the distinction between grave and ordinary-time evils. In their roles as pastors and confessors, at least some would have dealt with victims of child sex abuse in the past. But by the time they were making corporate decisions about how to deal with culprit priests, they were far removed from face-to-face engagement. Meeting with the victims personally would have awakened them to the ghastliness of the harms done. Refusal to do so allowed officials to remain aloof and to prioritize the Church's interests (both her reputation and material assets) as well as the sacred office of priesthood (and the well-being of their brother priests) over the intolerable harms suffered by their victims. Analogous reflection would commend a policy of requiring strategizing generals and Pentagon officials periodically to spend time with troops in the trenches, lest they forget that their sterilized term "collateral damage" refers to the degradation of human beings. Remember Job's friends whose face-to-face engagement of his suffering had them mourning with him, until their retreat into theory encouraged them to belittle his suffering and to blame the victim. Remember how their defense of God won them a rebuke from God. Where the worst evils are concerned, clear thinking and appropriate action demands that we keep compassion raw.

"Getting Real" about Human Agency

Theoretical Posits: I have it on good authority (from a leader in the field) that ethics likes to tell people what to do and how to be. Theories of moral right and wrong mean to be action-guiding. Virtue ethics bears witness to what it would be like to be a fine human being. Both make sense only if human agency is competent and capable, only if it is within our power to do or to become what they advise. Historically, how many ethical theorists forward a high view of human nature as a condition of the possibility of the moral life? Insisting that we can be accountable only for what is within our power, Stoics and Abelard posit an inner sanctum of self-control, untouchable by the chances and changes of what goes on outside. Peter John Olivi, Duns Scotus, and William Ockham insisted that (roughly speaking) incompatibilist free will is a condition of eligibility for moral assessment. Centuries later, Kant and Kantians insisted that "ought" implies "can."

Ethical theory purports to get to the heart of what is special about human agency: that is, that truly human actions (as opposed to involuntary movements such as respiration and digestion) are imputable to the agent for moral praise and blame. Aristotelians and Kantians suggest that what is distinctive is that human agency is rational agency, that human beings are autonomous and self-governing: human beings deliberate, apply principles, and issue dictates to themselves. Claudia Card and I have emphasized that what is distinctive about human beings is that we are persons. I have stressed meaning-making—organizing who one is, what one does and suffers around significant goals and relationships—as the central function of personal agency. Card is more expansive: a person has a distinctive point of view on the world into which she or he can invite others to enter. Persons are curious to explore, able to learn, and creative to invent. Persons are capable of forming personal relationships in which we give and receive love, are vulnerable to pain and open to joy.[14]

Reality Check: Getting real about human agency requires us to embrace the tension between the dignity of human nature and its fragility. On the one hand, among created goods, created personal agency deserves the greatest honor, enjoys the greatest entitlement to be nurtured and preserved. Its degradation or destruction and action (whether conscious or unconscious) to degrade or destroy it are among the worst evils.[15]

On the other, ethical theory's idealized pictures of human agency clearly fail to fit the facts. Aristotle frankly confesses: the badly brought up have scant chance at virtue. Kant is realistic enough to locate the free-willed agent in the *noumenal* rather than the *phenomenal* realm. In fact, the situation is much worse than they say. We are radically vulnerable to horrors. The honor code has it right: first-person horror participation shatters personal integrity.

First-person horror participation interferes with the person's meaning-making capacities by making it prima facie impossible for her or him to make positive sense of her or his life. Severe depression turns everything tasteless, leaves its victims unable to perceive anything as worthwhile. Schizophrenia twists interpretations of life experience into something bizarre. Soldiers return from theaters of war with PTSD. Traumatized brains and psyches are unable to anchor the horrors of war firmly in the past, so that vivid experiences float and interrupt as if they were clear and present dangers. First-person horror participation may merely stump and stalemate the search for constructive ways to go on. But it is often "mind blowing" to the extent that individuals find it difficult to function well enough to get through the day.

Horrors are not rare. History is a slaughter bench. The grim fact is that radical vulnerability to horrors is not accidental but rooted in our nature, in what we are and where we are: personal animals in an environment of real and apparent scarcity. Because we are material persons, we are highly vulnerable to abnormalities in our own biochemistry. Because we are personal animals, our personal capacities evolve through a developmental process which is itself easily disrupted. Even in adulthood, encounters with the worst evils can traumatize our psyches in ways from which it is humanly impossible to recover. Our big brains require us to be dependent for longer on at best neurotic adults whose adaptations shape our own. Even if we are reared up into the virtues we need to perform well in our social roles, those same virtues dispose us to limit in-group hostility and augment in-group cooperation in ordinary time. Investigations show that these tendencies do not easily generalize into universal human sympathy or carry over to life-threatening emergencies,[16] and that—given identifiable sociopolitical conditions—the vast majority of human beings can be persuaded to become active participants in mass killings.[17] Even if we are lucky enough to live in boring times, the truth remains that human beings are politically challenged. Limited imagination, deficient grasp of the properties of social systems, and fear of death and shortages, mean that humanly designed social systems spawn systemic evils, structures of cruelty that privilege some by degrading others. Yet, unless we are hermits, our sense of who we are and what we mean is fundamentally shaped by the social roles we fill and so tainted by complicity in and collective responsibility for human degradation.

Honest wrestling with problems of evil requires us to face up to the fact that horrors are deeply entrenched in the human condition in this world for reasons that are largely beyond our control. We cannot change human nature. We cannot radically remodel our environment. Nothing we can do guarantees against first-person participation in them. We can't reliably prevent them. Once they happen, there is nothing we can do to set them right. They are not the currency of retributive punishment, because worst evils are too bad even for the guilty.

Because the worst evils tend to twist, wreck, and ruin human agency, they are not the stuff of moral education either. Once human personalities are shattered, there is often nothing we can do to put Humpty Dumpty back together again. Whatever damages law courts may award, it is grotesque to suggest that we have adequate capital to compensate individuals for personal ruin.

Religion exists to help us grapple with evils from which only God can save us. But what is ethical theory to make of this? Claudia Card labors valiantly to bring the worst evils to our attention. When she realistically observes that not all intolerable harms are humanly preventable (e.g., natural catastrophes such as earthquakes, fires, floods, and death), her response is to restrict her category of atrocities to those that are culpably produced. She reckons that the others aren't relevant to her twin aims of supplementing blinkered theories of moral wrongness and of rallying us to political action.[18]

Ruth Barcan Marcus, in her article "Moral Dilemmas and Consistency,"[19] equivocates. Maintaining that moral dilemmas do not signal inconsistency within moral theory but bad fit with the circumstances, she urges that moral dilemmas serve a positive dynamic function of alerting us "so to arrange our lives and arrange our institutions as to minimize predicaments of moral conflict."[20] In the end, much as she does not want to see moral dilemmas as a tragic feature of the human condition, she admits that "however holy our wills or rational our strategies," "the contingencies of this world" may thwart our efforts and deny us complete success.[21] Theologically adequate ethical theories will join Card and Marcus in calling on us to work hard to prevent intolerable harms and, among other things, to uproot institutional structures that give rise to them. If we don't, things will get much worse. And no theologically adequate ethical theory will avert its gaze from what soteriology places front and center: by and large, we cannot save ourselves from the worst that we can suffer, be, or do.

Autonomy versus Perichoresis: In my judgment, getting real about human agency ought to make us consider replacing the ideal of human agency as self-determining autonomy with the theological model of perichoresis or functionally inclusive personality. Western Christian theology faces the fact that the human condition is not optimal. To say the least, we are challenged when it comes to thinking clearly about what ought to be done. We have difficulty pulling ourselves together, in keeping sensory appetites under rational control. The doctrine of Adam's fall is a biblically inspired hypothesis forwarded to explain how and why human agency got that way, when God initially created everything very good. Damage estimates vary, however. Like the ancient Stoics, Abelard, Olivi, Scotus, and Ockham remain optimistic. They envision a self-conscious ego that has it within its power—no matter what bodily states, emotional upheavals, sensory appetites, native inclinations, or external persuasions—to choose or not to choose, to choose for or to choose against what reason dictates. Apart from divine conservation and general concurrence, human free choice is a solo act. From Augustine forward, all agree that we need God's help. But their debates about what sort of help and what the help is for, are framed by the assumption that divine and human agencies are in competition: when it comes to causing human actions, God can make a greater only if we make a lesser contribution, and vice versa. Over the course of his Pelagian controversies, Augustine shifts from declaring "the will would not be will if it were not in our power" to "God works in us both to will and to do" to "our wills are more in God's power than in our own."[22]

Certainly, it is important for Western Christian theology to maintain many distinctions between divine and human agency. The divine essence is really distinct from human nature. The agent capacities that go with Godhead are radically (indeed, infinitely) superior to those that define human beings. Moreover, in only one case—the incarnation of the second person of the Trinity—do divine and human natures belong to numerically one individual substance. Metaphysically speaking, Jesus is God, but—metaphysically speaking—the rest of us are not God.

Nevertheless, the Bible suggests models, not of metaphysical union, but of functional partnership between humans and the divine. John's Jesus promises that the Paraclete and/or the Trinity will dwell in the disciple's hearts to teach them all things. Arguably, what John's Jesus has in mind is not merely information transfer at the cognitive level, but whole-selved education that sensitizes us to God's presence and teaches us how—*mutatis mutandis*—to see as God sees and to love as God loves. Just as with human infants and adult caretakers, the infant psyche starts as a booming buzzing confusion, which does not yet distinguish self from other and so is unable to recognize or conceive of the adult presence as personal presence; so the Trinity indwells, is omnipresent in human hearts, drawing out their capacity to be spiritual, long before and whether or not the human beings ever consciously recognize really present Godhead. Through daily interaction, human parents nurture children through a long period of ego development, rear up their children first into specifically human and then into individually distinctive capacities. Human parents hope to bring up their offspring to become adults with whom they can still be friends.

So also Godhead is agency enabling but headed toward friendship. Godhead does not aim at the impossibility of peer relationships, but at something more radical: a fundamental restructuring of our personalities so that what we say and do is directed not by the solitary autonomous ego but by lived partnership, by friendship with God at our core. The aim is for functional co-inherence in imitation of the Trinity. The Father, Son, and Holy Spirit live consciously, explicitly, and deliberately in such harmony and intimacy that there is one action and one will ad extra. John's Jesus illustrates the goal with his repeated claims: "I do only what the Father gives me to do; I say only what the Father tells me to say." The point is not that the Father bosses Jesus around, but that the human personality of Jesus has been formed and informed until Jesus and the Father share a common purpose and are in agreement about how Jesus is to carry out his role. Likewise, the post-Pentecost church leaders in the Acts of the Apostles have their personalities restructured to center on their partnership with the Holy Spirit. So also, St. Paul, whose core identity is taken over by his friendship with Christ: "I, not I, but Christ in me."

On this view, indwelling is not an emergency fix. Collaboration with divine indwellers is what we were made for. Functional co-inherence is a feature of our nature, part and parcel of God's original design. Echoing Irenaeus, we might say that a human being is assimilated to God in two phases. In the first, human being is made in God's image insofar as it is personal. In the second, the human being is reared up into Godlikeness until our personalities are restructured into an ever more conscious and deliberate cooperation with Godhead. Conversely, when horrors shatter human psyches, Godhead, all along the agency enabler and senior partner, moves over the fragments to reintegrate a core, to put Humpty Dumpty back together again.[23]

The perichoretic model keeps before us the fact that—for Christians—the human goal is not virtue, but holiness. To be sure, virtue is one way to shape human being into greater God-likeness. But it is not the only sort of cradle-to-grave holiness. Christian extremists like the desert ascetics had no interest in Aristotle's mean. They did not aim at becoming fine human beings. They bent themselves out of shape in all kinds of ways the better to see God. First-person horror participation can so damage human capacities as to put becoming a paragon of virtue out of antemortem reach. But Christian hagiography boasts of divine resourcefulness in partnering with human brokenness to let the light shine through. For those who participate in the worst, this is an interim consolation.

Likewise, the perichoretic model easily explains why human personality in all of its vulnerability should be so valuable. Human personality is a temple of the holy. What makes human beings holy is indwelling Godhead. This is what the dignity of human nature consists in: that it is made for functional partnership with God. Human agency can be twisted and shattered at its core. But indwelling Godhead does not abandon it. Once again, human agency is made for collaboration. Christians believe the promise that the holy is faithful to raise it up on the third (or at least, the last) day.

Grappling with Systemic Evils

Corollary to these two mandates is a third: we need to develop finer-grained understandings of systemic evil and collective responsibility. Here ethical theory and decision theory can provide analytical help, but the subject may have received more attention in theology than philosophy.[24]

Certainly, biblical religion recognizes that problematic evils are not restricted to the sins and sufferings of individuals. Systems have causal properties in the sense that how individuals are organized makes a significant difference to the consequences and significance of their actions. God created human beings to be systemically embedded, and that twice over. Human being is embedded in the system of nature, in this material world in which our kind emerged, this material world for survival in which our coping capacities evolved. Moreover, "human beings are political animals," embedded in the social systems into which we are born, in which we live and move and have our being. Because our actions are systemically embedded, and because our understanding of system dynamics is poor, human actions regularly have consequences we did not anticipate, much less intend. Because we are neither smart enough nor good enough to organize utopia, humanly devised social systems inevitably spawn systemic injustices. Yet, it is not only possible but easy for us to inhabit the upper and middle levels of our society while blindsiding its oppressive side effects.

Overall, double embeddedness means that our individual actions are inserted into systems that take over to give them unforeseen, unintended, and easily ignored consequences. This means that reasonable and well-meaning actions can have disastrous consequences, while apparent peccadillos get amplified into devastating harms. The traditional story of Adam's fall diagnoses the human predicament, when the primal pair's eating forbidden fruit plunges the human race into the world as we know it. For my part, I have contended that this double embeddedness lies at the root of our radical vulnerability to horrors.

There is more. The Hebrew Bible takes collective agency for granted. YHWH is a personal God who relates to Israel as to a corporate person. Because organizing society is so difficult, YHWH lays down guidelines, laws, and precepts. Over and over again, Israel's refusal to follow them gives rise to the systemic evils of idolatry and injustice. YHWH's modus operandi is to send prophets to tear away the veil of ignorance, to call attention to systemic evils, and to warn Israel to get busy and uproot them. When the powers that be and privileged classes are too attached to the status quo, when the evil-generating dynamics become too entrenched, YHWH whistles for some big power to come in and destroy the society. YHWH enforces a collective "timeout" from settled nation statehood before bringing the next generation back home to try again. Prophetic diagnoses make chilling reading as they showcase divine providence raining down indiscriminate collective punishment of the kind now forbidden by international law.

There is still more. Traditional Western doctrines of Adam's fall presume notions of collective responsibility according to which group membership imposes on individuals some kind of accountability for what the group does. The doctrine of original sin claims that—quite apart from anything individuals do—they are liable by virtue of their causal origin, simply because they are "family," biological descendants of Adam and Eve. At first, Augustine held that while we are not guilty for what Adam did before we were even a gleam in our forefather's eye, it is nevertheless appropriate that generation upon generation of offspring inherit parental penalties. Over the course of his Pelagian controversy, Augustine went further to embrace a doctrine of original guilt: that all of Adam's offspring deserve the punishments of ignorance and difficulty in this life and eternal torment in the next. Looking to the remedy, Anselm's satisfaction theory and some penal substitution theories of the atonement reverse the direction: justice can be served by one group member's bearing the costs of other members' shortcomings.

Already in the twelfth century, Abelard protested that an individual can be morally blameworthy only for what is within his or her power (as Adam's action was not for his descendants). Challenging any and all notions of collective responsibility has become a modern commonplace. If someone else can pay my monetary debts for me, does it make Kantian sense for anyone else to take my punishment? Surely, morally appraisable group action makes no more than metaphorical sense, since human collectives do not literally have minds and so do not literally form intentions.

My own sympathies lie on the other side. Surely, groups with decision procedures for setting institutional or social policies (e.g., nation-states, churches, universities, and business corporations) can be said to have intentions and purposes. Surely, they take actions that individual members could not do on their own. Surely, insofar as we identify with a group, we acquire ownership in the group's actions. For example, if—while living in Britain—I declare that I am an American, if I am foolhardy enough to go on to insist that (as I was taught in school) our entry into World War II secured the Allied victory, I am also obliged to own "our dropping atom bombs on Hiroshima and Nagasaki," even though I was too young in 1945 to do anything about it. Surely, if I frame my subjective identity largely in terms of performance in social roles, my meaning-making frame becomes implicitly tainted by the systemic evils of my society. Surely, my complicity deepens if I benefit from current social arrangements so much that I largely acquiesce in the injustices they cause. These convictions lie behind my own insistence that living in society inevitably makes citizens participants in the horrors of the systemic evils that they spawn.[25]

Obviously, my point here is not to persuade readers of my controversial positions, but to provoke some of us to work harder on these tricky questions, to clarify the relations between individuals and the systems in which they are embedded, to specify the conditions under which it makes sense to speak of group action, and to sort out the different kinds of moral assessments appropriate for individual members in relation to the actions of their groups. Because these issues infect both assessments of our non-optimal predicament and traditional estimates of what God might do about it, our wrestling with evil cannot be over until that homework is done.

Taking the Metaphysical Size-Gap Seriously

Metaphysical Excellence: Most contemporary discussions of problems of evil take it for granted that the perfect goodness at stake is God's moral goodness. Following J. S. Mill, they dismiss allusions to God's metaphysical excellence as changing the subject. In medieval philosophical theology, it was the other way around. God is posited as the ultimate explainer, the independent source of the being, excellence, and action of everything else. When Aquinas comes quickly (in *Summa Theologica* I, q. 6) to Divine goodness, it is metaphysical excellence, ontological completeness that he has in mind. Scotus argues that the ultimate explainer is an infinite being, with infinite goodness and maximal excellence. Anselm, Aquinas, and Scotus all think divine justice follows from divine metaphysical excellence, from God's being all perfection per se.

Where problems of evil are concerned, it is important to reclaim the thesis that Godhead is maximal metaphysical excellence, because it makes clear that Christianity—like Platonism and Neoplatonism—have value capital—that is, infinite excellence itself—that neo-Humeans cannot share. I have urged that what God is, is incommensurate excellence; that apt relation to it is incommensurately good for us. Aptly relating us to the good that God is, is one way for God to be good to us. A lively sense of the infinity of divine excellence is—I have claimed—key to taking horrors with full moral seriousness while allowing that participation in them can be balanced off or defeated.

Above Reproach?

The divine essence is maximally excellent. But God is also living and active. Problems of evil wrestle with what the Creator does and does not do. At the book's beginning, Job and his friends share the conviction that God is above reproach, immune from criticism. Being above reproach is not a moral category, but part and parcel of the honor code, which counts people above reproach either because their personal strengths are so great that there can be no deficiencies in their performance, or because they have sufficient power to enforce their will on others. When Job dares to accuse God, he "sins with his lips."

Later medieval theology maintained that God, as the primal source of the being and well-being of everything else, is the ultimate patron. Since patrons have no obligations to take on or to service clients, God has no obligations to creatures and creatures have no rights against God. Divine justice is not a function of fulfilling obligations to others but of consummate propriety in filling the patron role. Sticking within the honor code, problems of evil would not disappear but relocate. When the condition and/or character of clients falls short of announced divine purposes and objectives, this raises questions about whether there is enough to God to follow through and deliver, and threatens to put God to shame.[26]

Like Job's friends, many who wrestle with problems of evil take the proposition that "God is above reproach" to be foundational. Many proceed to draw the valid inference that "if God is above reproach, then it is not the case that divine actions and policies are subject to moral censure." The temptation is to slide from "it is not the case that divine actions and policies are subject to moral censure" to "divine actions and policies and—for that matter—their consequences are morally justified and that by morally justifying reasons." After all, doesn't etymology tell us that theodicy is justifying the ways of God to human beings?

Unfortunately, this sort of slippery slope threatens morality by identifying whatever happens in the world including the worst evils (e.g., genocide, torture, slavery, and human trafficking) as morally justified and justifiable—a result that most (nonconsequentialist) moral theories would condemn as morally outrageous and absurd. Further temptations lurk in the form of idolatrous slippery slope applications. Many human institutions—the Church, tribe or nation, the family—pose as above reproach. The slide from "not susceptible of moral censure" to "all policies and practices morally justified" readily assures us that the Church was morally justified in covering up the sex scandals, that my tribe or nation is morally justified in writing off whatever collateral damage self-preservation and collective aggrandizement require, and that taboos against exposing child-abusing parents are morally justified by the importance of the institution of the family.

In my judgment, we face a forced choice. If we say that God is above reproach, we imply that divine behavior needs no justification, that it is inappropriate—Calvin might say, "impudent," that is to say, shameless, another category that belongs to the honor code—either to ask or to offer morally justifying reasons for God's permitting or causing the evils of this world. It is even inappropriate to imply that God has any morally justifying reasons beyond our ken. If God is above reproach, our wrestling with problems of evil needs to shift ground. If we say instead that divine policies are morally justified, that God has these or those or the other morally justifying reasons, then we imply that God is not to be reproached, not because God is above reproach but because God has satisfied the conditions for moral justification. Take your pick, but don't equivocate. It is morally dangerous to try to have it both ways.

Focusing on the Ethics of Personal Relationships

Mainstream Christian theology insists that divine agency is intelligent voluntary agency, personal agency in the contemporary sense. Analytic philosophers wrestling with problems of evil mostly take it for granted that to be personal is to share eligibility for moral evaluation and to be networked by rights and obligations to other persons.

In my books on evil, I have joined my favorite medieval theologians in denying that God has obligations to creatures. This move has the theoretical merit of appreciating how a personal God is not simply—as Kantian Allen Wood once quipped—one more rational agent on a par with others. The metaphysical size-gap prevents all persons from being peers. The relevant parameter is not physical size (as in Dr. Seuss' *Horton Hears a Who*[27]), but personal capacities. Stay within the domain of human beings, and compare the personal competencies of adults and infants. As much as parents hope their babies will become, they are certain that infants are not yet their peers. So also and immeasurably more so, divine and human persons. The divine essence is infinite; the divine intellect and will are infinite, too. Where personal capacities are concerned, an infinite gulf yawns between the human and the divine.

Denying that God has obligations to creatures has the further merit of freeing us to focus on other issues. It puts us in a position to concede right away what piety protests: "God didn't have an obligation to treat us otherwise. God was within divine rights in treating us this way." Those who insist that God does have such obligations feel forced to spend their energy defending God, arguing that evils do not prove that God has failed in divine obligations or violated our rights. This is such a difficult task, that—having accomplished it to their satisfaction—they understandably feel that their job is done.

For the sake of argument, let me put my counter contention this way: either God has obligations to created persons, or God does not. Whichever way, the negative verdict "it is not the case that God has failed in divine obligations or violated our rights" should not be enough to put our wrestling with evil to rest. The perichoretic model casts God in the roles of agency enabler, aiming for a friendly if lopsided partnership. The deepest issue raised by participation in the worst evils is not whether God has violated our rights, but whether God is for us, whether God can be trusted to be good to us, whether God after all hates us, whether God has abandoned us or simply doesn't care.

The categories of rights and obligations are defensive lines in the sand that must not be crossed if social life is to be tolerable and possible. Rape violates a child's rights, whether the rapist is a stranger or a relative. Parental incest is much worse, because it involves betrayal of trust by the very persons the child was supposed to be able to count on for protection and nurture. Imprisonment for drug trafficking is hell, however you got there. But the indignity digs deeper when the person who testifies against you is someone you counted as your best friend. What was so difficult for the Bible's Job was not simply the pain and suffering and material ruin, but rather that such treatment was culturally understood as proof of divine disfavor. The worst of it was not even his wrecked social standing and reputation. Job's bottom line was different. In railing against God, Job is calling God to account for not behaving as a faithful friend.

Horrendous evils are prima facie life ruinous. Even if God was within divine rights in permitting or producing them, there is the leftover question of whether and/or how God means to be good to us after the worst has already happened. John Bishop and Ken Perszyk have pressed a still deeper question: whether a God who set us up for horrors by creating us in a world like this has exhibited perfectly loving relationality toward us.[28] Notice that the issue here is not Plantinga's pastoral question of how it is psycho-spiritually possible for participants in the worst evils to hold on to their trust in God. Instead, Bishop and Perszyk raise the morally prior question of whether a God who sets us up for horrors by creating us in a world like this, is trustworthy, whether God's track record in putting us in harm's way and not rescuing us takes God out of the category of people to whom it is reasonable to entrust oneself as to a parent or intimate friend. Such questions take us to the heart of relationship ethics, to the ethics of abandonment and betrayal, forgiveness and reconciliation.

Perhaps some take relationship ethics to be a subdivision of the ethics of obligation or in any event analyze personal relationships in terms of moral duties. I am a theologian, not an ethical theorist. I have no wish to pontificate about the architecture of ethical theory. The point that I want to urge in closing is this: we should not finish wrestling with problems of evil until we have explanations of how God can still be good to those who participate in the worst evils, of how God can still be trusted to be for them even though the worst has already happened, of how reconciliation and intimacy with God can be reasonable for them. This means attending to the ethics of intimate relationships in ways that, up to now, discussions of evil in analytic philosophy have rarely done.

Notes

1. John Bishop and Ken Perszyk, "The Normatively Relativised Logical Argument from Evil," *International Journal of the Philosophy of Religion* 70, no. 2 (2011): 109–126; "Concepts of God and Problems of Evil," in *Alternative Concepts of God: Essays on the Metaphysics of the Divine*, ed. Andrei A. Buckareff and Yujin Nagasawa (Oxford: Oxford University Press, 2016), 106–27. See also Marilyn McCord Adams, *Horrendous Evils and the Goodness of God* (Ithaca, NY: Cornell University Press, 1999), 12–13.

2. Claudia Card, *The Atrocity Paradigm: A Theory of Evil* (Oxford: Oxford University Press, 2002), 6–7, 60–64.

3. See Adams, *Horrendous Evils*, 5–6, 88–128.

4. Such queries were raised by Philip Quinn and Eleonore Stump at various meetings of the American Philosophical Association. Katherin A. Rogers makes clear how appalled she is at my suggestions in "The Abolition of Sin: A Response to Adams in the Augustinian Tradition," *Faith and Philosophy* 19, no. 1 (2002), 69–84.

5. Card, *The Atrocity Paradigm*, 3–5, 20, 55.

6. Ibid., 16.

7. Ibid., 8.

8. John K. Roth, "A Theodicy of Protest," in *Encountering Evil*, ed. Stephen T. Davis (Atlanta: John Knox Press, 1981), 7–37.

9. D. Z. Phillips, *The Problem of Evil and the Problem of God* (London: SCM Press, 2004), 41–46.

10. Marilyn McCord Adams and Stewart Southerland, "Horrendous Evils and the Goodness of God," *Proceedings of the Aristotelian Society: Supplementary Issue* 63 (1989): 297–323.

11. The better to steep oneself in twentieth-century atrocities, see Jonathan Glover, *Humanity: A Moral History of the Twentieth Century* (New Haven, CT: Yale University Press, 2000).

12. Phillips, *The Problem of Evil*, 42–43.

13. Card, *The Atrocity Paradigm*, 28. Card thinks this is especially important where political policy is concerned. Card's point applies all the more where divine government of the world is concerned.

14. Card, *The Atrocity Paradigm*, 80–81.

15. Ibid., 60.

16. For a discussion of local virtues, see Robert Merrihew Adams, *A Theory of Virtue: Excellence in Being for the Good* (Oxford: Oxford University Press, 2006), 144–99. See also Kathleen Taylor, *Cruelty: Human Evil and the Human Brain* (Oxford: Oxford University Press, 2009).

17. See James Waller, *Becoming Evil: How Ordinary People Commit Genocide and Mass Killing*, 2nd ed. (Oxford: Oxford University Press, 2007).

18. Card, *The Atrocity Paradigm*, 5, 13, 18–20, 55.

19. Ruth Barcan Marcus, "Moral Dilemmas and Consistency," in *Modalities: Philosophical Essays* (Oxford: Oxford University Press, 1993), chap. 9, 125–141.

20. Marcus, "Moral Dilemmas and Consistency," 127, 136.

21. Marcus, "Moral Dilemmas and Consistency," 140.

22. See Marilyn McCord Adams, "Genuine Agency, Somehow Shared: The Holy Spirit and Other Gifts," in *Oxford Studies in Medieval Philosophy*, vol. 1, ed. Robert Pasnau (Oxford: Oxford University Press, 2013), 23–60.

23. For a fuller discussion of this approach, see Marilyn McCord Adams, *Christ and Horrors: The Coherence of Christology* (Cambridge: Cambridge University Press, 2006), 144–69.

24. See, for example, Reinhold Niebuhr, *Moral Man and Immoral Society: A Study in Ethics and Politics*, 2nd ed. (New York: Scribner's, 1960); Edward Farley, *Good and Evil: Interpreting a Human Condition* (Minneapolis: Fortress, 1990); Gustav Gutierrez, *A Theology of Liberation: History, Politics, and Salvation*, rev. ed., trans. Caridad Inda and John Eagleson (Maryknoll, NY: Orbis Books, 1988); Emilie M. Townes, *Womanist Ethics and the Cultural Production of Evil* (New York: Palgrave Macmillan, 2006); Iris Marion Young, *Justice and the Politics of Difference* (Princeton, NJ: Princeton University Press, 1990).

25. For a helpful discussion of these questions, see Gregory Mellema, "Collective Responsibility and Qualifying Actions," *Midwest Studies in Philosophy* 30, no. 1 (2006): 168–75. See also Robert Merrihew Adams, "Responsibility for Outcomes," *Harvard Review of Philosophy* 21 (2014): 4–17.

26. For a more detailed account, see Adams, *Horrendous Evils*, 106–28.

27. Dr. Seuss, *Horton Hears a Who!* (New York: Random House, 2008).

28. John Bishop, "How a Modest Fideism may Constrain Theistic Commitments: Exploring an Alternative to Classical Theism," *Philosophia* 35 no. 3–4 (2007) 35, 387–402; "Towards a Religiously Adequate Alternative to OmniGod Theism," *Sophia* 48, no. 4 (2009) 48, 419–433; John Bishop and Ken Perszyk, "The Normatively Relativised Logical Argument from Evil," *International Journal of the Philosophy of Religion* 70, 109–26; Bishop and Perszyk, "Concepts of God and Problems of Evil" (forthcoming).

2 Kant, Job, and the Problem of Evil

John Hare

In HIS BRIEF WORK "On the Miscarriage of All Philosophical Trials in Theodicy" (1791), Immanuel Kant uses the story of Job to examine the problem of evil.[1] This work is not well known in the contemporary discussion of the problem of evil, but it fits the context of the present volume because Kant uses the tools of his moral philosophy to shed light on what kind of theodicy we should look for and what kind we should not look for. Since the idea behind this volume is to look at the sophisticated tools of moral philosophy to see whether we can make progress in thinking about the problem of evil, it is surely a good idea to look at the tools given us by one of modernity's greatest practitioners.[2] "On the Miscarriage of All Philosophical Trials in Theodicy" shows us how to start a Kantian reflection of this kind. Kant locates the proper limits of theodicy within his overall systematic epistemology, a notoriously disputed territory. This chapter is an attempt to describe a Kantian "transcendental theodicy" and then to suggest how this project might be carried further by someone not committed to Kant's system as a whole.

"Miscarriage" has a structure similar to Kant's *Critique of Pure Reason*. In the preface to the second edition of the *Critique*, Kant says "I have found it necessary to deny knowledge in order to make room for faith."[3] He follows this with eight hundred dense pages describing the limits of human knowledge, which only extends (simplifying somewhat) as far as the possibility of human sense experience. Students who take courses in the first *Critique* are familiar with the pattern by which it takes so long to get through this negative agenda that there is no time left at the end of the semester for discussing what Kant sees as the fruit of all this hard work, namely the faith (*Glaube*) for which room has now been made. It is not until "The Canon of Pure Reason" at A795=B823 that we get the positive doctrine (freedom of the will, immortality of the soul, and the existence of God) and are told, "If, then, these three cardinal propositions are not at all necessary for our *knowing*, and yet are insistently recommended to us by our reason, their importance must really concern only the *practical*."[4] Kant goes on to say that reason in its practical employment requires us to believe that we are "in the realm of grace," (a Leibnizian phrase) "where every happiness awaits us as long as we do not ourselves limit our share of it through the unworthiness to be happy."[5]

"Miscarriage" also proceeds through an elaborate critique of nine forms of "philosophical theodicy" and ends with the affirmation, drawn from reflecting on God's words to Job out of the whirlwind, that "God thereby demonstrates an order and a maintenance of the whole which proclaim a wise creator, even though his ways, inscrutable to us, must at the same time remain hidden—indeed already in the physical order of things, and how much more in the connection of the latter with the moral order (which is all the more impenetrable to our reason)."[6] At the beginning of his concluding remark at the end of the work, Kant comments, "Theodicy, as has been shown here, does not have as much to do with a task in the interest of science [*Wissenschaft*, from *wissen*, "to know"] as, rather, with a matter of faith [*einer Glaubenssache*]."[7] This is the same contrast between knowledge and faith that Kant uses in the preface to the first *Critique*, when he says that acknowledging failure in the sphere of knowledge leads to success in the sphere of faith. Moreover, the term "*Glaubenssache*" in "Miscarriage" may pick up the opening of the work, in which Kant says that theodicy is "the defending of God's cause" (*die sache Gottes*). He there goes on to concede that this defending or championing of God's cause "*might* be at bottom no more than that of our presumptuous reason failing to recognize its limitations."[8] Kant here acknowledges that such presumption is characteristic of philosophical theodicy—an attempt at justifying the ways of God to human beings within the sphere of knowledge—and he compares it unfavorably with a different kind of theodicy which starts from an acknowledgment of human ignorance and lies within the sphere of faith. The first is, according to Kant, no more than self-deceptive illusion. The second kind we will return to at the end of this chapter.

The structural parallel between the first paragraph of "Miscarriage" and the first sentence of another work, *Religion within the Boundaries of Mere Reason*, is also illuminating: "So far as morality is based on the conception of the human being as one who is free but who also, just because of that, binds himself through his reason to unconditional laws, it is in need neither of the idea of another being above him in order that he recognize his duty, nor, that he observe it, of an incentive other than the law itself."[9] In both *Religion* and the first *Critique* it is easy to get the impression that Kant's project is entirely destructive from a theological point of view. In *Religion* Kant looks as though he is saying that since we *are* free, and we *do* bind ourselves to the law, we do *not* need the idea of God.[10] But at the beginning of the third paragraph of *Religion*, Kant says that morality inevitably leads to religion.[11] How can this be? The answer is that Kant thinks human beings are not merely free, not merely rational, but also creatures of sense and creatures of need, and we desire our happiness in everything else we desire. Kant wants to make the point that it is rationally unstable for humans, being the combination they are, to attempt to lead a morally good life without believing in God as the supersensible author of nature.

So also at the beginning of "Miscarriage" Kant at first appears to deny the validity of theodicy. He says that the would-be advocate of God has to prove one of three things: either (1) that there is nothing counter-purposive (against the proper order of things, *zweckwidrig*) in the world, or (2) that if there is any such thing, it is not an intended effect but the unavoidable consequence of the nature of things, or (3) that it is the intended effect not of God but merely of rational beings, that is humans or angels.[12] Kant goes on to show that none of these three can be proved. But, characteristically, his conclusion is not that there is no theodicy, but that there is no proof. There is no "theodicy proper," which would be the result of a philosophical trial, "yet we cannot deny the name 'theodicy' to the mere dismissal of all charges against divine wisdom . . . if this is a pronouncement of the same reason through which we form our concept of God—necessarily and prior to all experience—as a moral and wise being."[13] As in *Religion* and the first *Critique*, the reasoning through which we form our concept of God as moral sovereign of the world is practical rather than speculative reasoning.

In "Miscarriage" Kant starts by disallowing a strategy that might at first glance seem identical to the strategy he eventually adopts himself. We may not, he says, dismiss the complaints of reason about counter-purposiveness simply "through a decree of incompetency of the tribunal of human reason," by saying that God is supremely wise and therefore all doubts must be dismissed as groundless.[14] Kant uses a legal analogy here. We are not allowed to claim *exceptio fori*, "an exception to the court"; in other words, we may not claim that the court (human reason) is not competent to conduct the trial. Such a claim "would immediately explain away as groundless, *even without examination*, all doubts that might be raised against it."[15] It is one of Kant's conditions for sincerity, which he is going to praise in Job as a paradigm, that before we submit ourselves to some doctrine, we should "test all claims" against it. We are not allowed, as it were, to finesse the need for this examination by simply declaring from the outset that no such claim is allowed.

Kant then proceeds to the examination of the claims of whatever is counter-purposive in the world against the wisdom of the world's creator.[16] He distinguishes three kinds of counter-purposiveness. First is the absolutely counter-purposive, "or what cannot be condoned or desired either as end or means."[17] This, he says, is the morally counter-purposive, evil proper (sin). The second kind is the conditionally counter-purposive, "or what can indeed never coexist with the wisdom of a will as end, yet can do so as means." This is the physically counter-purposive, ill (pain).[18] The third kind is counter-purposiveness in the proportion of ill to evil. Kant is notoriously a retributivist. He thinks that justice requires a strict proportioning of penalty and crime, and therefore that a just world (run by a divine moral wisdom) would have to be a world in which "everyone gets his due."[19]

The attributes of the world sovereign against whom the charges are being made can be specified in terms of these three kinds of counter-purposiveness. The three roles of the divine sovereign are like the three roles of human sovereigns, namely the role of legislator (making the law), the role of executive (running the world in accordance with the law), and the role of judge (judging our compliance with the law). The connection with the three kinds of counter-purposiveness is that the divine lawgiver has to be holy, "in opposition to the moral evil in the world," the divine executive has to be benevolent, "in contrast with the countless ills and pains of the rational beings of the world," and the divine judge has to be just, "in comparison to the bad state which the disproportion between the impunity of the depraved and their crimes seems to indicate in the world."[20] In each case there is something we find in the world that presents a *prima facie* objection against one of the three attributes. Why would a holy God allow moral evil? Why would a benevolent God allow pain? Why would a just God allow impunity of the wicked?

Kant then proceeds to lay out three philosophical attempts to rebut each of these three charges. He says that all nine of them fail. This is the destructive part of his project. He allows that there may be in time other attempts, but he thinks he has collected the main ones current up to his day.[21] Let's call the three charges "the objection from Holiness," "the objection from Benevolence," and "the objection from Justice" (capitalizing the names of the virtues in order to make it clear that it is God's virtues that are the basis of each objection). In each case, the three proposed theodical responses to each charge are sequential, making a claim in the first response, and then withdrawing to the position that even if that first claim fails, there is a second one, and even if the second fails, there is a third.

The first charge is that there is an inconsistency between a holy God and the moral evil in the world. The first attempt at rebutting this charge is to deny that there is any moral evil in the world, understood as contravention of God's law. Moral law is human wisdom, goes the response, not divine. Kant explains this further by quoting from Ovid, "the ways of the most high are not our ways (*sunt superis sua iura*)" (those on high have their own laws), and he may be thinking also of Isaiah 55:8–9: "For my thoughts are not your thoughts, neither are your ways my ways, saith the Lord. For as the heavens are higher than the earth, so are my ways higher than your ways, and my thoughts than your thoughts." Kant is contemptuous of this reply, which "can be freely given over to the detestation of every human being who has the least feeling for morality."[22] He does not object to saying that God's wisdom is incommensurable with our own. In discussing Job's encounter with God in the whirlwind, Kant says of the wise creator, "even though his ways, inscrutable to us, must at the same time remain hidden."[23] But what he dislikes in this first response is that it denies that God is a moral legislator. Throughout his corpus, Kant insists that we have to recognize our duties as God's commands.[24]

Actually, Kant ties God's holiness more intimately to the moral law than he needs to for the purpose of rejecting the first response. We could hold, unlike Kant, that the moral law withers away in the next life, where we enter into the love that is between the persons of the Trinity.[25] We could still hold that in this life we have to regard our duties as God's commands. We would then not be able to escape the first objection legitimately by saying that God is not, after all, opposed to the evil that we do.

The second response to the objection from Holiness is that even if there is moral evil, it is not to be held against God, because it is a necessary consequence of our finitude; God cannot create finite beings like us without allowing this evil. Kant thinks that this response is incoherent. If the "evil" that we do is simply the result of our finitude, we are not to be blamed for it; but if we are not to be blamed for it, it is not really "moral evil." Kant is consistent in holding that moral evil is imputable to us; for example he says "but this subjective ground must, in turn, itself always be a deed of freedom (for otherwise the use or abuse of the human being's power of choice with respect to the moral law could not be imputed to him, nor could the good or evil in him be called 'moral')."[26] This second response is unacceptable because it denies our freedom.

The third response to the objection from Holiness is that even if there is moral evil, and it is "a guilt resting on the human being," no guilt may be ascribed to God, "for God has merely tolerated it for just causes as a deed of human beings: in no way has he condoned it, willed or promoted it."[27] It is hard to understand Kant here. One problem is that he gives no examples of what kind of "just cause" he has in mind. One suggestion, from Karl Ameriks (in a private communication), is that Kant has in mind something like the tortures by the Inquisition, which seem like something humans have done wrong (and for which they are therefore guilty) but which also contributed causally to something Kant might think good, such as the Reformation.[28] But even without this example, the point of the response will be: "God brings good out of what we do wrong, and it may be (for all we know) that this particular good requires the wrong. But our agency is limited, because our knowledge of the future is limited, and we do not have access to the relevant good. God can use what we do because God knows things that we do not. This is not to say that God condones or promotes the wrong as a means to the good, but that God brings good out of it." This response requires saying also that there is a sense in which God does not even will it, and Kant points out that there is a difficulty here in seeing how a sovereign being, a "sole creator of the world," could be seen to be merely permitting things the divine will does not want to permit. Putting aside for the moment (we will return to it) the medieval scholastic distinction between God's antecedent and consequent will, Kant does not accept this response, because it does not treat us as responsible for the wrong we do, and so treats it merely as an "ill" rather than an "evil." If our actions are merely, as he puts it, "the effect of a higher being" for that being's own purposes, we are left in the same situation as with the second response.[29] That is, we cannot be held responsible, because we are not being treated as free agents. But for Kant this is unacceptable.

To the objection from Benevolence, there are again three theodical responses. The first starts from the premise that everyone would rather live than be dead. Does not this mean that however bad our life becomes, we still think there is more good in it than ill? Even suicides, so goes the response, agree with this to the extent that they postpone their self-killing; and when they carry it out, they are no longer there to count as a counterexample. Kant objects to this response on the grounds that it seriously underestimates the amount of our suffering.[30] Every human being of sound mind who has thought long and hard about the value of life would decline, he says, "to play the game of life once more."[31] This is not just true if the offer is a repetition of the same circumstances, but even any other circumstances a person chooses, "provided they are not of a fairy world but of this earthly world of ours."[32]

The second response is to concede that our lives contain more pain than pleasure, but to say that this is inevitable given our nature as animals. Kant objects that there is no necessity for God to create us at all. If it is true that our lives are inevitably miserable as a whole, surely a benevolent God would have refrained from creating us?

The third response is the most interesting. It is a variant of the "soul-making theodicy" often associated with John Hick.[33] God has put us here, the response goes, for the sake of a future happiness; we are to become worthy of that future glory precisely through our struggle with adversities.[34] Kant's objection is that even if it *is possible* that God could not have prepared us for the next life without putting us through the kind of trial to which most succumb, and the kind of life that is unhappy even for the best of us, we have no reason from our experience or understanding to think this is true.[35] The point about most people succumbing is an important one. Soul-making theodicies point to second-order goods like bravery and compassion that are produced out of misery, and which require the misery for their production. But there are also second-order evils, like depression and cynicism and withdrawal, and these also are produced out of misery. If the second-order goods are great enough to justify the misery, should it not follow that the second-order evils are great enough to de-justify it? And if Kant were right that most people succumb, then the de-justification would outweigh the justification.

Kant admits that we can cut the Gordian knot here. Like Alexander refusing to undertake the complexity of untying the knot, we can simply appeal to God's wisdom, and say that since God is benevolent, we should accept that all these trials must be necessary. But this is not a *theodicy proper*; it does not give a reason that we can evaluate within the domain of knowledge, rather than simply appealing to faith.

Kant spends more time on the objection from Justice. The first standard response to the apparent injustice of the world is to say that the evils we do are justly punished by the torments of bad conscience. Kant does in fact, as we know from elsewhere, believe that even the most hardened criminal retains the "predisposition to the good" that responds to the moral law.[36] But in "Miscarriage" he objects that the depraved person, even if he still hears the voice of conscience, is not much bothered by it, and "if only he can escape the external floggings for his heinous deeds, laughs at the scrupulousness of the honest who inwardly plague themselves with self-inflicted rebukes."[37]

The second response to the objection from Justice is reminiscent of the third response to the objection from Benevolence. It concedes that we see apparent injustice in the world, and the wicked seem to prosper. But the response is that this apparent injustice is itself meant to produce virtue, and the final result is "a glorious moral melody."[38] In other words, the suffering produces the virtue. Kant's reply is that this might be acceptable if we could see this result. But in fact what we see is that the good person's suffering is not "so that his virtue should be pure, but because it was pure."[39] The virtue produces the suffering. Again, we could postulate a future life in which virtue and happiness go together, and we know that Kant does in fact say that immortality is one of the postulates of practical reason.[40] But again, this would not be a philosophical theodicy, which is an exercise of speculative reason, within the domain of knowledge.

This appeal to a future life is taken up in the final response. Suppose we concede that there is not a "glorious moral melody," as far as we can tell in this life. May we then not appeal to the next life? Here the answer again depends on the nature of theodicy. As quoted earlier, Kant thinks that a theodicy "proper" belongs in the domain of theoretical reason, and there are no grounds within this domain for the belief in a second life that would rectify the injustice of this life. Indeed, it would be rational to conclude, based on our knowledge of this world, that another life would very likely be under the same laws as this one, and thus "the agreement of human fate with a divine justice is just as little to be expected there as here."[41]

Before we apply all this to the story of Job, we need to trace the connection Kant draws between two kinds of wisdom ("artistic" and "moral") and two kinds of theodicy ("doctrinal" and "authentic"). "Artistic" wisdom is the wisdom in the running of the cosmos that we can determine within the limits of our knowledge, namely a mutual proportioning of means and ends within nature. In the first *Critique* Kant is, in fact, optimistic about the prospects of a "physico-teleological" argument for the existence of a "highest architect of the world," though he does not think we can prove within the theoretical use of reason the existence of a "creator of the world" who would be "an all-sufficient original being."[42] "Moral" wisdom is the wisdom that governs the cosmos under moral law, and it is not accessible to our intuition.

Unfortunately we have no concept (in Kant's technical sense, i.e., within the limits of the human understanding under space and time) of how in the sensible world these two wisdoms are unified. We have no insight into how the supersensible (intelligible) world grounds the sensible world. The best we can reach is a *negative* wisdom of our own, which tells us that we do not know that there is no such unity and no such grounding. This negative wisdom is important because if we *did* know that there was no such unity and no such grounding, we could not legitimately believe in such postulates. Kant argues, as he does in all three *Critiques,* that in the absence of a veto from theoretical reason we may—and indeed we must—believe in this unity on grounds given by our practical reason.

The distinction between the two kinds of theodicy is that "doctrinal" theodicy is a philosophical inference within speculative reason from the utterances of the legislator (here understood as God's created world, since God creates by "speaking") to the legislator's will. Doctrinal theodicy thus argues from our access to God's *artistic* wisdom. By contrast, an "authentic" theodicy is made by the legislator himself. Kant understands the dismissal by practical reason of objections against the divine wisdom as "a divine decree," and so as issuing from God himself.[43] His reasoning can be spelled out as follows. He thinks this dismissal is a pronouncement of the same reason by which we form our notion of God as a moral and wise being. This is reason in its practical and not in its speculative employment. This reason legislates commands absolutely (it gives us a categorical imperative), and it can be considered the voice of God "through which he gives meaning to the letter of his creation." To put this in another way, the idea is that morality itself both tells us how we are to live and interprets the world in which that demand is to be carried out, by postulating that this world is run by a being who has the purpose of the highest good, the end that morality itself gives to us. Authentic theodicy argues from our postulation of a God with *moral* wisdom.

Kant concedes that there is a combination here that goes beyond our understanding. "For to be a creature and, as a natural being, merely the result of the will of the creator; yet to be capable of responsibility as a freely acting being (one which has a will independent of external influence and possibly opposed to the latter in a variety of ways); but again, to consider one's own deed at the same time also as the effect of a higher being—this is a combination of concepts which we must indeed think together in the idea of a world and of a highest good, but which can be intuited only by one who penetrates to the cognition of the supersensible (intelligible) world and sees the manner in which this grounds the sensible world."[44] Kant is a compatibilist about human freedom and physical causation, but a compatibilist of a rather odd kind. Most compatibilists are reductive, reducing our freedom to our desires and beliefs ordered in a certain way. Kant insists that our will is free to choose what is right, regardless of what we desire. But he also holds that our freedom is compatible with our actions being the effect of God's will, although we cannot penetrate into how this combination is possible, or how the sensible world is grounded in the supersensible. We humans do not have the kind of intuition required for this penetration—only God has it.

Kant finds authentic theodicy expressed allegorically in the story of Job. Job was, so the Bible tells us, "healthy, well-to-do, free, master over others whom he can make happy, surrounded by a happy family, among beloved friends—and on top of all of this (what is most important) at peace with himself in a good conscience."[45] This list of goods reveals Kant's own priorities. Making others happy and making oneself morally good is itself what he calls elsewhere "the matter of morality."[46] Then all these goods except for the crucial last one are snatched from Job, and he also has to suffer the "consolation" of his friends. Kant's main purpose is to distinguish the theodicies implicit in the supposed comfort given by Job's friends and in Job himself, as he is addressed by the voice from the whirlwind. The friends declare that Job's ills come from God's justice, as so many punishments for crimes committed. They cannot actually point to any such crimes, but they claim to know a priori that there must be some, for otherwise it would be impossible for God to punish Job in this way. Job protests his innocence, though he admits that he is a fragile creature, liable to error as all humans are. He says that he does not understand why God has done this, but that it is an unconditional divine decision, and "He has decided. He does as he wills."[47]

Kant contrasts the spirit of the two sides in this dispute. The friends speak as if they thought they could ingratiate themselves with God by their piety, or as if gaining God's favor were more important to them than the truth. They assert things where they have no insight, and pretend to a certainty that they cannot actually have. Job rebukes them for secretly wanting to flatter God into favor in this way.[48] He himself is frank about his lack of understanding, and he prays to God not to hide his face. Even so, "though he slay me, yet will I trust in him."[49] And then God does reveal himself, and deigns to lay before Job's eyes "the wisdom of his creation, especially its inscrutability."[50]

Strikingly, God reveals not just glimpses of the beautiful side of creation, but also harmful and fearsome things. One thinks of Rudolf Otto and the *mysterium* which is *fascinans* but also *tremendum*.[51] God shows Job things that appear to be purposive for their own sake but counter-purposive to other things, including human beings, and "incompatible with a universal plan established with goodness and wisdom." Kant does not indicate which "fearsome" things he has in mind, but he is surely referring to the descriptions of Behemoth and Leviathan in Job 40–41. What God reveals is something double, both an order and maintenance of the whole, and an inscrutability or impenetrability to our reason. This combination is a theme that again appears elsewhere in Kant. God is concerned, he supposes, to preserve our freedom. It may be providential that we cannot see God or prove God's existence with speculative reason; for "God and eternity with their awful majesty would stand unceasingly before our eyes," and we would end up conforming to the moral law from hope or fear, not from duty. It would be like a puppet show, in which "everything would gesticulate well but there would be no life in the figures." It is better that practical reason gives us our "first view into the realm of the supersensible, though only with weak glances."[52]

Job responds to the revelation from the whirlwind by conceding that he had spoken about things that were too high for him and that he did not understand (even though, as Kant points out, he did much better in this respect than his friends). In the final comparison, Job's friends might seem more pious, and Kant sarcastically notes that most ecclesiastical bodies in his time would applaud them.[53] But Job himself is the truly faithful one. He "did not found his morality on faith, but his faith on morality."[54] There is an echo here of the end of *Religion within the Boundaries of Mere Reason*: "the right way to advance is not from grace to virtue but rather from virtue to grace."[55] Kant is holding up for our admiration a "religion of good life conduct." His polemic is against people who think they can move from what they know about God independently of their moral commitments to a conclusion about what God requires of them.

Kant ends "Miscarriage" with a concluding remark about sincerity, which offers us a glimpse of Kant's view of conscience. But it is not directly related to our present purpose of describing Kant's view of the proper limits of theodicy. What can we keep from Kant's account even if we do not accept his overall systematic epistemology? Many of Kant's successors could not accept the view that we experience a world of "*phemonena*," of "things that appear," grounded somehow in a world of "*noumena*," of "things in themselves." Kant himself thought that this view was required by reason, but we may think of it instead as a translation of a metaphysical picture Kant inherited from Christianity and the various attempts in Christian history to achieve a synthesis with the various metaphysical pictures of Greek antiquity. We find this idea of a translation in Kant's *Religion* (though not the term 'translation'), where he proposes we think of revelation as two concentric circles, with the outer area of the larger circle representing historical revelation (the revelation to particular people at particular times and places) and the inside circle representing the revelation to reason (supposedly to all people at all times and places). In *Religion* Kant proposes to translate the central items of Christian doctrine from the outside circle into the language of the inside circle, using the moral concepts.[56]

But suppose we do not have access to a universal revelation to reason; there could still be translation into the language of morality, even if we concede that there may be different moralities for different people with different starting points. We can think of the epistemology here the same way. We need not suppose we have access to some "reason" that is neutral between Christian theism and its various competitors and universal to all people. We can still try to translate the biblical faith into language used by people outside our faith traditions, even though we concede that there may be different views of our epistemic position depending on our different starting points. If we start with a creator God, transcendent to creation, we will almost inevitably end up with some form of what Kant calls the distinction between "*noumena*" and "*phenomena*," at least with respect to our knowledge of God (God in Godself, *Deus in se,* as opposed to God in relation to us, *Deus pro nobis*). We will also have to form some view about the relation of this God to morality. Kant himself, at least in *The Critique of Practical Reason*, gives up the attempt to justify moral law's claim on us and proposes instead to simply start from the "fact of reason" that we are under the moral law.[57] He does not justify the fact of reason by saying that God gives us the law, but he does say that we should recognize our duties as God's commands. In "Miscarriage" he says that God "binds" us "under duty to obey him."[58] But it does not take a narrowly Kantian metaphysics or a narrowly Kantian morality to say that God gives us the moral law *and* runs the universe so that it makes sense for us to try to live by it.

To be sure, Kant tries to tie the Christian faith too close to morality (though he does not *reduce* the first to the second). He presents the next life as one in which we progress toward, though we never reach, holiness, and his conception of holiness is "the complete conformity of dispositions with the moral law."[59] I think we should say, rather, that most of what we know as the moral law will wither away. There will no longer be a context for prohibitions on lying, adultery, murder, and so on. Our relation to God there, and I think here in embryo, is one of union through knowledge and love, entering into the love that is between the persons of the Trinity (as Scotus says, *condiligentes*). Kant is wary of the kind of enthusiasm or fanaticism that is generated, in his view, by this kind of mystical language. Even if we disagree with him about this, however, we may still want to say that God gives us the moral law by command. This is all we need for what I call somewhat pretentiously a "transcendental" response to the problem of evil, which respects severe limits on our knowledge at least with respect to our knowledge of God.[60]

The central idea is that if we accept that we are under the moral law, and that God gives us this law, then we also have to believe that creation is the kind of place in which the attempt to live by the moral law makes sense.[61] The historical revelation already gives us what Kant calls "the moral concept of God," which derives from God's holiness as lawgiver, God's benevolence as ruler (preserver), and God's justice as judge.[62] Kant does not give a full argument in "Miscarriage" that these three sovereign roles have to be played by a single being.[63] They need not be by human sovereigns. All that is necessary for his argument is that the same law is being legislated, is the template for administration, and is the standard for judgment. But if we grant that it is the same being, this picture gives us something to say about the evil in the world, in the broad sense in which evil encompasses what Kant calls "ill" in addition to "evil proper."

We will not get a theodicy in the sense of God's reason for allowing some particular ill (such as Job's). That would extend beyond the proper limits of our knowledge, even if we think we know more than Kant thinks we know. The distinction between God in Godself and God in relation to us allows us to say that we do not have much "insight" into God's own mind except to the extent God reveals that to us, even if we are more generous than Kant about the continued possibilities of individuals receiving special revelation. But we will get a framework for thinking about the limits of the evil (in the broad sense) that God allows.

We can make another distinction, following the medieval scholastics, between God's antecedent and consequent will.[64] The consequent disposing will, Ockham says, is that "by which God wills efficaciously in positing something in being." But in antecedently willing from eternity that a given created will should act in a certain way, God does not determine the created will to act in that way. When Adam ate the apple, he was frustrating God's antecedent will, even though he was fulfilling God's consequent will. We might say, then, that evil in the narrow sense, or sin, is never permitted by God with the antecedent will, whereas ill can sometimes be so permitted. We can then ask whether, on the premise of our commitment to morality, we can conclude any limits on how much ill is permitted by God's antecedent will.

The transcendental response to the problem of evil proposes that there are limits produced by the requirement that the moral life make sense in the creation as it is established and maintained by the divine sovereign. What these limits might be can be illuminated by a couple of thought experiments. Suppose the gods set us up, as the Epicureans perhaps believed, for their own entertainment, rather as we now watch the soaps on television. Perhaps they gave us a moral sense because that made our subsequent agonizing more entertaining. But then the relationship between our moral striving and its results is determined by what makes an interesting plotline, not by our intentions. Or suppose there is an evil demon rather like the one Descartes imagines in the *Meditations*, except that this demon is interested in mucking up our moral lives instead of our cognitive lives. The demon arranges things so that when we try to do good, we actually produce harm roughly three quarters of the time. Surely in this case, as in the previous one, our commitment to morality would become rationally unstable.

The purpose of these thought experiments is to introduce the idea that if we accept Kant's principle that "ought implies can," we are committed to believing in two kinds of limit to evil (in the broad sense). We have to be able to will what is morally good and we have to be able to accomplish it reasonably often. These are limits on evil because the human heart cannot be so corrupt that it is incapable, given the (divine and human) assistance available, of what Kant calls a "revolution" that puts the morally good first and our own happiness second.[65] And the world cannot be so mired in evil that we cannot usually produce good even when we will it. These two limits on evil come from a consideration of God's legislative and executive roles.

Finally (but I think less securely), there is a third kind of limit that results from picturing God's role as judge. Perhaps Kant's retributivism is too strict here, when he claims we have to believe in the real possibility of the highest good, defined as "happiness . . . in exact proportion with the morality of the rational beings who are thereby rendered worthy of it."[66] Perhaps the implicit quantification is inappropriate. Still, if we are to believe ourselves accountable to the standard, we have to believe that it is the standard that is in fact operative. I cannot here get into theological questions about atonement, and the relation of God's justice and God's mercy. I have written about this elsewhere.[67] If we believe that how things ought to be is sustained by how things actually are over the whole span of creation, the commitment to morality will have implications about the final distribution of good and ill. Kant thinks immortality is, like the existence of God, a postulate of practical reason. His reason is that we seem not to be finished in our progress toward holiness when we die, and so not to be justly given eternal life with God.

We can add some thoughts from Marilyn Adams's chapter in support of this postulate. What she calls "horrendous evil" causes damage to our lives that justice would repair or defeat, and if we do not see justice in this life, we can hope for it in the next. Stephen Wykstra's chapter also connects in the following way. Kant stresses the hiddenness of God within the theoretical use of reason. But he also stresses that we can, so to speak, get inside God's mind at least to the extent (with "weak glances") that we have what he calls a "moral" conception of God. So we have what Wykstra calls "important access to sorts of goods that—jointly— both God passionately cares about and that God passionately wants us also to care about." Kant regards what he calls "the highest good" as a good of this kind.

These points about God's three roles are just a beginning of what a transcendental theodicy might look like, and all of them require more work. But this is a fruitful and currently underexamined strategy for thinking about the problem of evil.[68]

Notes

1. "On the Miscarriage of All Philosophical Trials in Theodicy," in *Religion and Rational Theology, The Cambridge Edition of the Works of Immanuel Kant*, trans. Allen W. Wood and George di Giovanni (Cambridge: Cambridge University Press, 1996), 19–37. Referred to as "Miscarriage," and abbreviated as *M*, for the German *Misslingen* ("miscarriage" or "failure"). Other translations of Kant from the Cambridge Edition include "Critique of Pure Reason" [KrV], trans. Paul Guyer and Allen W. Wood (Cambridge: Cambridge University Press,

1998); "Critique of Practical Reason," [KpV] and "The Metaphysics of Morals" [MdS], in *Practical Philosophy*, trans. and ed. Mary J. Gregor (Cambridge: Cambridge University Press, 1996); "Religion within the Boundaries of Mere Reason" [Rel], in *Religion and Rational Theology. Critique of Judgment* [KU] is translated by Werner S. Pluhar (Indianapolis: Hackett, 1987).

2. Kant is not "contemporary moral theory," as the title of this book prescribes. However, much contemporary theory is Kantian, and this whole family needs to be represented in an account of how moral theory should now be brought to bear on the problem of evil.

3. KrV, Bxxx.

4. KrV, A800=B828.

5. Ibid., A812=B840. In comments on this chapter, Jim Sterba, whose moral philosophy is broadly Kantian, professes himself unable to see why the justification or motivation for a morally good life should depend in any way on Kant's postulates of God and an afterlife where happiness is in proportion to virtue. Indeed he thinks that if I am motivated by the thought that God will make me happy if I do my duty, this undermines moral motivation. But Kant's point is that morality requires me to care for the happiness and the virtue of all those I affect by my action and those in relevantly similar circumstances to them and to me, and I therefore have to be able to believe that this combination of virtue and happiness is really (and not merely logically) possible for all of us. A defense of this argument would take me beyond the limits of this chapter. I have treated this matter a number of times elsewhere. See John E. Hare, *God and Morality* (Oxford: Blackwell, 2007), chap. 3, and Hare, *The Moral Gap: Kantian Ethics, Human Limits, and God's Assistance* (Oxford: Oxford University Press, 1996), chap. 3.

6. *M*, 8:266.

7. Ibid., 267.

8. Ibid., 255, emphasis added.

9. Rel, 6:3.

10. Merold Westphal takes this view in "Commanded Love and Moral Autonomy: The Kierkegaard-Habermas Debate," *Kierkegaard Studies*, 1998, 1–22.

11. Rel, 6:6.

12. *M*, 8:255.

13. Ibid., 264, emphasis on "proper" added.

14. Ibid., 256.

15. Ibid., 256, emphasis added.

16. Kant distinguishes here between moral wisdom and artistic wisdom. Artistic wisdom is displayed in the marvelous proportioning by which "means and ends reciprocally produce one another, as in organic bodies." But we are not entitled to move from this to moral wisdom, which has to be demonstrated entirely a priori.

17. *M*, 8:256.

18. The German for "evil proper" is *das eigentliche Böse*, and for "ill" is *Übel*.

19. *M*, 8:257.

20. Ibid.

21. Ibid., 263. The English translation of this passage gets the punctuation wrong, and this distorts the logic. In the first edition of *Religion within the Boundaries of Mere Reason: And Other Writings*, ed. Robert M. Adams (Cambridge: Cambridge University Press, 1999), a colon instead of a comma is put after "wisdom" and then, immediately afterward, a "for" is inserted before "then." I suspect that the comma after "undecided" needs to be put back in place, instead of a semicolon; there is a comma after *unentschieden* in the German.

22. Ibid., 258.

23. Ibid., 266.

24. See, for example, Rel 6:154; MdS 6:487. But there are many places where Kant says this. As to the complex question of whether Kant means the talk about God within practical reason to be regulative or constitutive, see Hare, "Kant on Conscience," in *Challenges to Moral and Religious Belief*, ed. Michael Bergmann (Oxford: Oxford University Press, 2014), 101–18. My view is that there are both regulative and constitutive uses within practical reason, and that Kant intends us to link up the first with the second.

25. See Hare, *God and Morality*, 105–11.

26. Rel, 6:21.

27. *M*, 8:259.

28. See Rel 6:186–87. An alternative suggestion is that the just cause is God's glory. See John Calvin, *Concerning the Eternal Predestination of God*, trans. J. K. S. Reid (Cambridge: James Clarke, 1961), 119: "In all [God's] works, the Lord has the reason of [God's] own glory." See also Kant, MdS 6:490: "It would make God's right itself, located in his *glory*, the end."

29. *M*, 8:264.

30. Susan Shell, *Kant and the Limits of Autonomy* (Cambridge, MA: Harvard University Press, 2009), 108. Shell shows that Kant is convinced by Verri that pain inevitably exceeds pleasure in human life. But this does not mean that life is given its value by the proportion of pleasure to pain in it.

31. *M*, 8:259.

32. Is Kant right about this? I do not know what most people would say in answer to such a hypothetical offer, but surely if we thought that there was too much misery to make another life on this Earth a good idea, we would not have children. Even if it is true that we would not repeat a life, this may have more to do with a sense that one life is enough than a sense that life contains more pain than pleasure.

33. John Hick, *Evil and the God of Love* (New York: Harper & Row, 1966).

34. *M*, 8:260.

35. Ibid., 260. Kant says, "This can be pretended, but in no way can there be insight into it."

36. Rel, 6:21: "that he holds this ground *qua* human, universally."

37. *M*, 8:261.

38. Ibid.

39. Ibid., 262.

40. See my earlier remarks about "The Canon of Pure Reason" in the first *Critique*, A795=B823. In our present text Kant says that this postulate would be a "decree of morally believing reason."

41. *M*, 8:262.

42. KrV, A627=B655. Kant is less optimistic in the third *Critique* (e.g., 5:453–54). He emphasizes there that we get from the moral argument a constitutive principle and from theoretical reason only a regulative one.

43. *M*, 8:264.

44. Ibid., 263–64.

45. Ibid., 265.

46. MdS, 6;385–88, 398.

47. *Job*, 23:13.

48. *M*, 8:266. See *Job*, 13:7–11, 16.

49. Ibid., 13:15.

50. *M*, 8:266.

51. Rudolf Otto, *The Idea of the Holy: An Inquiry into the Non-Rational Factor in the Idea of the Divine and Its Relation to the Rational,* trans. John W. Harvey (Oxford: Oxford University Press, 1950), 12–40.

52. KpV, 5:147.

53. "One alone excepted," he says, and he means the Berlin censors who retained their liberal policies even under the comparatively reactionary regime of Frederick William II.

54. *M*, 8:267.

55. Rel, 6:202.

56. Rel, 6:12.

57. KpV, 5:31–33.

58. *M*, 8:258.

59. KpV, 5:122.

60. I use the term "transcendental" because this response derives from reflection on the conditions of possibility for the moral life.

61. There is a version of this view in R. M. Hare's contribution to the so-called University Discussion, and in his paper "The Simple Believer," in *Essays on Religion and Education* (Oxford: Clarendon Press, 1992), 1–36 and 37–39. In the first of these, he talks about the *blik* or attitude about the world which makes me put my confidence "in my own continued well-being (in some sense of that word that I may not now fully understand) if I continue to do what is right according to my lights; in the general likelihood of people like Hitler coming to a bad end. But perhaps a formulation less inadequate than most is to be found in Psalm 75: 'The earth is weak and all the inhabiters thereof: I bear up the pillars of it'" (38).

62. *M*, 8:257. At MdS, 6:489 Kant makes the qualification, like Scotus, that we cannot strictly think of God's justice to us because justice is a reciprocal relation, and we cannot wrong God. See Scotus, *Ordinatio* IV, dist. 46, in *Duns Scotus on the Will and Morality*, ed. William A. Frank, trans. Allan B. Wolter (Washington: Catholic University of America Press, 1986), 183–91).

63. There is a partial argument at *M*, 8:257–58, "Justice indeed presupposes the benevolence of the legislator (for if his will were not directed to the well-being of his subjects, neither could he bind them under duty to obey him)."

64. Ockham, *Ordinatio* d.46, q.1, in *Opera Philosophica et Theologica*, ed. Juvenal Lalor, Stephen Brown, Gedeon Gál, Angelo Gambatese, and Michael Meilach (The Franciscan Institute, 1967–). Ockham is not a compatibilist, and in particular he does not accept the kind of compatibilism I earlier attributed to Kant. Kant is accordingly worried about the notion of God's permitting what God does not want to happen.

65. Rel, 6:47.

66. KrV, A814=B842, emphasis added.

67. Hare, *The Moral Gap*, chap. 8–10.

68. I am grateful to Karl Ameriks for extensive comments on an earlier draft of this paper.

3 Good Persons, Good Aims, and the Problem of Evil

Linda Zagzebski

A Metaethical Assumption in the Argument from Evil

Standard formulations of the argument from evil claim that an omnipotent being who is perfectly good would not permit, or probably would not permit, the
vast quantity and severity of evil in the world. These arguments almost always
have an implied assumption about the motivational structure of a good being.
J. L. Mackie, Michal Tooley, and William Rowe provide examples of the kind of
premise that reveals this assumption:

> 1a. A good being always eliminates evil as far as it can.[1]
> 1b. If God is morally perfect, God has the desire to eliminate all evil.[2]
> 1c. An omniscient, wholly good being would prevent the occurrence of any in-
> tense suffering it could, unless it could not do so without thereby losing
> some greater good or permitting some evil equally bad or worse.[3]

Although there are some differences among these premises, they all affirm a
connection between being a good person and acting with the aim of eliminating
evil.[4] Since the aim of preventing evil is almost always connected with the aim
of producing good, an initial formulation of the implied assumption is the
following:

> 2. A good person aims at producing good and preventing evil.

Michael Tooley's premise (1b) mentions desires rather than aims, but it is clear
from his version of the argument that he thinks of a desire to do x as something
that is sufficient to get a person to attempt to do x, so we may take it that Tooley
would accept (2).[5]

William Rowe's version (1c) specifies intense suffering as an example of the
kind of evil a good being would aim to prevent. Perhaps Rowe would be willing
to claim that a good being would aim to prevent suffering whether or not it comes
under the category of evil, and that possibility suggests that suffering and evil
have different conceptual connections to the motives of good persons. I believe

that the problem of suffering is a distinct and more difficult problem than the problem of evil, but for this chapter, I assume the most straightforward interpretation of (1c), according to which (1c) refers to suffering *qua* evil. So understood, (1c) implies (2).[6]

John Mackie's premise (1a) goes further than (2), stating that a good being always acts in a way that prevents or eliminates evil as long as it has sufficient power, but presumably Mackie believes that a good being aims at doing what it does, and so Mackie assumes (2). These days few writers on evil would go as far as (1a) as it is commonly recognized by all sides that a good being need not always prevent evils because there can be morally justifiable reasons to permit them. For instance, if there are evils that are outweighed by goods that cannot be obtained without permitting the evils, permitting those evils is not only compatible with (2), but follows from it. Rowe's version of the premise in (1c) acknowledges that explicitly. A well-known candidate for this category is the proposal that the good of free will outweighs all the evils that are produced through the exercise of free will. There are other possibilities, but in each case, if the proposed morally justifying reason for evil is the fact that some good states of affairs cannot be obtained without permitting evil, then (2) is assumed. Consequently, there is essentially no difference among the arguments of Mackie, Tooley, and Rowe with regard to their assumption of (2). Indeed, skeptical theists responding to the problem of evil typically assume (2) as well.[7]

Thesis (2) might appear innocuous because all it says explicitly is that two properties go together: the property of being a good person, and the property of aiming at producing good states of affairs and eliminating evil states of affairs. A being who has the first property has the second. But (2) raises a number of questions because good persons do much more than aim at producing good and preventing evil. Among other things, good persons attempt to *be* good persons and to *do* good acts, or at least to avoid evil acts, and the connection between being a good person and aiming to produce good and eliminate evil is not obvious. It is even possible that there can be a conflict between being a good person—having a good will and good motives—and aiming to do acts that have good consequences. A good person might aim to perform acts that have a certain character rather than to produce certain consequences, or a good person might act in a way that expresses a quality or state such as love, without aiming at producing good in the outcome. This means that we should not accept (2) until the connections among a good person, good acts, and good aims have been clarified.

But even if (2) is true, that does not tell us anything about why or how the property of being a good person is connected to the property of producing good and eliminating evil. If one property is more basic than the other, (2) does not tell us that. Here are two opposing possibilities, both of which are compatible with (2):

> 2a. A condition for being a good person is aiming at producing good states of affairs and preventing evil states of affairs.
>
> 2b. A condition for something being a good state of affairs and something else an evil state of affairs is that a good person aims at producing the former and preventing the latter.

The difference between (2a) and (2b) is striking, even though both are compatible with the thesis that a good person aims at bringing about good and preventing evil. According to (2a), aiming to eliminate evil is a more basic property than being a good person. The possession of the property of aiming to eliminate evil is a condition for the possession of the property of being a good person. But according to (2b), a good person aims to produce good and eliminate evil because what counts as producing good and eliminating evil is just what good persons aim to do. The property of being a good person is more basic than the property of aiming to eliminate evil.

To bring out the difference, consider this analogy. Moral philosophers of different kinds might affirm the following:

> 3. Virtuous persons act rightly.

But (3) is compatible with two very different views on the relationship between virtue and right acting:

> 3a. Virtuous persons are persons who act rightly.
> 3b. Right acts are acts that virtuous persons do.

(3a) makes the possession of the property of being virtuous derivative from the property of performing right acts. A right act is the more basic property. Right acts are determinable in advance of the determination of the virtuous persons. In contrast, (3b) makes the possession of the property of performing right acts derivative from the property of being a virtuous person. Being a virtuous person is the more basic property. What the right acts are depends on a prior determination of the virtuous persons.

Similarly, we could affirm (2) because we think (2a) is true. We might think that one of the things that makes a person good is that that person aims at eliminating evil states of affairs. Evil states of affairs can be determined in advance, and being a good person depends on having the right relation to those states of affairs. Alternatively, we could affirm (2) because we think (2b) is true. We might think that what makes an aim the aim of eliminating evil is that it is an aim to eliminate what good persons aim to eliminate. The goodness of persons is determinable in advance, and what makes a state of affairs evil is its relation to good persons.

(2a) and (2b) are by no means the only ways good personhood and the aim of eliminating evil can be connected in a way that is compatible with (2). The goodness of persons and the goodness or evil of the states of affairs at which persons aim could each be connected with some third thing, the goodness of which is more basic than either persons or states of affairs, such as good acts. Another possibility is that there is a general correlation between being a good person and having certain aims, with no deep connection between them at all (like the connection Jane Austen thought obtained between being virtuous and living in the country). There are many other possibilities that could explain the putative truth of (2).

Typical proponents of the argument from evil, as well as most of its attackers, assume (2) in the sense of (2a). That may not be explicitly stated, but it is indicated by the structure of standard arguments in which the hypothesis under attack is that there is a God who is perfectly good. Assuming that God is omnipotent, the apparent fact that God does not act with the aim of eliminating evil is taken to be grounds for retracting the hypothesis that God is perfectly good. In the dialectic of the argument, the evil of certain states of affairs comes first. The goodness of a person depends on that person aiming to eliminate these states of affairs. So well-known forms of the argument, including the arguments from Mackie, Tooley, and Rowe, proceed roughly as follows:

4. There are certain evils in the world, the evil of which is determinable independently of the goodness or evil of persons.
5. A condition for being a perfectly good person is that that person aims at preventing those evils in a way that is compatible with also aiming at producing good.
6. God apparently does not aim at preventing those evils.

(5) immediately entails (2a).

Notice that the argument from evil does not get off the ground if (2b) is used instead. With (2b), the apparent fact that a perfectly good God permits the states of affairs of this world would not be grounds for retracting the hypothesis that God is good. Rather, it would be grounds for retracting the judgment that those states of affairs are evil. Alternatively, if (2) is interpreted as merely asserting a correlation between the goodness of a being and the goodness of the states of affairs at which that being aims, then the existence of evil would be taken to be disconfirming evidence of that correlation. On another interpretation mentioned above, good persons and aims to prevent evils are connected by their connection to something else, such as good acts. With that interpretation, the argument clearly would need to be filled out with additional premises connecting the goodness of acts to good persons, on the one side, and to good aims, on the other.

So far these arguments from evil assume that a good person aims to produce good and eliminate evil, and what that typically means is (2a): a condition for being a good person is that that person aims at producing good states of affairs and preventing evil ones. The kind of condition intended in (2a) is most naturally interpreted as a metaphysical condition, but it might also be interpreted as epistemic. (2a) is problematic on both interpretations.

The Goodness of Persons and Their Aims: The Metaphysical Interpretation

The Goodness of Persons and the Pauline Principle

The advocate of the argument from evil presumably knows that theists believe there are firm grounds for the judgment that God is perfectly good; in fact, there is a tradition that identifies God with goodness itself. A person (or trinity of persons) is the exemplar of goodness. So even if (2b) is not true in general, it is much more plausible when the person in question is God. The aims of God could be the standard for what counts as good aims.[8] Nonetheless, the proponent of the argument says that the existence of evil shows that God fails (or probably fails) to satisfy a necessary condition for being good. As noted, the argument must assume that (2) is true in the sense of (2a). The property of being an evil state of affairs precedes—in a sense to be determined— the goodness of God. That is, whether or not it turns out that God is good, certain states of affairs are evil. A good person is (among other things) a person who aims at eliminating those states of affairs, and if God does not aim at eliminating those states of affairs, then God is not good, but those states of affairs are nonetheless evil.

Let us begin by taking (2a) in its most straightforward sense as a metaphysical claim about the relationship between the moral properties of persons and the good or evil of states of affairs. Interpreted this way, the metaphysical thesis implied by (2a) is the following:

7. The goodness or badness of persons derives from the goodness or badness of the states of affairs they aim to bring about or prevent.

According to (7), moral goodness or badness flows backward from the moral properties of states of affairs to the moral properties of the aims to bring about or prevent those states of affairs, and from there to the moral properties of the persons who have those aims as follows:

Persons ← aims ← states of affairs

Consequentialism is a familiar model of this way value is transferred. In a consequentialist value structure, the only things intrinsically good or bad are states of affairs of a certain kind. The moral properties of acts are derivative from the goodness or badness of the states of affairs to which those acts lead. The moral properties of persons derive from the moral properties of acts as follows:[9]

Persons ← acts ← states of affairs

This is not to suggest that an adherent of (7) must be a consequentialist. Indeed, (7) makes no reference to acts at all, and there are many views on the morality of acts compatible with (7). But consequentialism helps us picture the way value flows backward from what is intrinsically good or bad to what is derivatively good or bad, as in (7). This means that some well-known objections to consequentialism are also objections to (7).

One objection is the traditional Pauline principle: never do evil that good may come of it. As stated, the principle is obviously vague, but it identifies one of the most historically important problems with consequentialism—that consequentialism demands the performance of vicious acts in certain circumstances, the standard example of which is the killing of innocent persons to save many lives. Acts of that kind are said to be intrinsically evil. They do not derive their moral status from their consequences.

Notice first that it is not necessary to think that the Pauline principle has no exceptions to see the problem. If consequentialism ever morally requires what a morally good person would not do, there is a problem with consequentialism.

Second, notice that if acts can be evil intrinsically, that constitutes an objection to (7) as well as an objection to consequentialist ethics. Given that (7) says that the goodness of a person derives from the aim of producing good and eliminating evil, then the goodness of a person can require the aim of killing innocent persons to save other lives. If a good person would not kill or aim to kill an innocent person to save lives, then that person's goodness cannot always be derived from the aim of producing good and preventing evil states of affairs.

Third, this means that the general metaethical issue raised by the Pauline principle extends beyond the issue of whether there are intrinsically evil acts. The key insight of the Pauline principle is that the moral properties of acts do not derive (or do not always derive) from the value of states of affairs at which the agent aims. That is compatible with two distinct possibilities:

Possibility A. There are intrinsically good or evil acts, and the moral properties of persons derive from the moral properties of acts as follows:

Persons ← acts [states of affairs]

Possibility B. The moral properties of acts derive from features of persons, as follows:

Persons → acts [states of affairs]

In both cases the moral properties of persons and their acts are not derivative from the moral properties of states of affairs, but that does not settle the issue of whether the basic bearer of value is persons or acts. Let us look at both possibilities since they are both incompatible with (7).

In possibility A there can be an intrinsically evil act, or an act the evil of which does not derive from anything outside of the kind of act that it is. Standard examples are lying and intentionally killing the innocent. Why are such acts considered intrinsically evil? Suppose that lying is intentionally telling someone a falsehood. The badness of that act cannot derive from the badness of someone's believing a falsehood because even though believing a falsehood is not good, the badness of lying greatly exceeds the badness of someone's believing a falsehood. The badness of lying therefore cannot derive from the badness of the state of affairs at which the act aims. Similarly, intentionally killing an innocent person cannot derive from the badness of the loss of life of an innocent person since the badness of murder greatly exceeds the badness of the loss of life. In these cases the badness of the act is in the intentions of the agent. The will of the agent in an act of that kind is disordered. The act therefore does not derive its disvalue from the state of affairs at which the act aims.

The same point can apply to the intrinsic goodness of an act. Consider an act of intentionally giving someone else peace and comfort. The state of affairs of feeling at peace is good, but the value of the act of aiming at giving someone peace greatly exceeds the value of feeling at peace. Again, the value of such an intentional act cannot derive from the value of the state of affairs at which the agent aims.

In possibility A the moral properties of a person who performs an act derive from the moral properties of the acts the person performs. The moral properties of some of those acts are intrinsic. It follows that the moral properties of persons do not derive exclusively from the goodness or badness of the states of affairs at which those persons aim. (7) is therefore false.

Possibility B also arises from the focus on intentions in the Pauline principle, and the insight that the goodness or badness of an intentional act cannot derive from the value of the state of affairs at which the act aims. But it does not follow that the value of such an act must be intrinsic. Possibility B focuses on the intuition that there is a close connection between persons and their acts, and in fact, the act is a category partly defined by what is going on in the mind of the agent.

What a person does unintentionally is not the same kind of act as what that person does intentionally, even if the consequences are the same, and that difference makes a moral difference. The focus on intentions in acting also leads to the distinction between what one intends and what one foresees, and that leads to a moral difference between the good or evil of what one does intentionally and the good or evil of what one lets happen. For moral theories that focus on the good or bad of outcomes, this distinction is not relevant.

What a person intends to do expresses love, hate, respect, honor, pride, envy, or other personal states that arguably have intrinsic value or disvalue. If so, when a person intentionally kills an innocent person, the badness of the act derives from the fact that such an act expresses dishonoring of innocent human life, which is a disordered quality of the person. In this picture, the personal quality of dishonoring innocent human life is intrinsically bad, and any act that expresses dishonor of innocent human life is bad derivatively. It is bad because it expresses an intrinsically bad state. This view leads to the same position as the view that there are intrinsically bad acts—namely, that there are acts whose badness does not derive from the badness of the intended outcome. Either way, (7) is false.

The picture of the flow of value given in the diagrams of A and B deserves attention in discussions of the source of the value of acts. Acts can be (i) intrinsically good or bad, (ii) good or bad because of their connection to the states of affairs they aim to bring about, or (iii) good or bad because of the qualities of persons that are expressed in such acts. An act is the bridge between a person and the world. An intentional act is rooted in the psyche of the agent, and it affects the world through an intentional structure. It is not controversial that there are properties of good or bad throughout the entire structure, but there are many different ways value can flow within that structure, and I think that it is by no means obvious that value does not flow as depicted in diagrams A or B.

My view of the Pauline principle, then, is the following:

i. It need not be an absolute principle to constitute a threat to the view that the only thing intrinsically good or evil is states of affairs.
ii. It constitutes a threat to more than the consequentialist view that the value of acts derives from the value of consequences. It is also a threat to (7), for if it is implausible to say that the moral properties of acts derive from the value of consequences, it is also implausible to say that the moral properties of persons derive from the value of the states of affairs they aim to bring about.
iii. One need not insist that there are intrinsically bad acts to see the problem in claiming that the value of acts derives from states of affairs. The value or disvalue of an act could be intrinsic, but even if it is extrinsic, it could derive from properties of persons rather than consequences.

If (7) is presupposed in many arguments from evil, the Pauline principle is a threat to the validity of these arguments. Improved arguments would shift the focus to the claim that a good person would not act in ways that God acts, or alternatively, would act in ways that God does not act. The fact that there are evil states of affairs in the world is not sufficient to establish such a claim.

Integrity and Predicting Consequences

There is another well-known problem with consequentialism that applies to (7). Bernard Williams argues, in his well-known critique of utilitarianism, that consequentialism demands agents ignore their self and the story of their lives when doing so has better consequences. Personal projects, plans, and values must be overridden when dictated by the utility calculus. One's personal values include many things that are distinctive of the individual person, such as taking care of one's children, developing loving relationships with particular individuals, embarking on a career in philosophy, developing one's talent for music, taking up a hobby such as gardening or genealogical research. Each of these projects involves an extended commitment of time, resources, and energy that could otherwise be used to maximize good from an impersonal viewpoint. If utilitarianism demands of a person the sacrifice of these deep commitments for the sake of the consequences, then utilitarianism attacks integrity in one of its senses.

Williams formulated this objection as a problem for utilitarianism, but notice that it also applies to (7) because it is an objection to consequentialism as a principle of practical reasoning. The problem is that if the moral status of persons derives from the value of the consequences at which they aim, then it does not matter what a person honors, loves, and cares about as long as she aims to produce good and eliminate evil. But we define ourselves in part by what we care about and how we design our lives around the things we care about. However, according to (7), the way we define ourselves is irrelevant to our moral status except in so far as we define ourselves in a way that lines up with the utility calculus. So the Williams objection from integrity is not simply an objection to a certain way of evaluating the morality of acts; it is an objection to a certain way of evaluating the moral status of persons.

The Williams objection applies to the problem of evil because God has a life, a fact that is easy to ignore in an argument about the motives of a good being rather than a good person. Scripture reveals that God has plans, although presumably not all divine plans are revealed to humans. Still, theodicies have been developed that refer to a divine plan for a life of mutual sharing between God and his creatures. For instance, Marilyn Adams has in several places offered a Christological approach to the problem of evil, in which the story by which Christ defeats the horrors of human life is a component of a narrative of the divine life. The stories of individual human lives and the life of the Church are held together by the Christological narrative, and that narrative is a component of God's plan for his own life.[10] In a different way, Eleonore Stump's extended reflections on Biblical narratives reveal the way evil and suffering are components of a larger divine narrative in which God desires union with humans. The integrity objection to utilitarianism is connected to narrative defenses like theirs because they clearly think of God as a person, a person whose life is designed by God himself. That life includes the desire to merge his life with the lives of creaturely persons who are also designing lives. Why such a person as God would design a life in which his creatures must suffer is a serious problem, but it is not the problem that a good person aims at producing good and preventing evil. To assert, like (7), that a good person must aim solely to produce good outcomes is to fail to understand the structure of a life and what makes it good as judged by the person who designed the life. Similarly, defeating evils in a life is not a matter of producing goods that outweigh the evils. Evils in a life are elements in the organic narrative structure of a life, the goodness of which is not an outcome of the process of living. If the integrity objection applies to ordinary human beings, it applies all the more to the Creator, whose design for his life in communion with his creatures cannot be superseded by a demand to calculate the value of the outcome of each divine choice.

In summary, (2a) can interpreted as offering a metaphysical condition for the possession of the property of goodness by persons. Interpreted that way, (2a) arises from a view of value given by (7), the thesis that the moral properties of persons derive from the goodness or badness of the states of affairs at which persons aim. Two important objections to consequentialism are also objections to (7). One objection is that the prohibition on intentionally killing the innocent requires that the morality of acts does not always derive from the value or disvalue of the states of affairs to which the acts lead. The Pauline principle is a traditional way to express this prohibition, and it need not be understood as absolute nor even require the view that there are intrinsically evil acts to pose a problem for (7). The second objection is that utilitarianism attacks the integrity of persons. This also can be formulated as an objection to (7) because the problem is not just that utilitarianism sometimes requires the agent to put aside her deepest projects and commitments, but that any theory that makes the moral status of persons derivative from the value or disvalue of states of affairs ignores the moral importance of distinctive features of individual persons. Indeed, it ignores what a person is.

The Goodness of Persons and Their Aims: The Epistemic Interpretation

A proponent of (2a) can treat it as a statement of an epistemic condition rather than as a metaphysical condition. She might think that it is easier to identify evil states of affairs than it is to identify good persons, and a criterion for thinking that some person is good is that that person aims to eliminate what we take to be evil. That interpretation of (2a) makes the evil of states of affairs prior to the goodness of aims in the order of discovery rather than in the metaphysical order, and she might affirm (2a) in its epistemic interpretation regardless of her position on the metaphysical interpretation of (2). Whether or not aiming at eliminating independently identified evils is a condition for *being* a good person, reasonably believing that some person aims at eliminating independently identified evils may be a condition for reasonably *believing* that that person is good. So understood, (2a) is the following thesis:

7. A condition for reasonably judging that some person is good is that one reasonably judges that that person aims to produce good and prevent evil.

If we are more confident about our ability to identify evil states of affairs and people's aims than of our ability to identify good persons, it is reasonable to make our identification of good persons conditional on our prior identification of good and evil states of affairs, and our judgment of whether someone aims to produce or eliminate those states of affairs.

So consider the following set of potential beliefs:

    i. God is a good person.
    ii. *X* is an evil state of affairs.
    iii. God does not aim to prevent or eliminate *X*.

The proponent of (8) says that (ii) and (iii) have epistemic priority over (i). One reasonably ought to make a judgment such as (ii) and (iii) in advance of a judgment about God's goodness. Given certain background assumptions, including assumptions about God's knowledge, power, and the other goods that God can produce and evils that God can eliminate, (8) says that judging (ii) and (iii) is grounds for judging the negation of (i), or at least for being skeptical of (i). Belief (i) is treated as epistemically less well-grounded than (ii) and (iii) because the grounds for any judgment of God's goodness include judgments like (ii) and (iii).

How do people reasonably form the belief that God is good? By looking at the created world, seeing that it is mostly good, and seeing that God aims to eliminate the evils in it? That can be one of the ways. But they can also come to believe that God is good in other ways: through Scripture and tradition, religious experience, or the teaching authority of the Church, for example. These reasons for believing (i) are independent of beliefs about the existence and quantity of evils in the world, and beliefs about God's aims. The belief in (i) might be very well grounded, or it might not be. It might be reasonable to be confident in it, or it might not be. But whether (i) is reasonable is not settled by making the prior judgments (ii) and (iii).

Those who see (2b) as an epistemic principle will do the reverse and will say that (i) and (iii) have epistemic priority over (ii). Reasonably judging (i) and (iii) is grounds for skepticism regarding (ii). Another possibility is that someone uses (i) and (ii) as grounds for skepticism regarding (iii). Yet another possibility is that a person denies (2) in any form, in which case she may not even detect a tension among the beliefs (i) through (iii).

Most people, however, are probably in none of these positions. They do not use (2a) as an epistemic principle, nor do they use (2b), even though they think that there is a sense in which (2) is true. Indeed, for many theists, the judgments (i), (ii), and (iii) are, to some extent, formed independently. Beliefs in (i) may be based on Scripture, religious experience, and the teaching of religious authority. Likewise, beliefs about the existence and quantity of evil in the world are generally grounded in experiences and natural dispositions that are independent of the belief that God is good. The belief (iii) typically depends on observations of the world and a number of beliefs about the psychology of a good person that are independent of beliefs (i) and (ii). Given the kinds of grounds these beliefs have, both (2a) and (2b) are questionable as principles of moral epistemology. In any case, (2a) deserves more critical attention. Without that principle, our judgment of a person's goodness may be better grounded than our judgment of his aims together with our judgment of what is evil.

Conclusion

To summarize, the standard versions of the argument from evil assume

> 2. Good persons aim to produce good and prevent evil,

where the context of the argument makes it most natural to interpret (2) as

> 2a. A condition for being a good person is aiming at producing good states of affairs and preventing evil ones.

The kind of condition intended in (2a) can be either metaphysical or epistemic. Interpreted metaphysically, the thesis assumed in (2a) is

> 7. The goodness or badness of persons is derivative from the goodness or badness of the states of affairs they aim to bring about or prevent.

Two objections to consequentialist ethics are also objections to (7). First, the Pauline principle that one should not do evil to produce good is both an objection to the view that the moral properties of acts derive from the moral properties of their consequences, and to the view that the moral properties of persons derive from the moral properties of the states of affairs at which persons aim. There may be acts a good person would not do either because of the kind of act that it is (possibility A) or because the act expresses qualities a good person does not have (possibility B). Second, the famous integrity objection by Bernard Williams arises from a view of persons as having the moral right to design lives the goodness of which is not an outcome at which they aim. A good person lives a good life, but a good life is not solely a function of how good a job that person does in aiming to produce the best outcome.

If instead (2a) is interpreted epistemically, the thesis assumed is the following:

8. A condition for reasonably judging that some person is good is that one reasonably judges that that person aims to produce good and prevent evil.

(8) is a principle in moral epistemology that makes the judgment

i. God is a good person

derivative from the judgments

ii. *X* is an evil state of affairs,

and

iii. God does not aim to prevent or eliminate *X*.

I have not argued that (8) is false, only that it is far from obvious.

Some of the most subtle theodicies reveal problems with (8). Narrative theodicies can weaken (8) by revealing ways in which we find out the goodness of God without reference to God's aims. But in addition, narratives can sometimes reveal divine aims we would not have considered otherwise, and they can reveal goods and evils that we would not have independently identified. For instance, although we might have thought of the good of union with God and the evil of separation from God, we might not have thought of suffering as a sharing in the divine life, and we might not have thought about the difference between eliminating evil and defeating evil without a narrative account of divine and human life.

If we accept these arguments, then narrative insights on the nature of a good person and a good life are connected with the denial of (7) and (8), and reveal the weakness of a central assumption in standard arguments from evil.

Notes

1. See, for instance, J. L. Mackie, "Evil and Omnipotence," *Mind* 64, no. 254 (1955): 200–12.

2. See, for instance, Michael Tooley, "The Problem of Evil," *Stanford Encyclopedia of Philosophy* (Summer 2013). http://plato.stanford.edu/archives/sum2013/entries/evil/.

3. See, for instance, William L. Rowe, "The Problem of Evil and Some Varieties of Atheism," *American Philosophical Quarterly* 16, no. 4 (1979): 335–41.

4. I say "person" to make it clear that these arguments are not about good beings like stars and flowers, but about beings who act intentionally.

5. That is implied by another of Tooley's premises: "If evil exists and God exists, then either God doesn't have the power to eliminate all evil, or doesn't know when evil exists, or doesn't have the desire to eliminate all evil." This implies that a being with the desire to do *x* in

Tooley's sense would aim at doing x, and would succeed in doing x if he had the requisite power and knowledge.

6. I argued for that claim in *Divine Motivation Theory*. Good and evil are opposed conceptually, but suffering and good are opposed in a different way, a way that goes to the heart of human experience. When we see horrible suffering, we think, "A loving God would not permit that!" In my opinion, it is much easier to handle alleged conceptual incoherence than to respond to the problem of suffering. Linda Trinkaus Zagzebski, *Divine Motivation Theory* (Cambridge: Cambridge University Press, 2004).

7. This is a point stressed to me by Jim Sterba.

8. There is more than one way a consequentialist can evaluate a person's motives and intentions. Motives and intentions can be assessed directly by their consequences, or they can be assessed indirectly by the consequences of the acts to which they lead. For instance, some motives generally have good consequences even though they are not well correlated with the performance of right acts as determined by the consequences of the acts. For a discussion of the way motives can be evaluated by the utilitarian, see Robert Merrihew Adams, "Motive Utilitarianism," *Journal of Philosophy* 73, no. 14 (1976): 467–81.

9. See J. J. C. Smart and Bernard Williams, *Utilitarianism: For and Against* (Cambridge: Cambridge University Press, 1973).

10. See Marilyn McCord Adams, *Christ and Horrors: The Coherence of Christology* (Cambridge: Cambridge University Press, 2006).

4 Does God Cooperate with Evil?

Laura Garcia

THE QUESTION "DOES God cooperate with evil?" has an obvious answer for most theists, certainly for those who conceive of God as a being that exists necessarily and is essentially omnipotent, omniscient, and morally perfect. Since cooperating with an evil act is immoral, necessarily, God does not cooperate with evil acts. However, the Catholic theological tradition is nearly unanimous in claiming that God does cooperate with evil in certain ways.[1]

St. Thomas Aquinas in his treatise *De Malo* (*On Evil*) asks whether acts of sin come from God. Surprisingly, his answer is yes: "Augustine says in his work *On the Trinity* [III, 4, n. 9] that the will of God causes every species and movement. But acts of sin are indeed movements of free choice. Therefore, the acts come from God."[2] Germaine Grisez follows suit in the third volume of his comprehensive treatment of moral theology: "In God's absolutely good act of sustaining the creatures he has chosen to create, he accepts as side effects all the wrongdoing and other evil in the universe [see CCC, 310–12]. . . . So, good people sometimes may and even should cooperate in others' wrongdoing."[3]

On their face these claims seem to conflict with the belief that God is morally perfect, providing an opening for an argument from cooperation in evil against the goodness of God. Arguments from evil have been the most frequent and formidable weapons in the arsenal of atheism, and the suggestion that God cooperates in the evil actions of human beings seems to surrender the cause before the battle begins.

The problem for theism posed by God's cooperation in evil is distinct from that raised by God's permission of evil. In ordinary use "the problem of evil" refers only to the latter, which generally takes the following form: A perfect being would not allow certain evils to exist, but these evils do exist; therefore, there is no perfect being. This is the standard argument from evil. It asks whether God, by hypothesis a perfect being, could be morally justified in permitting evil, especially evil caused by human actions. While philosopher Alvin Plantinga has demonstrated that evil is not logically incompatible with the existence of God,[4] the argument in its current form claims that the kinds of evil humans cause and experience make it improbable that there is a God. This is known as the evidential argument from evil.[5]

The question here, however, is a different one, namely, whether God cooperates in evil by creating and sustaining free creatures and their actions in existence. It seems that an affirmative answer to this question yields a new logical argument against the existence of God (where "God" is shorthand for "a perfect being"). This is a more serious form of the problem of evil than the concern over whether God is justified in permitting evil. If God causally contributes to evil acts it follows that he permits them, but the reverse is not true. Further, the argument against God's existence from his cooperation with evil is a logical one (though not a priori since it includes one empirical premise). It might be stated as follows:

1. There is a perfect being. (assumption for the sake of the argument)
2. A being that cooperates in evil acts is not morally perfect. (by definition)
3. Evil acts occur. (empirical observation)
4. Evil acts occur only if the perfect being cooperates with them. (1)
5. The perfect being cooperates with evil acts. (3, 4)
6. The perfect being is not a perfect being. (2, 5)
7. Therefore, there is no perfect being. (1, 6—reductio ad absurdum)

Given the importance of divine moral perfection for traditional theism, perhaps philosophers of religion should devote more of their attention to the view, common even among traditional theologians, that God in some way causes the evil actions of his creatures.

Analyzing the concept of cooperation in evil seems to fall squarely within the province of philosophy. The principles involved depend on deeper theoretical claims and incorporate theories of causality, intentions, actions, shared agency, and double effect theory. Yet the subject has been treated almost exclusively by Catholic moral theologians. Attempts to explicate the standard doctrine of cooperation in evil are hindered by the absence of a canonical statement of it. A further obstacle is that theologians working from the same philosophical and theological tradition sometimes employ the same terms to define very different categories of cooperation in evil. On the other hand, since most theologians central to the twentieth-century development of its principles draw on the moral theology of Thomas Aquinas, the basic approach and central distinctions are consistent across these explications.

Cooperating with evil is a feature of specific actions, and moral judgments about particular cases normally appeal to principles drawn from one's moral theory. I operate here out of a virtue theory in which the primary virtue is benevolence or good-will. According to that theory, the intentions of the agent are crucial to deciding the morality of a specific act, whether carried out by single person or a group of persons working together. Since what an agent intends does not normally include every effect of his or her act, the doctrine of double effect has an important role to play in distinguishing the intended from the unintended and the permissibility of the intended.

A Virtue Theory of Ethics

Virtue theories in moral philosophy focus on intentions as the key to evaluating human acts as virtuous, vicious, or morally neutral.[6] One such theory, extensively developed and defended by J. L. A. Garcia, treats benevolence or love as the fundamental virtue from which the others derive. On this view, the welfare of the recipient of a morally significant act wholly determines the act's moral status. Any benefits the agent derives from the act are morally irrelevant. Finally, only the agent's intentions—the input to the act—are relevant to its moral evaluation. I refer to this as the motivation-based virtue theory or MVT.[7]

Priority of Motivations

MVT treats intentions and other motivations behind a human act as the crucial ingredients for determining whether the act is virtuous or vicious. It considers the actual or expected consequences of an act irrelevant to that determination, and so is incompatible with every form of consequentialism. MVT claims that there are some absolute or exceptionless moral norms, such as that it is always wrong to enslave a person, it is always wrong to take the life of an innocent person, and so on (where it is understood that these acts are done intentionally). Here I limit my discussion of MVT to its understanding of the role of intentions in evaluating actions.[8]

The most fundamental moral principle of MVT is that the only proper attitude toward other persons is respectful concern or benevolence. This kind of concern involves having a certain stance toward others: wishing them well, desiring or favoring their genuine good, taking pleasure in benefits they receive, caring about their welfare, and so on. We might divide these kinds of psychological states into three categories:

1. Affective—such as appreciating others' value as persons, feeling compassion and empathy
2. Appetitive—such as wanting, seeking, or hoping for others' welfare, desiring to help them
3. Practical—such as intending, choosing, and planning to do things that benefit others

Intending to do something that affects other people should be motivated by these kinds of psychological states, or at least not by other states incompatible with them. It is important to bear in mind that one may fail morally even by refraining from acting, since failing to act may stem from insufficient concern or even contempt for another person or group. This understanding of the centrality of benevolence is echoed by David Beauregard, who argues that charity is especially relevant to the moral questions that arise in bioethics: "This central Christian virtue includes the two minor virtues of mercy and beneficence. The former is essentially 'grief for another's distress,' a kind of pity and compassion. The second may be defined as 'doing good to someone,' and so may be loosely equated with care."[9]

There are several advantages to MVT over competing moral theories. First, the benevolence and respectful concern it places at the heart of virtue are attitudes we naturally and fundamentally want and hope others will have toward us. Even if they do not know us personally or there is nothing they can do to help, we hope others will feel compassion for us when we are suffering or be pleased to know that we are doing well. Second, MVT reflects the ordinary meaning of terms like "desirable" as what is good to desire and "valuable" as what is good or appropriate to value. Third, our ordinary judgments about other's actions are based on the attitudes and desires those actions reflect rather than on their results or mere correspondence with duty.[10] MVT appeals to the common intuition that humans' most basic need is to be loved. We want others to care about us even if their efforts to help us fail. Similarly, while it is important to fulfill our duties toward others, we feel betrayed if a friend who seemed genuinely to care about us turns out to be motivated not by affection but only by a sense of obligation.

A fourth consideration supporting MVT is the pretheoretical assumption that only factors within a person's control are relevant to the moral evaluation of his or her actions. The consequences of an action, especially the long-range consequences, are outside the control of finite, human agents. In fact, sometimes even attempts to perform basic acts like straightening one's glasses do not succeed, due to paralysis, injury, or external force, and more complicated plans can be thwarted in all kinds of ways. Hence, we cannot guarantee that our attempts to help others will in fact do so. What we can control are our attitudes and intentions in acting. By implication, then, these psychological states are the proper locus of moral evaluation for human actions.

Finally, MVT can explain the centrality in classical virtue theory of the four cardinal virtues, as these are aspects or preconditions of desiring the good of others for their own sake. Justice is presupposed by benevolence since treating others unjustly is deeply incompatible with wishing them well. Courage, temperance, and fortitude are necessary for making the good of others one's main priority, since they free us from operating primarily from our own appetites, desires, and emotions. Some of the virtues on Aristotle's list are not included in MVT, however. Magnanimity and pride, for example, seem to involve a rather self-satisfied appraisal of one's own excellence. MVT also adds to the classical view virtues such as compassion, benevolence, attentiveness, and so on.

According to MVT, vicious or evil actions deviate in some way from the re-spectful concern we owe to others. An agent acts more or less viciously depend-ing on the distance between benevolence and the motives behind his act. These motives can range from the less vicious—inattention, indifference, neglect, and callousness, to the more vicious—envy, greed, vengeance, and hatred. Intending to gossip about Edna is more vicious than listening to gossip about her even though both are morally wrong.

Aristotelian virtue theory claims that the good all humans necessarily seek is happiness or self-realization. The exact nature of that end is the subject of many a philosophical treatise, but Aristotle and Thomas characterize it primarily as ful-filling humans' natural desire for knowledge, the perfection of our highest fac-ulty. For Aristotle this is knowledge of divine things while for Thomas it is the beatific vision. However, Thomas does include some role for the body and for friendship with others, which is closer to Socrates' (and perhaps Plato's) vision of the afterlife.

The motivation-based virtue theory differs from Aristotle and Thomas on this point. MVT characterizes the ultimate end as participation in loving rela-tionships in which each party is motivated by genuine love for the other. In the next life this might take the form of loving appreciation for others and joy in their company. There is a role for the intellect in this view, since it involves judgments about what would contribute to the genuine good of the other and how best to promote it. But MVT contends that although human beings naturally seek truth, their deepest desire is to love and be loved. On this account, the ultimate end of persons is love, which includes but transcends knowledge of truth.

Some might characterize this difference as a disagreement about the means for attaining the ultimate end where that end is still happiness or self-fulfillment. After all, both theories treat moral virtues as the key to human flourishing. But while Aristotle focuses on those virtues that serve reason's quest for truth, MVT focuses on virtues that serve the heart's capacity for love. While proper love of self is included in MVT, the ultimate goal of virtuous persons is not their own flourishing but that of others. In fact, MVT warns against acts of kindness to others that are ultimately motivated by a desire for one's own good. This would be self-defeating in any event, since genuine love for others precludes treating them in any respect as a means to an end outside themselves.[11]

Morally Significant Roles

Further analysis is needed to determine what loving concern requires of us in our day-to-day interactions with others. MVT holds that the shape of a given person-to-person relationship, that is, the role we occupy in another person's life, gives specific content to our moral obligations. Not every social role is morally significant, of course, but moral significance enters the picture whenever our attitudes toward others coincide with or depart from the concern and kindness we owe them. Relationships with obvious importance for the moral life include the roles of spouse, parent, child, teacher, friend, coworker, citizen, and membership in the human family.

We also play a role with respect to ourselves, which requires us to act from positive regard for our genuine good, including acquiring attitudes and habits that will free us to serve other individuals and the common good. Our understanding of the moral requirements of our various roles may lead to practical dilemmas but these are not genuine moral dilemmas. No one is morally required to do the impossible. One's inability to serve everyone's needs at the same time is another of the factors outside one's control. In cases of conflict among our roles, we must reflect on the priority among them and the probable impact of our choices on our most central relationships.

To take an example, suppose Helen is a married woman with four children who works full-time at a local medical clinic. Helen's interest in the well-being of her husband and children rightly takes priority over her concern for extended family members, friends, acquaintances, and colleagues. While each of these role relationships requires a stance of charity toward the others, her children deserve more of her care, attention, and energy than, say, the Red Sox (though in Boston the Sox enjoy a level of devotion bordering on hyperdulia).

Helen's intentions and attitudes toward her children, in light of her crucially important role in their lives, should be consistent with a deep commitment to their genuine good and thoughtful attention to how she can advance it. If the moral obligations associated with her role as a mother should conflict in some way with what is expected of her as a friend or colleague, clearly the needs of her children should take priority. Her role in their lives is permanent and indispensable in a way that her role in the lives of the others is not. Further, her inability to serve the well-being of everyone at once is not a moral flaw but an inevitable result of her finitude. Finally, moral assessments of self and others must recognize that what we primarily and fundamentally owe to others is respectful concern rather than a specific way of reflecting that concern in our actions.

Intentions

Individual Intentions

We turn now to a more detailed discussion of intentions and their role in vicious acts, keeping in mind that intentions are the essential ingredients in determining whether an agent who acts in a certain way is cooperating in an evil act. Perhaps the most popular analysis of intentions defines them as mental states that settle the question of what to do; they express a decision to bring about an action or realize a plan.[12] Intending something involves planning or committing to doing it. Intentions follow on deliberation about what to do and the choice of an available option (where the option might be to do nothing). Choosing is a mental act while intending is a state of an agent—the state of intending to perform a particular action, carry out a plan, or achieve a goal.

This understanding of intentions captures their role in initiating, sustaining, and guiding actions and it includes a role for both the intellect and the will in human acts. The intellect considers what would be good to achieve and ranks or orders alternative actions or plans that are possible means for attaining that good. The good or end of an agent's act is defined by what she aims at, such as doing well on a job interview, getting the dog off the couch, or protesting against a local developer who wants to pave paradise and put up a parking lot.

Alternative definitions of intentions, in terms of beliefs, reasons, or desires, fail to capture this interplay between reason and will. If intentions are analyzed in terms of desires alone, where one's strongest desire or strongest combination of desires is one's intention, the will is blind—it is moved not toward a good apprehended by reason but by passions and appetites alone. Even if the agent is conscious of her desires and aware of their influence on her action, on this analysis her intellect is not what moves her will. On the other hand, if intentions consist only of reasons for acting or beliefs about what would be good to do, the will is idle—it can be moved only by a desire for a good. As Thomas puts it, the will is an appetitive power, not a power of the intellect.[13]

Deliberations about what to do are guided by reason but they are also affected by other mental states (anticipation), physical states (intoxication), and external circumstances (excessive party-fication). Factors like these can influence the intellect as it deliberates about what to do and so affect the agent's intention. Unless they overwhelm his ability to reason, however, the intellect can evaluate their importance and aptness for achieving the intended end. Reason is commonly capable of ignoring or dismissing non-rational factors in its deliberation, though of course it can also be overcome by them. To whatever extent a person's intentions are necessitated, however, they are not properly his intentions and so not subject to moral evaluation.

In his discussion of human action in the *Summa Theologica*, Thomas describes two ways in which the will is free: "Man can will and not will, act and not act; again, he can will this or that, do this or that."[14] The first is the freedom to act or refrain from acting and the second is the freedom to choose among genuinely open alternatives. Since free actions are ordered to a good and every finite good has some limits or imperfections, each can in principle be either recommended or rejected by the intellect. This means that reason's recommendation does not compel the consent of the will. Thomas further insists that "the will is mistress of its own act . . . but this would not be so, had it not the power to move itself to will.

Therefore, the will moves itself."[15] This is one of his strongest endorsements of human self-determination. In free acts, then, the will actualizes itself to intend an act or commit to a plan of action aimed at some good.

Shared Intentions

Since cooperation in evil involves sharing the vicious intentions of another agent, we turn to consider shared intentions or group actions. Abraham Sesshu Roth, author of the entry on shared agency in *The Stanford Encyclopedia of Philosophy*, offers a helpful overview of contemporary theories of shared actions.[16] It is a subject that offers endless opportunities for chisholming,[17] but the account Roth describes as the intuitive or simple view seems perfectly adequate. The common sense theory models joint agency on individual agency: when I act as an individual, I intend what I am doing, so when I participate in a shared activity, I intend what we are doing.[18] Another way to describe the shared intention is that when I participate in a shared activity, I intend that we do something together or that I do something with you. Roth calls this the "we-intentions view" but I refer to it as the minimalist account of group intentions or MAGI.

A first objection to MAGI is that it is not just simple but simplistic. I cannot intend that we act in a certain way, since other people's intentions are private mental states outside of my control and I can only intend what is within my power to achieve. Therefore, MAGI is a nonstarter. But there is no reason to think that my intending that we do A presupposes that I can intend for someone else. My intention might be simply to do A with my friend. This intention may presuppose that my friend also intends (or will intend) A, but it need not be part of my intention to control her mind or lobby her into doing A.

One way to act on an intention that we do A is to ask another person to help with A. Suppose Ann wants to wallpaper her kitchen and Lynn offers to help. They make a plan to tackle the project on Saturday. Now Lynn intends that she and Ann will wallpaper Ann's kitchen on Saturday and Ann intends that she and Lynn and will wallpaper her kitchen on Saturday. (Substituting for the indexicals here would make for awkward prose but make it more obvious that they share an intention.) Probably neither intends to wallpaper solo (in fact, no sane person would try it at all), so neither intends simply to wallpaper Ann's kitchen.

Of course, an intention that we do A is subject to the same kinds of interference that plague intentions that I do A. Ann may change her mind because she cannot find the right pattern or Lynn may decide to come clean about her sorry wallpapering record. The fact that neither can intend for the other does not mean that they cannot both intend the same thing, namely, working together to wallpaper the kitchen.

A further objection to MAGI is that it does not sufficiently connect the individual intentions to the joint project. As Roth puts it, "Even if our intentions coincide on the action and the plural subject in question, if there is no agreement on how to go about it, or if we each fail even to accord any significant status to the other's intentions, there would be no intention or action shared in this instance."[19] This seems unobjectionable but its relevance to the MAGI view is not obvious. If Ann and Lynn both intend that we will wallpaper Ann's kitchen, where they mean the same thing by "we" and by "wallpaper Ann's kitchen," it seems to me that they share an intention vis-à-vis the wallpapering activity.

If Ann changes her mind and decides not to wallpaper after all, then for the moment they no longer have the same intention and will no longer be doing the previously intended shared activity. This hardly entails that their original plan was not a shared intention to wallpaper Ann's kitchen. Similar considerations apply to the scenario in which Lynn and Ann have different ideas about how to paste up the wallpaper. Then although their intentions about pasting up the wallpaper in a certain way do not coincide, this does not vitiate their joint intention to wallpaper. Differences about the means are resolved along the way. Since, as we shall see, intentions are defined by their ends, it is the ultimate goal of an activity that the agents must share. The means are secondary and may be substituted for or dispensed with as the plan proceeds. Even individual intentions to engage in an activity rarely include every detail; rather, the means will be chosen and adjusted as the activity unfolds.

Rival theories of shared agency usually begin from two or more individual intentions to do A and then develop criteria for weaving them together in such a way that the individuals can be said to be working as a group on the same plan, project, or activity. The individual intentions are called "participatory intentions," taking the form "I intend to do A." Since the participatory intentions have to converge on the same action in the right way in order to count as a shared intention, these theories require additional principles to ensure that the goals of each member of a group mesh with those of the others.

Consider a circle of friends in which each has a participatory intention to paint a house in its entirety (or contribute to painting it). Unfortunately, some want to paint it yellow and others want to paint it brown (maybe because the house next door is yellow). Since they do not agree on the means for painting the house, the joint activity is stymied—the participatory intentions do not mesh into a common group intention. Similarly, if the friends arrive at the site to find that the house has numerous gables and balconies, some may decide against all of the means and hence against the end. It may be that some members of the group had a tepid level of commitment to the project in the first place or are not particularly skilled at house painting. Perhaps these folks adopt a revised intention, to paint the siding of the house and not the trim, but that intention is not shared by the rest of the group.

One way to avoid such problems is to interpret participatory intentions as conditionals of the form: "I intend to do A on the condition that you intend likewise." Of course if you also have a conditional intention then neither of us actually intends to do A. We might call this the date night conundrum, characterized by conversations like:

"What do you want to do?"

"Whatever you want to do."

"But I want to do what you want to do."

and so on ad infinitum. Nothing happens unless someone chooses to act unconditionally.

Another suggestion is that participatory intentions are predictive: "I intend to do A as long as I can reasonably expect that you will be committed to A as well." Again, it follows that my intention to do A is conditional, not on your actually committing to do A but on the probability that you will commit to it: "I intend A as long as (only if?) I think you will also intend A." But suppose I am really into A and will do it with or without you. Then my intention to A need not involve any prediction about whether or not you will do A, though I may hope you will. Perhaps I have two tickets to a Red Sox game and ask if you would like to go. My present intention is to go to the game with you, but that intention does not depend on any prediction as to whether you will share it. I might find out that you are (gasp!) a Yankees fan.

It seems, then, that premising an individual's participation on what others intend does not achieve the desired results. Perhaps instead we should think of participatory intentions as subject to certain rational constraints that accompany the participatory intention and prevent the kind of intractable conflict that plagued the house-painting project. Presumably, this will require a delicate balance between preserving the voluntariness of group participation and ensuring that participants' intentions connect in a way that enables the project to go forward.

One theory along these lines interprets participatory intentions to do A as committing one to whatever means to A are agreed on by the group (perhaps by majority vote). This proposal draws on an analogy between individual and group deliberations. If I commit to A and determine that B is the best way to achieve A, it is irrational for me not to commit to B. Similarly, or so the argument goes, if I intend to participate in group activity A and the group decides that B is the best way to achieve A, it is irrational for me not to intend B.

But surely commitment to a joint project does not commit one to the means that get the most votes from the group. If Julie does not know when she commits to A that she will be required to commit to B as well, she cannot have intended B in intending A. She may be physically incapable of B or have moral objections to it. Hence, the claim that participatory intentions are subject to these quasi-logical constraints is simply implausible. In fact, it is not obvious that even a person's own belief about the best means to an intended end make it irrational not to intend those means. Sometimes recognizing what one is up against is a reason to rethink the whole idea.

If rational constraints do not succeed in keeping members of a group on task, perhaps we should think of participatory intentions as subject to moral constraints instead. One possibility is that a participatory intention to A commits one to a genuinely joint activity, where A is a genuinely joint activity only if each member of the group publicly commits to A and is explicitly accepted into the group by every other member. Further, in committing to A one incurs a serious moral obligation to the others in the group and cannot withdraw from it unless every other member agrees to it.

My guess is that few people would sign up for group activities under these conditions. But the bigger problem for this theory is that it cannot be implemented. If no member of the group can be admitted without the explicit consent of the other members, there is no way to initiate a group activity. Perhaps one begins with an alpha member whose own commitment to A is appropriately unconditional. While the strict normative conditions imposed on participants may ensure each commits unreservedly to A and all of its subparts, it is hard to believe that run-of-the-mill group activities demand anything like that level of commitment. Surely joining a pickup soccer game does not require of every player an open agreement to take part that must be accepted by each other player. Maybe this means soccer does not count as a genuinely shared activity, but it seems the vast majority of our joint activities are more like playing soccer than joining a secret society.

My (admittedly novice) opinion is that the project of trying to construct shared intentions from individual intentions is a doomed enterprise. Instead of treating a participatory intention as a two-way relationship between an individual and an intention, we should conceive of it as a three-way relationship among an individual, an intention, and another person or group. MAGI understands shared intentions as just such a three-way relationship, having the form "I intend that we do A" or "I intend to do A with you." For MAGI, the focus is on doing something together, not simply doing something. Commitments to shared activities involve two or more persons who intend that we will do A together, where 'we' might be completely specified, indeterminate, or yet to be announced and A could be anything from taking a walk to advancing world peace.

How does this apply to the moral questions raised by actions that help another person carry out an evil plan? When does intending to act in a way that assists an evil act become, in effect, a shared intention? Also, are contributions limited to the means for carrying out an evil act ever morally permissible?

The Traditional Doctrine of Cooperation in Evil

Cooperating in evil sounds like a bad thing to do, so it is difficult to see how there could be any morally permissible version of it. Dictionary definitions of "cooperation" list such synonyms as "concurrence," "agreement," and "consent," so cooperating in an evil act appears to include some kind of endorsement of it. In its ecclesiastical Latin origins, "to cooperate" means to work together or act jointly for the same end. In other words, it is an instance of shared agency.

While Doctors of the Church, like Augustine and Thomas, address some of the moral issues involved in cooperation with evil, they do not employ the terminology and categories of the doctrine in its present form. Some of those categories were introduced to deal with moral questions raised by technological and cultural developments in the 1960s and 1970s with respect to contraception, abortion, and research that destroys embryonic human beings. It is no accident, then, that the most readily accessible current explanations of cooperation in evil appear in the publications of the National Catholic Bioethics Center (NCBC). Unfortunately, the brief explanations offered there sometimes raise as many questions as they answer.

In his 1956 textbook on medical ethics, theologian Edwin F. Healy developed one of the most comprehensive expositions of the received doctrine on cooperation with evil. His work is also one of the earliest to be devoted to medical ethics, preceding the founding of the Hastings Center (1969), the Kennedy Institute of Ethics (1971), and the NCBC (1972). Philosopher Paul Ramsey, sometimes called the father of medical ethics, published his first book on the subject in 1970.[20] Healy's accomplishment is all the more impressive in that he ties the doctrine of cooperation to Thomas's thought in a way that is accessible to those unfamiliar with Thomistic metaphysics and moral philosophy.

Healy begins with the following definition: "Cooperation [in evil] . . . means concurrence with another person in an act that is morally wrong. This concurrence may be accomplished in either of two ways: by acting together in doing something that is morally wrong or by supplying another with what is helpful to him in doing something that is morally wrong."[21] The first sentence defines cooperation in evil *simpliciter*—it is concurring with another in an evil act. The second introduces the first and most important distinction in the doctrine of cooperation—acting together in doing something wrong versus supplying something helpful to the agent in doing something wrong. Acting together is called "formal cooperation" while supplying something useful is "material cooperation." These categories are exhaustive and mutually exclusive; any act that cooperates with evil does so formally or materially, and no act cooperates in an evil act both formally and materially. While a particular agent may cooperate both formally and materially in evil, those designations would have to apply to distinct acts.

Formal Cooperation

Formal is distinguished from material cooperation by the intentions of the cooperator. The "form" in "formal cooperation" refers to the relationship between the form (or intention) behind an agent's evil action and the intention of the one who assists that act in some way. The matter of an act consists of the material means required for realizing the agent's intended evil end or carrying out her evil plan. Formal cooperation is in turn divided into explicit and implicit formal cooperation in evil.

EXPLICIT FORMAL COOPERATION

Explicit formal cooperation is an instance of joint agency or shared activity in which the cooperating party shares the intention of the perpetrator regarding her immoral act (plan, project, etc.). Peter Cataldo and John M. Haas of the NCBC offer this definition of explicit formal cooperation: "Formal cooperation is assistance provided to the immoral act of a principal agent in which the cooperator intends the evil. The assistance need not be essential to the performance of the act in order for the cooperator to intend the evil of the principal agent's act."[22] This definition closely resembles that provided by Henry Davis in his 1945 work, *Moral and Pastoral Theology*: "Cooperation is formal when A helps B in an external sinful act, and intends the sinfulness of it, as in deliberate adultery."[23] The context of both statements makes it clear that they are intended to apply to acts of explicit rather than implicit formal cooperation.

Both of these definitions describe the cooperator as intending the evil or sinfulness of the act, but since the evil or immorality of an act is not something a person can intend, the exact nature of explicit formal cooperation is difficult to determine. Healy's brief description of formal cooperation is an improvement, since it includes the key element of shared agency—acting together in doing something wrong. The cooperation is with the other person's intention to do something immoral, which explains why explicit formal cooperation in evil (as an expression of a vicious intention) is always wrong. In the MAGI theory of shared agency, the cooperator here intends that we do A together, and so concurs with the bad intention of another.

IMPLICIT FORMAL COOPERATION

A person accused of formal cooperation in evil may protest that she did not intend the evil act itself but only one of the means for achieving it. However, intending to bring about something as a means to an end is also intending the end. Deliberately supplying something useful for another's evil act, then, amounts to a participatory intention with respect to that act. This may be obscured by the fact that the cooperator in this case seems to intend only the means and not the end, but intending the end is implicit in her intending a means precisely because it is a means to that end. This is called implicit formal cooperation in evil.

While the will can be directed toward a means as well as an end, Thomas claims that an agent need not aim at both in the same intention because the means and the end are different goods: "Since the end is willed in itself, whereas the means, as such, are only willed for the end, it is evident that the will can be moved to the end without being moved to the means; whereas it cannot be moved to the means, as such, unless it is moved to the end."[24] One can intend a means to an end for its own sake (or the sake of some other end) or precisely as a means to the intended end. In the first case, intending the means is distinct from intending the end, but in the latter case the agent intends the end in and through intending the means, so there is only one intention. If David intends to get cash at the ATM to buy tickets to a play tonight, his intention to go to the ATM incorporates his further intention to buy the tickets and both are for the sake of the end—seeing the play. If he takes out the cash but does not see the play, we would conclude that he never really intended that end.

Clearly it makes no moral difference whether one's intending an evil end is explicit or implicit. Hence, formal cooperation in evil is never permissible. In some cases the cooperator's contributory act might even be more vicious that that of the primary agent, who may not understand the moral gravity of her intention. Formal cooperation is one of the few categories in the doctrine of cooperation with evil that admits of a clear definition.

Material Cooperation: Immediate and Mediate

Material cooperation in evil is providing assistance to the agent of an evil act while not sharing that agent's ultimate intention. Even if one intends something that contributes to the wrongful act or supplies a helpful means to the intended end, one does not share the agent's intention to act for that end. If a cooperator intends some means as a means to the success of an evil act, she cooperates formally in it; if she intends the means for their own sake or the sake of some independent good, she cooperates only materially.

Drawing on Healy's definition, we may characterize material cooperation as "concurrence with another in an act that is morally wrong . . . by supplying another with what is helpful to him in doing something that is morally wrong." This definition is appropriately general in that it focuses on the two factors that separate material from formal cooperation: what the cooperator intends—to assist an agent who is bent on doing something evil, and what kind of assistance is being offered—something helpful to that agenda.

Material cooperation is divided into two main categories: immediate and mediate. Most treatments of this topic settle for defining immediate material cooperation since mediate cooperation can then be characterized as any material cooperation that is not immediate. Immediate material cooperation in evil is the category closest to formal cooperation and, as the term suggests, involves supplying a means to the evil end that is particularly useful or effective. Heribert Jone, in a 1963 textbook on moral theology, offers the following definition: "[Immediate material cooperation is] concurrence in intending an act which directly tends to produce the evil act, though without intending the evil act."[25]

Jone adds: "[Such cooperation] is always wrong, and some would add 'even when done under grave moral duress.'"[26] He does not take a firm position on acts carried out under serious pressure, such as threats to one's life or family. Perhaps he is reluctant to contradict Charles McFadden, who just two years earlier categorically condemned all acts of immediate material cooperation: "Even though one is not interested in seeking the immoral objective and is motivated by purely extrinsic factors," McFadden warns, "no reason, however grave, would ever allow a person to participate actively, as a partial efficient cause, in the immoral act itself."[27]

NCBC ethicist John Di Camillo concurs with McFadden on this point, but adds a note of sympathy for the person who caves in under pressure: "When individuals are forced under duress (e.g., at gunpoint) to cooperate in the intrinsically evil action of another, they act with diminished freedom. Following Church teaching, the matter of their action remains objectively evil, but they do not intend this object [the form of their action] with true freedom. In such cases, the matter remains objectively evil as such, but the subjective culpability of the cooperator is diminished."[28] Note that the cooperator's culpability is diminished but not eliminated, since he retains the freedom to refuse to cooperate. The reduction in culpability is presumably due to the power of the temptation to do whatever it takes to avoid being shot in the head.

Nonetheless, Di Camillo agrees with Jone and McFadden that all immediate material cooperation in evil is morally wrong. It differs from formal cooperation only in that the cooperating agent rejects (or at least does not share) the primary agent's intention. In implicit formal cooperation, the agent intends some means to an evil end precisely because it furthers that end, while in immediate material cooperation she intends the means knowing it will assist the agent but not intending it to serve that end. The judgment that acts of immediate material cooperation in evil are vicious is also consonant with MVT, since it condemns actions that contribute something material to an evil act, even if the contributing agent's own ultimate end is a good. Assisting an evil act is itself an evil act, and one may never act viciously even as a means to a very great good.

Deciding which acts fall into the category of immediate material cooperation in evil is another matter. We will begin with Jone's characterization of immediate cooperation as "concurrence in intending an act that directly tends to produce an evil act."[29] The phrase "tends to produce an evil act" is a bit puzzling. An agent's act can only be produced by her own will. Since it is impossible for the act of one agent to produce the act of another, it is also impossible for one agent's act to tend to produce another's act. We will assume, then, that by "tends to produce" Jone means "tends to assist or further."

Even on this interpretation, however, the definition fails to capture the right set of actions. An act that merely tends to assist an evil act might, on a given occasion, be very unlikely to do so—performing the act in those circumstances would neither further nor tend to further another's evil action. Yet on Jone's definition that act falls into the category of immediate material cooperation. The reverse is also true. An act that normally does not tend to further an evil act might do so in a given case, and yet it would not be an act of immediate cooperation on Jone's definition. This difficulty suggests that acts of cooperation in evil should be assessed on the basis of their actual relationships to evil acts rather than on their typical relationships to such acts.

Charles McFadden characterizes acts of immediate material cooperation as those in which a person "does render some aid because of some personal benefit that will be derived or because of some loss which will thereby be avoided."[30] While motivations like these may characterize some acts of material cooperation, others may well be guided by other motives and aimed at other ends, such as overcoming capitalist oppression or preventing a race riot. Like Jone, McFadden fails to capture all and only those acts of material cooperation that qualify as immediate material cooperation in evil.

In an article addressing institutional cooperation in evil, Peter Cataldo and John Haas adopt the opposite approach, defining immediate material cooperation indirectly as material cooperation that is not mediate: "If one merely makes possible the evil act of another then the cooperation is said to contribute a nonessential circumstance."[31] Acts of immediate material cooperation, then, contribute an essential circumstance of the evil act. This definition is not especially illuminating, however, since the distinction between essential and nonessential circumstances is, if anything, even murkier than that between mediate and immediate cooperation. More substantively, a person who merely makes an act possible does not seem to cooperate with it at all and a person who contributes a nonessential circumstance may still cooperate quite closely with an evil act. A material means does not have to be essential in order to be very helpful to an evildoer.

Finally, the claim that one's contribution is essential to the act of another person is puzzling at best. Could not someone else make the same contribution? Perhaps the essential feature is not the cooperator, then, but the specific means he supplies. Supplying an essential means would count as immediate cooperation and supplying a nonessential means would be an act of mediate cooperation. But since there are many ways in which a particular object or state of affairs can be essential to another, these terms also require clarification.

Perhaps a cooperator's act is essential to an evil plan only if refraining from the act would have prevented the evildoer from carrying out his plan. Unfortunately, this places almost every act of material cooperation into the mediate (or nonessential) category. Even if someone's contribution to an agent's evil plan is substantial, it may still be that refraining from that act would do nothing to prevent her from carrying out her plan. Often enough, in fact, there is nothing one can do to prevent another person from acting viciously. If it is permissible to assist someone's evil plan as long as refusing to do so would not change the outcome, many obvious acts of immediate material cooperation in evil will receive a moral pass.

Taking a cue from the previous proposal, we might ask not whether the evil act could occur without the cooperator's act but whether it would occur without it; that is, if the cooperator had not performed that act, would the evildoer still have carried out her plan? This raises the bar slightly for acts of mediate cooperation, since it might be that while the primary agent could carry out her plan without a specific person's help or contribution, she would not choose to do so. A down side of this proposal is that judgments about what another person would do in hypothetical situations require a great deal of familiarity with that person's character and motivations. Without such knowledge, it will be next to impossible to apply this criterion in specific cases.

In general, parsing the immediate/mediate distinction in terms of the essential/inessential distinction fails to capture the morally relevant feature of these categories. The goal is to determine which material contributions to a plan of action are always illicit, leaving the others in moral limbo for the time being. The relevant relationship is the closeness or proximity of a certain means to an intended end and so requires a difficult but objective determination. But the relationship between an evildoer's actual and hypothetical intentions involves a subjective and highly tentative determination, which leaves the moral status of the cooperator's act more or less up for grabs.

While other versions of the immediate/mediate distinction avoid the theoretical conundrums of the above proposals, they give up in clarity what they gain in simplicity. For example, immediate/mediate has been parsed as direct/indirect or proximate/remote.[32] But these terms are virtually synonymous with immediate and mediate so they do not move the discussion from the starting line. This is a problem inherent in definitions involving linear concepts. Choosing any point along an uninterrupted continuum as the key to a morally important distinction is bound to seem arbitrary and at least partially subjective. Thus, many of the important categories in the traditional theory of cooperation in evil resist precise definitions. No attempt to define immediate material cooperation in evil is entirely satisfactory and none has garnered the support of a majority of scholars. I call this the problem of the criterion.

"Permissible" Mediate Material Cooperation

Let us assume that the problem of the criterion can be resolved in some way. The next order of business for the traditional doctrine is to distinguish between morally permissible and impermissible acts of mediate material cooperation. The traditional doctrine on cooperation in evil declares that some acts of mediate material cooperation are morally permissible. Given the moral significance of this claim, we now need a criterion for distinguishing between the materially cooperating sheep and goats.

Virtually every theologian who endorses the possibility of legitimate cooperation in evil is also committed to exceptionless moral norms regarding the sanctity of human life, the nature of marriage, the right to religious freedom, and the like. In principle, material cooperation in evil of any kind seems to lend itself to just such an exceptionless norm, that is, that every act of material cooperation in evil is wrong. This makes the exception for certain acts of mediate material cooperation all the more puzzling.

THE DOUBLE EFFECT PROPOSAL

One strategy for defending that view, adopted by Germaine Grisez and several others, introduces the principles of double effect theory to distinguish between legitimate and illegitimate mediate material cooperation in evil. This approach holds some initial promise, since double effect principles apply to actions aimed at a good outcome that are also expected to bring about certain unintended negative results—pain, loss, suffering, and so on.

The doctrine of double effect applies to actions in which both the intended end and the intended means for achieving it are good but the agent foresees or expects that the action will have some bad effects as well. The theory dictates that for such acts to be morally licit they must meet the following criteria:[33]

1. The intended end must be good in every respect, and any subintentions (means to that end) must also be good.
2. Only the good effect is intended, not the bad effect.
3. The bad effect is not a means to the good effect.
4. The intended good is proportionately valuable enough to justify allowing the bad effect.

Normally the bad effect involves nonmoral goods like the suffering of the innocent, loss of life or property, personal anguish, and the like. However, traditionalists on cooperation in evil, including Grisez and Anthony Fisher, claim that
even when an action's bad effects include offering mediate material assistance to
another's evil act, the agent may still be morally justified in performing it. This
claim falls outside the ordinary purview of double effect theory, but Grisez thinks
it can be successfully defended by employing the principles of that theory.

Recall that principle (1) requires that the agent's intentions and subintentions
in acting must be good without qualification. Assume for the time being that
some acts are good in this sense even though they have the unintended effect of
providing mediate material assistance to an evil act. Principle (2), that only the
good and not the evil effect must be intended, is already guaranteed by the fact
that we are dealing with mediate rather than immediate material cooperation.
Also, since the assisted evil act is (presumably) not a means to the good end, the
action passes principle (3). The only remaining criterion is (4), that the good effect must be "proportionate" to the bad effect, that is, it must be great enough to
justify permitting the action's bad effect of (perhaps among other things) furthering an immoral act. Grisez interprets the fourth principle as requiring a positive
answer to the question: "Is it reasonable to perform the act given its negative
consequences?"

Since some acts of mediate material cooperation seem to pass the first three
tests, then, it remains only to weigh their good effects against the bad effect of fa-
cilitating another's evil act. Anthony Fisher, Bishop of Parramatta in New South
Wales, has devoted much of his career to describing and defending the traditional
doctrine on cooperation in evil and most of his exposition of it is clear and useful. But in an essay that begins with an overview of the doctrine, he declares that
human existence is rife with acts of cooperation in evil that cannot be avoided
and may even be morally required:

> Even Christ's little band paid taxes some of which were no doubt used for
> wicked purposes; despite his entreaties, when Jesus cured the sick some of
> them went on to sin more; after repeatedly evading his persecutors, Christ
> eventually allowed himself to be arrested, thereby occasioning his false trial
> and a terrible execution. All sorts of wickedness goes on in our society, and we
> finance it through our taxes, elect leaders who allow it and fail to do much to
> change things. More immediately, almost anything we do can be an occasion,
> opportunity or means for someone else to do something wrong. To avoid all
> cooperation in evil would require that we abandon almost all arenas of human
> activity . . . and could well constitute a sin of omission.[34]

In my view, none of these examples qualifies as cooperation in evil. Paying taxes
and electing state officials may be partial preconditions of a state's bad actions and
policies, but they neither concur with those policies nor do anything specifically
to assist them. Taxes fund many important services that citizens are called on to

support, which is why we are encouraged, even by Jesus's teaching, to pay taxes. The fact that the state uses some of the money it receives for evil does not make an individual taxpayer complicit in all of its policies or procedures. Jesus's curing of sinful people did permit them to continue to live and so continue to sin, but surely he did not cooperate with their later sins by curing their illnesses. Finally, one hardly knows what to make of the claim that by allowing himself to be arrested, Christ cooperated with the agents of his passion and death. In fact, as the term "allowing" indicates, this was merely permitting an evil, not cooperating with it. More generally, the things we do that others use as occasions for evil are at best preconditions or permissions of those acts, not contributions to them.

Fisher is more careful in his definitions of the various categories of cooperation in evil. Like Grisez, he employs the doctrine of double effect to sort morally permissible from impermissible acts of mediate material cooperation. Arriving at the fourth principle of that doctrine, he advises, "when considering whether to engage in an action which has the foreseeable effect of assisting someone else's wrongful purposes, we must ask ourselves how important are the benefits expected from this action, how probable, how lasting, how extensive and for whom? What kind of loss or harm would result? . . . People with dependents, for instance, have more to lose from refusing to do certain procedures, than do people with no dependents."[35]

This last phrase appears to undercut what has gone before. Fisher's moral theory bases judgments about an action's permissibility on whether the intention behind it is virtuous, in complete independence from the consequences, circumstances, or pressures on the agent. But since principle (4) of double effect theory calls for a judgment on the proportion between the good to be achieved and the evil to be permitted, Fisher appeals to a cost/benefit analysis in order to justify acts of mediate material cooperation in evil that would otherwise be ruled out tout court. As the problem of the criterion makes obvious, the size of one's contribution to an evil act does not seem particularly significant for moral theory, except perhaps for determining how vicious the intention behind it is.[36]

The traditional doctrine of cooperation, at least on its face, holds that even when one does not share the intention of an evildoer, it is always wrong to knowingly supply something useful to her in carrying out her plan. As far as I can see, it follows from this claim that even mediate material cooperation in evil is impermissible. If acting for the sake of a good has the further effect of assisting a moral evil, the good intention does not suffice to justify the act. This problem occasions a certain amount of hand-wringing in the traditionalist literature. The usual strategy is to insist that, given the countless negative consequences of furthering an evil act, it is extremely unlikely that any act of this kind will be permissible.

The undisputed master of that strategy is Germaine Grisez, whose list of potential bad effects goes on for pages:

> Interaction with wrongdoers tends to generate psychological bonds and interdependence. Thus, cooperation often leads to opportunities and temptations to engage in further cooperation. . . . In this way, material cooperation often is an occasion of grave sin. . . . [Further], what a material cooperator is doing can: have bad moral effects on the wrongdoer, scandalize third parties, lead to disharmony between the cooperator and the victims of the wrongdoing, impede the cooperator from offering credible witness against the wrongdoing, and/or impede the cooperator from carrying out his or her vocation in other respects. . . . Cooperation by "good" people reassures sinners and encourages them to be obdurate.[37]

Grisez concludes that very few actions could have positive effects significant enough to outweigh the many foreseeable negative effects of cooperating with evil. In fact, it is unlikely that there are any morally permissible acts of mediate material cooperation in evil. While I agree with his conclusion, I find it troubling that Grisez is willing to base it on consequentialist considerations rather than on matters of principle. If material cooperation in evil corrupts both the cooperator and the evildoer, causes scandal, and encourages others to sin with a good conscience, why continue to insist that it is sometimes permissible?

It is a pity that these lengthy and often edifying discussions serve only to muddy the waters on both cooperation in evil and double effect theory. If one surrenders the principle that every instance of material cooperation in evil is impermissible, one can hardly prevent more superficial calculations of their consequences from bestowing a blessing on acts of dubious moral acceptability. It is hard to imagine that every conscientious ethicist will be able to apply Grisez's exhaustive list of relevant considerations to every act they evaluate. Worse still, anticipating the total effects of a particular act and assigning a weight to each is notoriously problematic. Even among the likeminded, judgments about concrete cases can differ wildly.

To take just one example, in distinguishing licit from illicit mediate material cooperation Henry Davis states, "mediate cooperation is proximate [and so impermissible], if the help given is very intimately connected with the act of another, as to hold a ladder for the burglar as he climbs up to a window for the purpose of burglary. Mediate cooperation is remote, if the help given is not closely connected with the other's act, as to purchase tools for a burglar."[38] It is almost certain that most defenders of the received view would call both of these acts instances of formal cooperation in evil. Given this level of disagreement, it is no surprise that Davis concludes "great varieties of opinion . . . on any given case except the most obvious are inevitable, and there is no more difficult question than this in all of moral theology."[39]

Acts of material cooperation in evil include the intention to assist an evil act in some way. (If the assistance is inadvertent it is not cooperation in evil.) One co-operates materially in an evil act in order to achieve a good end. Thus, the assistance is not a mere side effect of one's action but one of its subparts, so the act violates double effect theory's first principle. Presumably, in acts of this kind the good one intends cannot be achieved without also assisting the wrongful act. Hence, assisting that act is an integral part of one's plan, a means to the intended good, which violates the third principle of double effect.

More generally, double effect theory cannot be used to justify acts with morally impermissible effects. Its purpose is to determine when it is morally licit to act for a good end when that act will also bring about some amount of nonmoral evil. In order for her act to pass the third double effect criterion, it must be clear that, if the agent could achieve the good end without also causing the bad effects, she would choose to do so. This is a way of demonstrating that the bad effects are not willed as a means to the good that is sought. In acts of material cooperation, however, assisting an evildoer is accepted precisely because (we presume) there is no other way to achieve the good.

In fact, even though acts of material cooperation in evil do not share another's evil intention, they provide the kind of assistance to an evil act that is universally condemned when considered sufficiently substantive, even when the agent is under serious duress. How then can it be that when the assistance is judged to be relatively negligible, consequentialist considerations can trump the presumption of moral turpitude? I contend that the strategy of using double effect theory to justify some acts of material cooperation results in applying proportionalist criteria to the most important distinction in the entire theory—that between licit and illicit acts of cooperation in evil. I call this the problem of creeping consequentialism.

While we can expect some imprecision in the field of ethics, as Aristotle famously noted, confusion about which, if any, acts of mediate material cooperation are permissible is fatal to the received view. Combined with the slippery nature of linear concepts, the problem of the criterion, and creeping consequentialism, it is next to impossible to provide a systematic and coherent analysis of cooperation in evil.

The Narrow Theory

An Ontology of Actions

Closer attention to St. Thomas's action theory might help resolve some of the problems that plague the traditional view. His account borrows from Aristotle's hylomorphic theory of substance, according to which every individual being is composed of form and matter. The form is the principle that gives the thing its nature or essence, determining the kind of thing it is, and the matter is what receives the form and, because of its concreteness, individuates members of that kind. Every human being has the same form, but humans are composed of matter as well.

A proper or adequate definition of a kind includes its genus, the closest general category to which it belongs, and the essential property that distinguishes it from other species in that genus. For humans, the genus is animal and the specific difference is rationality, that is, the power to grasp general concepts, consider several means for achieving an end, and choose freely among them. As animals, individual humans are embodied, and being embodied is essential to the kind of thing they are. This means that humans can exist only as individuals; the form or species has no independent existence of its own.[40] Aristotle describes the form and matter of a substance as its formal and material causes, where "cause" is understood as whatever brings something about, either by effecting it in some way or by serving as one of its constituents.

Substances come to be from the union of matter and form.[41] The form of a substance determines both the powers it has and the end it seeks (or tends toward). The natural powers of things are present even when they are not actualized—indeed, even if they are never actualized. A cat has by nature the power to spring almost instantaneously from a crouched position, but a very lazy cat might never exercise that power. Some powers are passive, such as the capacity to breathe, while others are active, such as the ability to dunk a basketball. When a substance brings something about by exercising of one of its powers, it is an efficient cause of that thing.

The end, or ultimate goal, of a substance is its full realization as that kind of thing or the fulfillment of its telos. Of course most natural things are not conscious of their end but strive for it by instinct or other internal principles. Aristotle refers to the end of a substance as its final cause. This cause precedes the acts of a substance only in the sense that it is present and therefore operative in the form of that substance. For Aristotle, the formal, material, efficient, and final causes cover the entire causal territory and so the entire ontological makeup of an individual substance.

While Aristotle does not apply this causal analysis to accidental features of substances, Thomas finds it a useful paradigm for an ontology of human acts. Of course, since actions are not substances, the hylomorphic theory applies to them only by extension or analogy. Thomas defines a (voluntary) human act as an actualization of the power of the will. Since the will is guided by reason in choosing an end, specific acts are defined by the agent's intention in acting, what she seeks to do or accomplish. Thus, formal cooperation in evil involves sharing the agent's intention and so becoming a joint agent of the evil act.

The matter of an act consists in the physical means for performing the act or achieving the intended goal. These are the materials or ingredients the agent intends or comes to intend as means to her end. While they include the brain states and bodily movements of the agent, they also include whatever external objects or contributions the agent needs for achieving her end. As we have seen, aiding someone in an evil act by supplying or bringing about one of these means (or an acceptable substitute) is material cooperation in evil.

The efficient cause of an act is whatever brings it about, so the efficient cause of a human act is the will of the agent. Thomas claims that the will, as an appetitive power, always aims at a good, or at least at a perceived good. This "perceiving" is a contribution of the intellect. Reason considers various goods achievable by the agent and determines their relative attractiveness, attainability, and so forth, but the will determines which to pursue. Thomas holds that even evil acts aim at a good, but they go awry in some way—preferring a merely apparent to a genuine good, seeking a good at the wrong time, in the wrong way, and so forth. Since no one can will for another person, however, there is no category of efficient cooperation in evil.[42] Attempts to influence someone to choose an evil act do not produce that act and so are not efficient causes of it, though they are vicious acts in their own right.

The end or final cause of an act is its realization, the content of which is determined by the agent's intention. Since the final cause of an act is incorporated into its formal cause, we will not treat it as a separate category of cooperation in evil. However, some Catholic theologians, inspired by certain remarks of Thomas, define the end of an act as its object, which is something like the act taken in isolation from both the intention behind it and the effects that follow it. On that interpretation, "object" refers to the objective dimension of the act—what it is in itself, so to speak. Examples might be killing an innocent person, stealing a thousand dollars, or sneaking into the movies.

One reason to offer an agent-independent definition of an act is that it allows for a certain formulation of exceptionless moral norms along the following lines: some acts (or objects) are always wrong and doing them is always immoral, independently of their consequences and of the agent's intentions. However, this overlooks the difference between intending an evil act simpliciter and intending it for the sake of a further end. While an act may be immoral independently of an agent's ultimate end, it cannot be immoral independently of an agent's end in acting—his immediate intention. Refilling the same Burger King coffee cup instead of buying another one is morally questionable but only when done intentionally. If one is sleepwalking or deeply preoccupied when standing in front of the coffee urn, the fact that the act is wrong to intend does not suffice to make one's present act immoral. More generally, the object of an act makes it vicious only if that object is intended.

Having described the main ontological features of human acts, Thomas offers a brief account of the process involved in acting intentionally. The process involves five stages:

1. Apprehension of an end
2. Desire for the end
3. "Counsel" or deliberation regarding the means to the end
4. Desire for the means
5. Intending to act for the means

If deliberation concludes that there is a single means to the desired end then choice and intention are simultaneous—in fact, Thomas says, they are identical. In these cases step (5) simply follows step (4). When more than one means is available, desire for the end requires a choice among the means before the agent intends one of them. In these situations there are six steps, since deliberation about the means leaves one's options open, so it must be followed by choice of one of the alternatives and then desire for that means, followed by intending the means.

At first blush this seems far too complicated an account of typical garden-variety actions, which are rarely accompanied by the depth of reflection the theory seems to require. Perhaps major or difficult decisions follow some such pattern, but grabbing the car keys on the way out the door or petting the cat seem relatively step-free. Thomas might reply that the steps involved in acting often occur almost instantaneously and may be outside the conscious awareness of the agent. If my husband asks why the keys are in the refrigerator, I might be able to recapture my train of thought, including where it went off the rails, but it is doubtful that I was aware of that process at the time.

Implications of the Narrow Theory

Given this ontology of actions, the narrow theory offers the following definition of cooperation in evil:

> To cooperate in the evil act of another person is to endorse, assist, or further that act either formally or materially.

Since its formal and material causes are the only constituents of an evil act to which another can contribute, sharing an agent's bad intention (the formal cause) or assisting its realization (the material cause) are the only ways to cooperate with that act.

The narrow theory concurs with traditionalists in judging that any act that shares an agent's vicious intention is impermissible, since it participates in the very feature (the intention or end) that determines the moral quality of an act. The material cause of an act, as we have seen, consists of the means for carrying it out.

Here the narrow theory departs from the received view, since the narrow theory claims that every act that contributes materially to the realization of an evil act is morally impermissible. However, the material cause is limited to supplying or helping provide a means that is an ingredient in the agent's plan as he or she conceives it (or a means that serves the same purpose as such an ingredient).

Acts that merely make an evil act possible (e.g., delivering the paper that has a news article about wealthy neighborhoods, clerking at the hardware store where a criminally minded person purchases certain handy tools, failing to leave the lights on while on vacation) are not as such cooperation in evil. Likewise, permitting an agent to perform an evil act is not a way of cooperating in it, since permitting it does not entail that one shares the agent's intention nor does it provide material assistance. Failing to intervene when one witnesses an evil act or failing to take measures to prevent or hinder it may be blameworthy, but they are not as such ways of cooperating in that act.

The narrow theory holds that the moral evaluation of an act depends on the agent's intentions and the psychological states that motivate that act. A person who adopts another's intention to perform an evil act and/or assists him in doing so is, in effect, a joint agent of that act, and acting as a joint agent of an evil act is always wrong. Obviously, this view requires some knowledge of an agent's motivations and we have no direct access to others' psychological states. Still, we can and do form reasonable judgments about a person's motives and intentions by observing his past actions, speaking with him or others who know him, and so on.

The same goes for determining the degree of a person's moral responsibility for a particular cooperative act. Such judgments are based on the knowledge we have about the cooperator and the circumstances of her act. Moral accountability can be vitiated or lessened by many factors; insufficient knowledge of the relevant moral principle and lack of freedom in acting are the main candidates here. These factors help to decide how vicious the agent was in performing the act, but they are irrelevant in determining whether the act is something vicious to intend.

The narrow theory has several advantages over the traditional theory:

1. It focuses on the agent's intentions as the proper locus of moral evaluation.
2. It avoids linear concepts in defining the fundamental categories of cooperation in evil.
3. It solves the problem of the criterion by specifying the ontological boundaries of actions.
4. It eliminates the need for lengthy and complicated assessments of acts of mediate material cooperation.
5. It avoids creeping consequentialism.
6. It accommodates the intuition that all acts of cooperation in evil are vicious, differing only in how vicious they are.

Difficulties in assessing an act's degree of viciousness are common to every moral theory, since "degree" is an inherently linear concept. However, rather than appealing to consequences or other empirical features of the act, the narrow theory presupposes MVT's claim that the agent's intentions are the proper focal point of moral theory. They are decisive for determining both that an act is vicious and how vicious it is. The latter determination is based on the psychological states that motivate the act and their distance from the care and goodwill owed to the person or group on the receiving end of it. This in turn is specified by looking to the agent's role(s) in the life of that person or group.

Objections to the Narrow Theory

Defenders of the traditional doctrine would deny that cooperating in evil is always vicious, since some (mediate material) cooperation in an evil act can bring about a great good, perhaps even a good that outweighs the evil resulting from the perpetrator's act plus the cooperator's acceptance of it. However, the previous discussion of such cases concluded that intending an act that will foreseeably contribute a constituent in an evil plan makes one an accomplice in that plan and so is never permissible. Anticipated positive consequences of an act are irrelevant to deciding its moral status; that decision rests solely on the attitudes, motivations, and intentions behind the act.

A second objection to the narrow view is that failing to act for a good can be blameworthy even if one could attain it only by assisting an evil act. Appeals to this claim are sometimes used to justify programs that distribute needles to heroin addicts or condoms to married men with AIDS. While the ends in view are praiseworthy (preventing infections and deaths from the use of shared needles, preserving a couple's intimacy), to provide something that facilitates immoral acts (continued drug use, sex divorced from its inherent meaning) is to cooperate in such acts and ultimately to undermine the genuine good of those one is trying to help.

A third objection is that moral dilemmas sometimes require us to choose a lesser evil, which may include cooperating with an evil act as an unintended side effect of one's actions. This objection rests on the false assumption that there are genuine moral dilemmas (as opposed to apparent ones). Failing to benefit a person or group is not wrong when doing so would require acting viciously in some way. Far from being a lesser evil, refraining in such circumstances is morally required. On the other hand, intending to assist another's evil act is always morally wrong, even if it brings significant benefits to others—indeed, even if it also benefits the victims of the act. The moral dilemmas objection, by justifying some acts of cooperation in evil, exposes its advocates to creeping consequentialism.

Divine Cooperation in Evil

Preconditions of Evil Acts

We are now in a position to apply the narrow theory of cooperation in evil to our main topic: does God cooperate in evil? Defenders of an affirmative answer to this question often support their view with examples of especially vicious acts that humans have been allowed to commit. Since the theistic assumption is that God (as a perfect being) sustains in existence free human agents, their powers, and the acts that exercise those powers, it seems that he cooperates with their acts, including their evil acts. This yields the argument described in the introduction to this essay, which concluded that there is no perfect being. Since the argument is logically valid, which is to say the conclusion follows necessarily from the premises, perfect-being theism survives only if the argument is unsound, having at least one false premise.

Proponents of the traditional theory of cooperation might reject the second premise: a being that cooperates in evil acts is not a morally perfect being. Given the traditionalist claim that preconditions and permissions of evil acts are possible ways of cooperating with them, even a perfect being may in principle cooperate with evil. In fact, since God's creative act brings about every precondition of every evil act and no event in the universe occurs without his permission, the traditional view entails that God is the cooperator in evil than which none greater can be conceived. It seems to me that this approach effectively surrenders perfect-being theism, an outcome that warrants serious attention to alternative theories of cooperation in evil.

At this point, it is only fair to add that Thomas appears to accept the broad view, though appearances may be deceiving in this case. When he considers God's contribution to evil acts in the *Summa Theologica*, Thomas lists only their preconditions: "Whatever there is of being and action in a bad action, is reduced to God as the cause; whereas whatever defect is in it is not caused by God, but by the deficient secondary cause [i.e., the will of the human agent]."[43] He elaborates on that account in his treatise *On Evil* when addressing the question, "Do acts of sin come from God?"

> Since God is by his essence being, for his essence is his existence, everything existing in whatever way derives from himself. . . . Acts of sin are evidently beings and classified in the category of being. And so we need to say that the acts are from God [in this respect]. . . . We trace what regards the activity of those with the power of free choice to God as the cause, while only free choice, not God, causes what regards the deordination or deformity of those with the power of free choice. And that is why we say that acts of sin come from God, but that sin does not.[44]

This passage indicates that Thomas rejects the claim that God cooperates materially in evil acts. Rather, he intends only the good—the existence of finite persons with the freedom to seek the genuine good of others or only satisfy their own desires and appetites.

While God is the primary cause of human acts, he does not support or assist their turn toward evil or vice. Human acts have a secondary cause—the will of the agent. God makes evil acts possible, but contributing to the preconditions of an evil act is not cooperating in that act. The conditions obtaining when a person chooses do not determine whether she acts viciously or virtuously, so providing one or more preconditions of an act is not a way of cooperating with the agent's vicious intention. My quarrel with the argument from cooperation in evil, then, is with the fourth premise: evil acts occur only if the perfect being cooperates with them. While a perfect being must be said to provide all of the preconditions of evil acts, this does not entail that he cooperates with them.

To summarize, the formal cause of an evil act is the agent's intention or end. Since God does not share any wicked intentions, he does not formally cooperate in any evil acts. The material cause of an evil act consists of the means or objects required to realize the agent's intention and only those means. It does not include background conditions or general circumstances that allow the act to occur, such as gravity, oxygen, continued existence, and available victims. Human agents can intend only what they believe they can bring about, so while the agent of an evil act may presuppose that various background conditions will continue to obtain, those conditions are (generally speaking) not within her power and so are not ingredients in her plan.[45]

Permission of Evil Acts

Even if God does not further the evil acts of his creatures, it might be argued that he cooperates in evil by permitting them to occur. However, recall that a further implication of the narrow theory is that permitting an act is not a form of cooperation with it. It is possible to permit an evil act to occur without either sharing the intention of the agent or assisting with any of the means for its execution. In some cases, a person's permitting an evil act may be a precondition of its success but, as we have just seen, preconditions do not belong to the act itself.

A possible objection here is that there could be circumstances in which a person's permitting an evil act is part of the agent's plan and so cooperates with it in some way, either formally or materially. For example, a security guard at a biology lab might assist a break-in by refusing to trip the alarm and doing nothing to stop the perpetrators. In this situation, however, the guard is not simply permitting the break-in to occur but also aiding it (cooperating with it) by deserting his post and failing to fulfill the responsibilities of his job. It is hard to imagine that he would do so willingly unless he shared the intentions of the perpetrators, which would make him a formal cooperator in their plan. Even if his permitting the break-in were not a case of cooperating in evil, it would be morally vicious on other grounds. On the other hand, a passerby who witnesses the break-in and fails to do anything about it is clearly not cooperating with it. His inaction may be morally objectionable, but not on the grounds that he furthers an evil act.

Even though God sustains persons and their powers in being, evil acts occur only if he permits them. God does not cooperate in the will's turn toward evil. Therefore, the argument against God's existence from divine cooperation in evil is unsuccessful. This conclusion has important implications not only for theology and philosophy of religion but also for moral and political philosophy. A criterion that distinguishes cooperation in evil from preconditions or permissions of evil provides a principled way to separate genuine from ersatz examples of cooperation. Questions about what qualifies as cooperating with evil are not limited to Catholic individuals and institutions. They are also relevant to current concerns about contributing to global warming, a culture of violence, racial stereotypes, rampant consumerism, exploitation of workers, and many other ills. Addressing these questions will require further work on the relationships between individuals and institutions and whether institutions can cooperate in evil.

Postscript: Is God Justified in Permitting Evil Acts?

One of the most troubling issues for perfect-being theism is that it is difficult to know what justification, if any, God might have for permitting evil acts. The evidential argument from evil maintains that it is improbable on the evidence available to us that God is justified in permitting the kinds of evil acts humans have committed.[46] This is the problem of evil in a more familiar form, but it is not the topic of this chapter.

My present view is that William Alston's response to the evidential argument is eminently sensible.[47] Alston points out that our knowledge of the kinds of goods that exist and the possible connections between them and the evil acts that God permits is limited at best and does not include any detailed knowledge of God's mind or of a life beyond this one. Given these limitations, our evidence is a frail reed on which to hang an indictment of divine goodness. In claiming that God can have no good reason for permitting evil actions, Alston notes, "we are taking the insights attainable by finite, fallible human beings as an adequate indication of what is available in the way of reasons to an omniscient, omnipotent being."[48] This is the problem in a nutshell. There is simply no reason to think that we are in a position to know whether God has good reasons for permitting humans to choose evil. In my view, this makes the evidential argument from evil an academic exercise. But that is a project for another day.

Notes

1. Throughout this essay I use "cooperation *in* evil" and "cooperation *with* evil" as equivalent concepts. Since a human action may be simple or complex, I refer to such an action variously as an act, action, plan, undertaking, and so forth.

2. Thomas Aquinas, *On Evil*, ed. Brian Davies, trans. Richard Regan (New York: Oxford University Press, 2003), Q. III, a. 2.

3. Germaine Grisez, appendix 2 in *The Way of the Lord Jesus*, vol. 3, *Difficult Moral Questions* (St. Bonaventure, NY: Franciscan Press, 1997).

4. See Alvin Plantinga, *The Nature of Necessity* (New York: Oxford University Press, 1974). The argument also appears in more accessible form in Alvin Plantinga, *God, Freedom, and Evil* (New York: Harper & Row, 1974).

5. Several inductive arguments from evil appear in Daniel Howard-Snyder, ed., *The Evidential Argument from Evil* (Bloomington: Indiana University Press, 1996). These include William L. Rowe, "The Problem of Evil and Some Varieties of Atheism" and "The Evidential Argument from Evil: A Second Look"; Paul Draper, "Pain and Pleasure: An Evidential Problem for Theists" and "The Skeptical Theist"; Bruce Russell, "Defenseless"; and Richard M. Gale, "Some Difficulties in Theistic Treatments of Evil."

6. Some believe that St. Thomas denies that any actions are morally neutral, since he divides all free actions into good and evil. However, he explicitly states that some actions are morally neutral "such as when a man strokes his beard, or moves his hand or foot" (*Summa Theologica* II–I, Q. 18, a. 9). Presumably neutral acts fall within the category of good actions because of some nonmoral way in which they are good, but I leave these matters to scholars of St. Thomas's thought.

7. I would like to thank Professor Garcia for his contributions to and comments on this explication of the theory. For a helpful overview of MVT see J. L. A. Garcia, "Norms of Loving" in *Christian Theism and Moral Philosophy*, ed. Michael Beaty, Carlton Fisher, and Mark Nelson (Macon, GA: Mercer University Press, 1998), 231–59.

8. For an example of this view see Hugh J. McCann, "Settled Objectives and Rational Constraints," *American Philosophical Quarterly* 28, no. 1 (1991): 25–36.

9. David Beauregard, "Virtue in Bioethics" in *Catholic Healthcare Ethics: A Manual for Practitioners*, 2nd ed., ed. Edward J. Furton, Peter J. Cataldo, and Albert S. Moraczewski (Philadelphia: The National Catholic Bioethics Center, 2009), 27.

10. Immanuel Kant's moral theory requires that one's motivations in morally significant actions should be limited to respect for the moral law as a dictate of reason; nonrational psychological states are at best irrelevant and at worst pernicious. In his contribution to this volume, however, John Hare offers an interpretation of Kant's work that suggests he may have actually endorsed a kind of virtue theory centered on benevolence.

11. Kant and others qualify this norm, allowing acts that treat another person as a means to an end as long as she is not treated merely as a means to an end. In my view, while another's work or abilities may be useful to achieving an end, persons themselves are not means to those ends and should not be treated as such. The grocery store clerk, postal worker, cab driver, and flight attendant have an intrinsic dignity that is therefore necessarily independent of the services they render.

12. These functions of intentions are enumerated in Robert Dunn, "Intention" in *Routledge Encyclopedia of Philosophy*, ed. E. Craig (London: Routledge, 1998). Available at http://www.rep.routledge.com/article/V018SECT2.

13. St. Thomas, *Summa Theologica* I, Q. 83, a. 3.

14. St. Thomas, *Summa Theologica* II–I, Q. 10, a. 2.

15. St. Thomas, *Summa Theologica* II–I, Q. 9, a. 3.

16. Abraham Sesshu Roth, "Shared Agency," *Stanford Encyclopedia of Philosophy* (December 2010): section 1. http://plato.stanford.edu/entries/shared-agency/.

17. See Daniel Dennett and Asbjørn Steglich-Petersen, *The Philosophical Lexicon* (2008). http://www.philosophicallexicon.com/. This collection of tongue-in-cheek definitions incorporates the names of various philosophers of the past and present. This example is inspired by the work of the late Roderick Chisholm, who was known for delivering minute and painstaking analyses of epistemic concepts. Hence, "to Chisholm" is "to make repeated small alterations in a definition or example. 'He started with definition (d.8) and kept chisholming away at it until he ended up with (d.8″″″″).'"

18. Roth, "Shared Agency."

19. Ibid.

20. Paul Ramsey, *The Patient as Person: Exploration in Medical Ethics*, 2nd ed. (New Haven, CT: Yale University Press, 2002). The first edition appeared in 1970.

21. Edwin F. Healy, *Medical Ethics* (Chicago: Loyola University Press, 1956), 101. In interpreting Healy and other theologians of the pre-Vatican II era, I rely especially on Peter O. Pojol, "Cooperation in Evil: Limits and Latitude" (PhD thesis, Weston School of Theology, 2006).

22. National Catholic Bioethics Center (NCBC), "What Is the Principle of Cooperation in Evil?" http://ncbcenter.org/document.doc?id=139.

23. Henry Davis, *Moral and Pastoral Theology*, vol. 1, *Human Acts, Law, Sin, Virtue* (London: Sheed & Ward, 1945), 341.

24. St. Thomas, *Summa Theologica* II–I, Q. 8, a. 3.

25. Heribert Jone, *Moral Theology*, trans. Urban Adelman (Westminster, MD: Newman Press, 1963), 87.

26. Jone, *Moral Theology*, 87.

27. Charles McFadden, *Medical Ethics*, 6th ed. (Philadelphia: F. A. Davis, 1967), 360. Jone was probably familiar with the fifth edition, published in 1961 and reprinted in 1962 and 1963. McFadden's text was considered the definitive treatment of Catholic medical ethics from 1946 through the Second Vatican Council.

28. John A. Di Camillo, "Understanding Cooperation with Evil," *Ethics & Medics* 38, no. 7 (2013): 1.

29. Jone, *Moral Theology*, 87.

30. McFadden, *Medical Ethics*, 329.

31. NCBC, "What Is the Principle of Cooperation in Evil?"

32. This approach is exemplified by the NCBC document "What Is the Principle of Cooperation in Evil?"

33. From Edward J. Furton and Albert S. Moraczewski, "Double Effect" in *Catholic Healthcare Ethics: A Manual for Practitioners*, 2nd ed., ed. Edward J. Furton, Peter J. Cataldo, and Albert S. Moraczewski (Philadelphia: The National Catholic Bioethics Center, 2009), 23–26.

34. Anthony Fisher, "Cooperation in Evil: Understanding the Issues" in *Cooperation, Complicity, and Conscience: Problems in Healthcare, Science, Law and Public Policy*, ed. Helen Watt (London: Linacre Center, 2005), 29.

35. Ibid., 54.

36. Even here, the importance or helpfulness of the means provided is relevant only in helping determine the viciousness of the agent's motives in acting.

37. Germaine Grisez, *Difficult Moral Questions* (Chicago: Franciscan Herald Press, 1983), appendix 2. http://www.twotlj.org/G-3-A-2.html.

38. Davis, *Moral and Pastoral Theology*, 341.

39. Ibid., 342.

40. For a recent defense of this ontology of substances that engages the current literature see David S. Oderberg, *Real Essentialism* (New York: Routledge, 2007).

41. More precisely, substances result from the union of prime matter and a substantial form.

42. McFadden sometimes describes material cooperation as doing something that is a "partial efficient cause" of an evil act, but in this context the phrase is misleading. What one supplies is rather a partial material cause of the act.

43. St. Thomas, *Summa Theologica* I, Q. 49, a. 2.

44. St. Thomas, *On Evil*, Q. III, a. 2, emphasis mine.

45. If a precondition were such an ingredient, it would no longer be simply a precondition but a partial material cause of her act.

46. The evil brought about by free agents is usually called moral evil, while suffering and pain from other causes is called natural evil. Both problems must be addressed in some way by those offering a theodicy. Here we consider only the moral problem of evil.

47. William Alston, "Some (Temporarily) Final Thoughts on Evidential Arguments from Evil" in Daniel Howard-Snyder, ed., *The Evidential Argument from Evil* (Bloomington: Indiana University Press, 1996), 311–32.

48. Alston, "Final Thoughts," 321.

5   The Problem of Evil

Excessive Unnecessary Suffering

Bruce Russell

I. The Best Version of the Argument from Evil

Here is what I think is the strongest version of the argument from evil against the existence of an all-knowing, all-powerful, wholly good God.

> 1. If God exists, he would not allow excessive, unnecessary suffering.
> 2. But there is excessive, unnecessary suffering.
> 3. So God does not exist.

By "allowing unnecessary suffering" I mean "allowing suffering the allowing of which is not needed to bring about greater good or to prevent greater evil."[1] To allow *excessive*, unnecessary suffering is to allow *way more* than is needed to bring about such good or to prevent such evil. Like Peter van Inwagen, I use the term "evil" to mean "bad things." As van Inwagen says, the problem of evil is really the problem of bad things.[2] Suffering is in itself a bad thing regardless of whether it results from evil intentions or natural causes, and the issue is why God, if he exists, would allow so much suffering of innocents.

The word "excessive" appears in premise (1) because van Inwagen and others have argued that God could allow *some* unnecessary suffering.[3] I am not completely convinced by these arguments, but my aim is to offer a version of the moral premise (the first premise) in the argument from evil that all theists can accept. Then the central question will be whether there is sufficient reason to believe that premise (2) is true. That epistemic question is, and should be, the focus of attention for both atheists and theists.

In the past I have argued the following: we have observed massive amounts of terrible suffering of innocent children, and we can see no reason why God, or any wholly good person, would allow all that suffering if he knew about it and could prevent it. The best explanation of all that suffering is that there is no adequate reason to allow it, not that God exists and allows it for reasons beyond our ken.

If theists assert that the God-explanation is better, or at least not worse than, the atheist's explanation, they will be led to skepticism about the age of the earth.

Some Creationists believe that the Earth is about six thousand years old; hypo-thetical Young Earthers, about one hundred years old. (Bertrand Russell fa-mously raised the possibility that it is only five minutes old.) The Creationists and Young Earthers will argue that God created the Earth recently with all its signs of age (deep river valleys like the Grand Canyon's, fossils, cave paintings, etc.) for reasons beyond our ken. They might even suggest a reason why he would do that: it is better to have people learn the lessons of history through the *apparent* rather than the *real* suffering of innocent humans and animals in the past. It is true that if God did this some people created around the time that the Earth was actually created (six thousand or one hundred years ago, or even five min-utes ago) would have false memories of having committed heinous crimes and having lost loved ones, and that is not a good thing. But it is much better to have a world like that than one where millions and millions of innocent people and animals have suffered for millennia. If we are in no position to judge that there is excessive, unnecessary suffering, then we are in no position to judge that Cre-ationism and Young Earthism are false. But surely we are in a position to judge these views false. So Skeptical Theism leads to unacceptable forms of skepticism.

Before turning to recent attempts by Skeptical Theists to argue that their view does not lead to unacceptable forms of skepticism, I want to consider a defense of the version of the argument from evil that I offered above that I do not think is successful.

II. An Inadequate Kantian Defense of the Argument from Evil

The Skeptical Theists do not argue that we are justified in believing that the sec-ond premise in the argument I gave above is false. They just think that we are in no position to judge whether it is true or false. They are skeptical; they think we should suspend judgment about the truth or falsity of that premise. Here's why.

They think that we are in no position to judge whether there are no goods of which we are unaware (goods beyond our ken) whose realization requires God to allow all the terrible suffering we see, and so in no position to judge that a wholly good being would not allow such suffering for the sake of such goods. Further, we are in no position to judge that allowing all the suffering of innocents that we see is not needed to bring about goods of which we are aware of. Hence, we are in no position to judge that (2) is true, that is, that there is excessive, unnecessary suffering. For all we know, God's allowing all the suffering we see is needed either to bring about goods we are aware of, or ones that we are not aware of.

The intuitive idea behind the atheist's defense of the argument I gave is that it is *always wrong* to treat someone as a mere means and *no amount of good of any sort* (nor the prevention of any sort or amount of evil) could morally justify treat-ing a person as a mere means. No good being would allow the little girl in Flint (whose case I discussed in my first essay on the problem of evil)[4] to be brutally beaten, raped, and then murdered so that her mother's boyfriend could exercise his free will or so we could learn a lesson from the heinous crime. No good being would allow the Swinsons to drown little Ariana by pouring water down her throat because she was not eating properly.[5] There *could not be* goods so great that they could make failing to intervene to stop these despicable actions morally permissible. There is an absolute Kantian prohibition against allowing harm to some in order to benefit, or prevent harm to others, for that would be using them as mere means.

But Derek Parfit has given a couple of examples that should make us think that it is sometimes morally permissible to use someone as a mere means. My favorite concerns an egoist who saves a drowning child only in order to receive the money her distraught parents promise to give him. He treats the child as a mere means, as his road to riches. But he does not do wrong when he saves the child. He lacks virtue and has bad intentions, but his action is not wrong.[6]

Perhaps the correct principle is what Parfit calls the *Harmful Means* principle:

> It is wrong to impose a serious injury on someone [such as cutting off a leg] as a means of benefitting other people [say, to save their lives].[7]

Parfit's statement of the principle can be generalized to say that it is always wrong *to harm*, or to *allow harm*, you could easily prevent as a means to realizing some greater good or preventing some worse evil. The egoist who saves the drowning child does not violate this principle because he *does not harm* the child he saves.

But there is the famous example of a big guy stuck in the mouth of a cave, face pointing inwards, that counts against the *Harmful Means* principle.[8] He and five friends have been exploring some caves, and he gets stuck in the mouth of the cave when he tries to back out. Now if nothing is done he and the five other spelunkers will drown because water is rising in the cave, and he will act as a human plug. You are outside the cave and realize what is going on. You have a stick of dynamite and can blow the big guy free, which will kill him but save the five. He will not die immediately and will suffer more if you blow him up than if you let him drown. Though it would be hard to do, I think that it would be morally permissible, even obligatory, for you to blow the big guy free. However, the *Harmful Means* principle implies that it would be wrong of you to do that because you would be harming him (remember, he will suffer more if blown up than if he drowns) as a mere means to benefit others.

So the atheist cannot argue that no amount of good *could* justify harming someone, or allowing harm to befall them, in order to benefit others or prevent greater harm from befalling them. Here is an example where harming the big guy would be morally justified because it is the only means of saving the five from a panicked drowning. So maybe there are goods that we are unaware of that justify God, if he exists, in allowing the brutal treatment of Ariana Swinson and the little girl in Flint, and millions of other children who have suffered similar fates. Perhaps God foresaw that these little girls would lead horrible lives if he did not allow their admittedly brutal deaths at the time they occurred, and they were compensated by being brought in union with him at that time instead of having to suffer for many years on Earth and only then being united with God. And perhaps there are other goods that we are unaware of involving the little girls, the mother, the boyfriend, and even those of us who have become aware of these heinous acts, that morally justify God's allowing these evils to occur. In short, even if the *Harmful Means* principle is true, it is not absolute. It is a principle of *prima facie*, not all things considered, wrongness. It allows for exceptions if greater harm can be prevented, or greater good brought about, if someone is harmed (or allowed to be harmed) as a mere means to benefit (or prevent harm to) others.[9] That opens the door for the theist to respond and claim that we are in no position to judge that it would be wrong of God, if he exists, to allow all the terrible suffering we observe, for his allowing it may be among the permissible exceptions to the *Harmful Means* principle.

III. Saving Hypotheses

A. A Falsifiable Story That We Are Justified in Believing False

Perhaps the best approach for the theist to take against abductive versions of the problem of evil like the one I have given is one that Steve Wykstra has been pursuing of late. It involves coupling an empirically indeterminate core form of theism with various specifying hypotheses to yield a specific version of theism. Wykstra illustrates how scientific theories often contain an indeterminate core that is conjoined with various supplemental hypotheses which change in the light of new observations. For instance, in the past scientists defended the core wave theory of light against objections by modifying their view of the nature of the ether through which they believed light travels.[10] Empirical observations disconfirmed that theory if the ether in which light is assumed to travel transmits longitudinal rather than transverse waves but not if the waves are transverse. So they adopted a different auxiliary hypothesis about the nature of the ether while still accepting the wave theory of light.

Irving Copi gives an example of how someone can defend the view that the Earth is flat even in the face of the observation that the bottom half of a ship sailing away on the seas disappears from sight before the top half. That can be explained if light waves travel in long, shallow upward arcs even if the Earth is flat. So if you adopt an auxiliary hypothesis that says that light travels in big arcs rather than in straight lines you can save the flat earth hypothesis in light of the observation about how ships disappear from sight.

Of course, an auxiliary hypothesis cannot save a theory if there is reason to believe it is false. The hypothesis that light travels in transverse waves through the ether, and the hypothesis that it travels in long, shallow arcs, will not save the relevant theories if there is independent reason to believe they are false. Suppose that on the assumption that there is no afterlife, the best explanation of all the suffering we see implies that there is no God who allows it for reasons beyond our ken, but that if there were God and an afterlife it is just as likely that there would be all the earthly suffering we see as there would be if there were no God nor afterlife. Let S=all the earthly suffering we see. Let T=theism is true. Let L=there is life after death. Let P stand for the probability of something. Then P(S/T) might be less than P(S/~T), but P(S/T&L) not less than P(S/~T) (assuming that we are considering epistemic probabilities and we have not yet realized that T implies L, or at least makes L likely). Still, if (L) is unlikely itself, say, because it introduces the necessity of immaterial souls or the transmission of a person's material body to some material resurrection world upon that person's death, then it would not be reasonable to accept (T&L). Insofar as T itself implies L, or makes L very likely, then if L is very unlikely, so is T. Suppose it is very unlikely that Clark Kent saved one person in San Francisco and a minute later saved another person in New York. However, assume that it is not at all unlikely that he saved these two people *if* he is Superman *and* can fly at the speed of light. Suppose it is very unlikely that anyone is Superman; to atheists the existence of God is like the existence of Superman. Now add that Superman can travel at the speed of light; suppose it is even an essential property of Superman that he can travel at that speed. In other words, suppose it's true that *if* someone is Superman, then he can travel at the speed of light. That makes the hypothesis that Superman exists even more implausible. Likewise, suppose it's true that *if* God exists, there is an afterlife. But if it is unreasonable to think that there is an afterlife, then there is even more reason to think that God does not exist. A saving, or supplementary, hypothesis can be a sinking hypothesis![11]

Perrine and Wykstra write about expanding core theism by conjoining it with "specifying claims (such as the fallenness of nature, the depravity of humanity, the importance of free will, etc.)"[12] In *The Problem of Evil*, van Inwagen offers what he calls a defense against the problem of evil. A defense, unlike a theodicy, offers some hypothesis that, *for all we know*, is true and that makes the relevant evil compatible with the existence of God, while a theodicy argues that we know, or are at least are justified in believing, that such a hypothesis is true. To say that a hypothesis is true *for all we know* means that we are not justified in believing it false, even if we are also not justified in believing it true. Suppose we interpret van Inwagen as offering auxiliary hypotheses to save core theism against the challenges that the problem of evil poses (though I do not think that this is what he intended[13]) and, in particular, against the challenges the global problem of evil poses which looks at the vast amounts of horrible suffering ("horrors" for short) in the world, especially that experienced by innocent children.

Here's van Inwagen's story that he claims is, *for all we know*, true. There was once a sort of paradise on Earth after God miraculously changed man's primate ancestors into rational beings with free will. These early humans then exercised their free will, rebelled against God, and became separated from him. Once this occurred humans lost their preternatural powers that enabled them to protect themselves from wild beasts, disease, and natural disasters. Before their separation from God, they could tame wild beasts with a look, cure disease with a touch, and foresee natural disasters and thereby protect themselves from their destruction.[14] After the separation, they became decrepit with old age and mortal, and lacking perfect love, they harmed others out of jealousy and greed and other motives founded in their egoism inherited through the genes of their ancestors. God allowed, and continues to allow, the world to become a chaotic place where bad things happen by chance even to good people as his only hope of getting humans to freely return to him.

In summary, van Inwagen's defense is that, *for all we know*, there was something approaching paradise on Earth for rational human beings who were miraculously created by God. Then there was a fall due to man's rebellion against God caused by the imprudent and immoral exercise of his free will. No longer having "a representation of perfect love in the Beatific Vision" before their minds, humans were unable to control their selfish motives.[15] But now God has a plan for redemption, "a plan to restore separated humanity to union with himself," that involves horrible suffering of even innocent humans and animals, where that suffering itself serves no purpose (though apparently his plan of *allowing it* serves the purpose of encouraging people to want to reunite with him).[16] Van Inwagen says that innocent people suffering for no reason "is part of what being separated from God means; it means being the play thing of chance."[17]

Van Inwagen claims that *for all we know* the story he tells is true, but I think we are justified in believing it is false. And if that is the case, his story cannot serve as a saving auxiliary hypothesis for a version of expanded theism. Further, Perrine and Wykstra's hope of conjoining core theism with "specifying claims (such as the fallenness of nature, the depravity of humanity, the importance of free will, etc.)" looks less promising as a path to saving theism since van Inwagen's claims are about just those things.

But we are justified in believing that van Inwagen's story is false. First, some of what van Inwagen says seems contrary to evolutionary theory. He claims that our pre-human primate ancestors suddenly became rational as a result of God's miraculous intervention in nature. But according to evolutionary theory, advantageous traits in a population develop gradually as members of a species with less desirable traits do poorly in the competition for survival and reproduction.[18] Further, he claims that our ancestors lost their preternatural powers. But why would that happen since they would give those who possessed them an advantage when it comes to survival and reproduction? Part of the story that van Inwagen tells does not make sense from the standpoint of evolutionary theory.

And his story does not make sense from the standpoint of morality. Why would a wholly good God allow innocents at the time of the fall to suffer and also allow their descendants to suffer, including their innocent offspring? Did later children have original sin? But that makes no sense. My children are not guilty because I committed a crime. The descendants of the original sinners are not guilty because they are the descendants of such people. Perhaps allowing innocents to suffer is the only way *to encourage* those who have turned away from God to reunite with him. Suppose that were true. Is it morally permissible to allow those innocents to suffer terribly? We don't see any reason that would justify allowing that to happen, but maybe there are reasons beyond our ken for God to allow this. Still, if we are not justified in believing there *are* such reasons, this cannot serve as a saving hypothesis. You can't save the flat earth hypothesis by arguing that light rays *might* travel in long, shallow arcs. You need reason to believe they do.

Further, van Inwagen's story does not make sense given what we know of human psychology. If adult children are estranged from their parents, often the best way for the parents to restore the relationship is *not* to allow the children, and *their children,* to suffer terribly. Reconciliation is more likely if the parents show genuine concern and compassion for their estranged children and grandchildren by doing what they can to relieve their suffering, by helping them out, not by simply looking on and having the children wonder why their parents have not intervened on their behalf.

So given what we know about the world and human nature, we are justified in believing that the three main parts of van Inwagen's expanded free-will defense are false. It is not reasonable to believe that rationality arose in the way his story claims and that preternatural powers were had and then lost. It is not reasonable to believe that a wholly good, omnipotent, and omniscient God would allow all the horrors that have befallen the innocent who did not rebel against him. Finally, it is not reasonable to believe that God would adopt the harsh plan of redemption that van Inwagen proposes. Van Inwagen's story cannot serve as a saving hypothesis when conjoined with core theism. Van Inwagen claims that the story he tells is "consistent with what we know of human prehistory," that it is "a possible story," and that "it was the sort of story that *could* be true, that it represented a real possibility, that it was true for all you knew."[19] The first two parts of the last

claim are true, but it does not follow that it was true *for all you knew.* For the latter to be the case, we could not be justified in believing the story is false, but we
are. It is certainly a long way from being a story that we are justified in believing
which it must be to be an auxiliary hypothesis that can save core theism. It is not
even a story that it is as reasonable to believe as to disbelieve; it is not even a story
that warrants suspension of judgment.

B. Unfalsifiable Saving Hypotheses

Wykstra might respond in two ways to my objections to van Inwagen's story.
First, although van Inwagen's story may not serve as a good saving hypothesis,
there are other better candidates. Second, if atheists are going to argue that their
hypothesis better explains the evil in the world than the theist's hypothesis, they
need to consider the *total evidence,* taking into account not only the most obvious and awful examples of evil but also of good.[20]

Wykstra thinks the move from what he calls naive or shallow theism to deep
theism is motivated by an awareness of the depth and breadth of animal and
human suffering in the world, currently and throughout history.[21] The naive theist thinks that what God values and disvalues, what weights he gives to goods and
bads, and the connections between the two in the actual world, is on the surface,
easily discernible by humans on a little reflection. However, after becoming aware
of the extent and awfulness of the suffering in the world, the naive theist comes
to see that it is not so easy to discern God's purposes. So the saving hypothesis of
the deep theist is that we do not know all of what God values and disvalues, nor
do we know what relative weights he assigns to those values and disvalues. Finally,
we do not understand how evils in the actual world are connected to goods that
God values. We have some knowledge of what God values and disvalues, etc., but
our understanding, compared to his, is like the understanding of a young child
to that of his parents.[22]

One problem with this hypothesis of ignorance is that it is a retreat into mystery. Suppose some people believe in gremlins. Suppose people report seeing
them do nice things that are seemingly incompatible with their nature. A believer
in gremlins, a "gremlinite," might explain away the apparently disconfirming
observation by offering the saving hypothesis that gremlins are very clever beings and so we often cannot discern their reasons for doing, or failing to do, what
they do.

Further, Wykstra's saving hypothesis (that God would know much more than
we can grasp about goods and bads and which bads to allow for the sake of which
goods) should be assessed in light of the famous exchange between Antony Flew,
R.M. Hare, and Basil Mitchell more than a half century ago.[23] In Flew's parable,
a Believer will not let any evidence count against his belief that some gardener

tends a plot in the jungle where many flowers and many weeds are growing. Given his acceptance of the positivist's theory of what makes a claim cognitively meaningful (that is, meaningful and either true or false), Flew concluded that the Believer's claim is cognitively meaningless. We need not accept that theory of meaningfulness to make the more modest claim that the Believer's assertion that there is an invisible, intangible, empirically undetectable gardener who tends the plot is *meaningful but unjustified.*

The Perrine/Wykstra defense against the argument from evil faces a dilemma: either the auxiliary hypotheses that are conjoined with core theism are falsifiable or they are not. If, like van Inwagen's story they are falsifiable, there is good reason to think they are false. On the other hand, if they are like Wykstra's auxiliary hypotheses and are unfalsifiable, then the special theism that results from conjoining them with core theism is unjustified for the same reason that the Believer's view that there is an invisible, intangible, empirically undetectable gardener who tends the plot is unjustified. If a belief is justified, it must be either by *a priori* or empirical evidence, but neither Flew's Believer nor Wykstra's deep theist is justified in either of these ways in holding the beliefs they do. In particular, the deep theist is neither *a priori* nor empirically justified in believing that *there is* a God who allows all the horrors we observe for reasons beyond our ken.

Suppose, instead, the deep theist is justified *a priori* in believing that *if* there is a God, he would likely allow evils for reasons we would be unable to grasp, reasons beyond our ken. This should bring us back to Mitchell's parable, the parable of The Stranger. In that parable, a member of the resistance in an occupied country meets The Stranger. The Stranger tells the partisan that he is on their side and urges this man "to have faith in him no matter what happens." Later, The Stranger is observed sometimes helping members of the resistance but at other times "handing over patriots to the occupying power." Sometimes the partisan asks for help from The Stranger and receives it; at other times, he does not. When Wykstra urges Paul Draper and other atheists to attend to the *total evidence*, not just to the massive amount of terrible suffering experienced by the innocent, he is like the partisan who urges his friends to look at *all* The Stranger has done, not just to what appear to be betrayals of the resistance. In the situation of the parable, that is sound advice, but it would not help the partisan's case to assert that *if* The Stranger is on their side but very, very clever, he will sometimes act in ways that seem to help the resistance and sometimes in ways that seem to be betrayals of the resistance. His friends readily accept that conditional but think that there is so much evidence of betrayal that it is not reasonable to believe that The Stranger is on their side. Further, in the parable it is assumed that the partisan has met The Stranger and spent a night in conversation with him. That is the basis of his trust. Whether anyone has had comparable "meetings" with God is questionable. So the evidential situation of all of us is more like that of the friends than of the partisan.

There are other features in the parable of The Stranger that make it disanalogous to our actual situation regarding the evil we observe. First, we can understand why The Stranger might do what appears to be against the interests of the resistance, for he is a finite being who has limited power. But that excuse could not apply to God's allowing excessive, unnecessary suffering. Further, it seems legitimate for atheists to ignore good things that happen in the world, for many of the evils we observe do not seem necessary to bring about those goods, or to prevent greater evils. No matter how much good there is in the world, God would not allow excessive, unnecessary suffering. So we can ignore that good if we have reason to believe that there is such suffering.

Consider the following analogy. Smokey the Bear is against forest fires, and we observe a forest fire that it seems he could easily have prevented if he exists. It also appears that allowing it to burn was not needed to prevent even worse fires in the future or to help rejuvenate the forest. After reflection, we can see no reason why, if Smokey exists, he would have allowed this fire to burn. That gives us adequate reason to believe that Smokey does not exist. It does not matter if there are other fires that have been put out by sudden, intense downpours and still others that have been allowed to burn that have helped a forest rejuvenate and flourish. It's enough to disbelieve in Smokey that this fire was allowed to burn for no apparent reason. Similar reasoning applies to disbelief in God: there is reason to believe that he would not allow *all this terrible suffering of innocents* regardless of what other good things there are in the universe or what other bad things seem to have been inexplicably prevented.

IV. How Young Earthers Can Take Advantage of Expanded Theism

Contrary to what I have just argued, suppose, for the sake of argument, that we are justified in believing that the combination of all the good and evil that there is in the world is likely on some version of expanded theism. That is, assume that $P(O/T\&H_1)$ is fairly high. Let Y = the Earth is young (maybe six thousand years old, maybe a hundred, maybe only five minutes). Let O^* = there are deep river valleys, fossils that are very old according to scientific means of dating, cave paintings that are very old, etc. Let H_2 = it is better to have a world that appears to be very old but is not than one that appears very old and is because people in the former world can learn the lessons of (apparent) history without a good deal of suffering while people in the latter world cannot. Then the Young Earthers will claim that $P(O^*/T\&H_2)$ is fairly high.

I do not think anyone can reasonably dispute O^*, so let's consider H_2. van Inwagen himself writes:

> But it seems clear that a world in which horrible things occurred *only* in night-mares would be better than a world in which the same things occurred in real-ity, and that a morally perfect being would, all other things being equal, prefer a world in which horrible things were confined to dreams to a world in which they existed in reality.[24]

No doubt van Inwagen would argue that other things are not equal between a dream world and the real world because real free choice is possible only in a real world.[25] But the Young Earthers could agree and then respond that that is why God *eventually* created the real world, about one hundred years ago! He just did not want people to come into the world unprepared and without information available to them that would permit them to avoid certain horrible consequences of their contemplated actions. Defenders of the Young Earthers can argue that what most people take to be our world is significantly better than a dream world but, also, that their hundred-year-old world is significantly better than what most take to be our world.

Van Inwagen would probably reply that the hundred-year-old world is not significantly better than what we take to be our world because it would contain what he calls massive irregularity, that is, it is a world "in which the laws of na-ture fail in some massive way." He thinks that, *for all we know*, massive irregular-ity "is a defect in a world, a defect at least as great as the defect containing the patterns of suffering found in the actual world." And he says, "A world that came into existence five minutes ago, complete with memories of the unreal past, would on that count alone be massively irregular—if indeed such a world was meta-physically possible."[26] He would probably say something similar about the hundred-year-old world I imagined.

But while we can see how a world in which, say, the law of gravity often fails would not be as good as one in which it does not, the sort of massive irregularity we would find in a hundred-year-old world does not seem so bad. There will be no more harm, or frustration, in that world than in ours resulting from people forming and then trying to execute life plans, or even particular actions, and then failing. The only difference between the hundred-year-old world and what we take to be our world is that it began much later. There seems to be no disadvantages to the hundred-year-old world compared to the world as we usually conceive it to be. And it has the advantage that people can learn from the apparent past with-out creatures having to endure the real suffering that a real past would involve.

Nevertheless, one might hold that "massive deception is inconsistent with the nature of a perfect being,"[27] even if a hundred-year-old universe is much *better* than what we take to be the actual world. But why is massive deception inconsis-tent with the nature of a perfect being? Suppose a group of people in Nazi Germany could have saved thousands of Jews by engaging in some massive deception, say, by hiding them in an underground city and then lying to the Nazis when they asked if they were hiding Jews. That massive deception seems morally permissible, even obligatory, if those people were sure that they would not be caught and punished. So if God exists, it would have been morally permissible, even obligatory, for him to massively deceive the Nazis regarding the whereabouts of the Jews since he would not fear being caught and punished, or any other bad consequences.

I have defended what I called H2, the hypothesis that it would be better to have an Earth that is hundreds of years old with apparent signs of age and lessons that can be learned from an apparent human and natural history than an Earth that is actually billions of years old whose history is just like the apparent history of the young earth but with enormous amounts of actual horrible suffering of innocents. I take it as intuitively obvious that we are not justified in believing Young Earthism and H2=(Y&H2) on the total evidence, E, that is, (Y&H2/E). I argued earlier that if we took van Inwagen's story as an auxiliary hypothesis it would not be reasonable to accept a version of theism that conjoined theism with that story because that story is not itself reasonable. In fact, it would be difficult to find any "specifying claims (such as the fallenness of nature, the depravity of humanity, the importance of free will, etc.)" that would qualify as reasonable saving hypotheses when conjoined with core theism. However, even if someone could come up with a specifying hypothesis, H1, that is as reasonable as H2, it would not show that it is reasonable to accept (T&H1) on the total evidence. That is because, intuitively, it is not reasonable to accept (Y&H2) on the total evidence, and (T&H1) is a relevantly similar world view.

Some might think that (T&H1) has an epistemic advantage over (Y&H2) because that form of expanded theism is compatible with science (with cosmology and geology) while expanded Young Earthism is not. Of course, the Young Earthers differ from most people, including the expanded theists, in their view about how old the universe is, but they accept the scientific method when applied to what happens after the beginning of the universe (which is also true of scientists even if they disagree about when that beginning occurred), all the same laws of nature as standard science, etc. They just think it began much later than science claims. But what makes their hypothesis a poor one is not that difference. It is a poor one for two reasons: (1) it is like the hypothesis of the invisible, intangible, unsmellable, etc., gardener in that there is no way in principle to falsify it; (2) it posits immaterial beings whose reasons and methods of causing things to happen in the material world are necessarily beyond our grasp (beyond our ken). It is a hypothesis of mystery. The same objection would apply to a gremlin theory in which invisible, intangible, unsmellable gremlins exist and are appealed to in order to explain as yet unexplained phenomena, assuming that nothing in that gremlin theory is inconsistent with ordinary science, apart from introducing empirically indiscernible entities whose ways of interacting with the physical world are a mystery.

Another objection is that we could not learn from the past if expanded Young Earthism were true because given the deception involved, we could not be justified in believing that God is not deceiving us now. But the Young Earthers can hold that God gave us reason to believe in an apparent past that is just like the actual world, that is, a past with apparent laws of nature with the same content as the laws of nature in the actual world that now exists, and with persons who have the apparent psychological nature that actual humans now have. That is why we can learn from the apparent past, and we have no reason to distrust God just because he deceived us about the age of the earth or the universe. He did that for good reasons at least some of which we can grasp.

V. The G. E. Moore shift

Skeptics sometimes argue:

> 1. If I know I have a hand, then I can rule out skeptical hypotheses such as that I am a handless being deceived by an evil demon, a handless human in The Matrix, or a handless brain-in-a-vat (a BIV).
> 2. But I cannot rule out those skeptical hypotheses.
> 3. So I don't know that I have a hand.

Such an argument can be generalized to conclude that I don't know anything about the external world. G. E. Moore argued to the opposite conclusion by accepting (1) and then arguing:

> 2*. I know I have a hand.
> 3*. Therefore, I can rule out the skeptical hypotheses.

The theists might try something similar. I argued above:

> 1A. If God exists, he would not allow excessive, unnecessary suffering.
> 2A. But there is excessive, unnecessary suffering.
> 3A. So God does not exist.

But the theist might accept (1A) and then argue to the opposite conclusion:

> 2B. God exists.
> 3B. So God has not allowed excessive, unnecessary suffering.

Of course, there have been many attempts to argue for (2B). Here I am just going to object to an argument from Plantinga's theory of warrant that concludes that we are warranted in believing that God exists and relies on the claim that we have a *sensus divinitatis*.

For Plantinga, warrant is what is required to turn true belief into knowledge.[28] According to Plantinga's theory of warrant, warrant is a function of a person's cognitive faculties that are aimed at producing true beliefs, when those faculties are functioning properly and are being exercised in an appropriate environment, that is, in an environment for which they were designed or are suited, say, as a result of evolution. More specifically, his view is: S is warranted in believing P if, and only if, (i) S's belief that P is the result of S's cognitive faculties that are aimed at producing true beliefs (not at beliefs that have survival value or some other pragmatic benefit) functioning properly, (ii) S's belief that P is formed in an appropriate environment, that is, in an environment for which those cognitive faculties were designed or suited, say, as a result of evolution, (iii) those properly functioning cognitive faculties are reliable in that environment.[29]

Plantinga might go on to argue that we have a *sensus divinitatis* that sometimes functions properly and in certain circumstances satisfies the three conditions specified in his account of warrant. Perhaps when he looks at a flower, a sunset, or a majestic snow-capped mountain on the basis of his *sensus divinitatis* he immediately forms the belief, "God created that," and according to his theory, is thereby warranted in his belief.

Of course, someone might claim to have a *sensus gremlintis* or *leprechaunitis* that also satisfies Plantinga's three conditions of warrant, but they would not be justified in believing that there are gremlins or leprechauns, nor justified in believing that they were warranted in holding that there are gremlins or leprechauns, if they were not justified in believing that they have such a sense. Similarly, no one would be justified in believing propositions that imply that God exists on the basis of having a *sensus divinitatis,* nor justified in believing they were warranted in accepting those propositions, unless they were justified in believing they had such a sense. I see no reason for thinking that any of us has a *sensus divinitatis.* So even if Plantinga's theory of warrant were correct, it would not get him very far.

But his theory is not correct. After offering his "first approximation" to a theory of warrant, he offers the following account of the necessary conditions of warrant.

> A belief has warrant for me only if (1) it has been produced in me by cognitive faculties that are working properly (functioning as they ought to, subject to no cognitive dysfunction) in a cognitive environment that is appropriate for my kinds of cognitive faculties, (2) the segment of the design plan governing production of that belief is aimed at the production of true beliefs, and (3) there is a high statistical probability that a belief produced under those conditions will be true.[30]

I am not sure why Plantinga does not consider (1)-(3) sufficient for warrant as he did in his "first approximation." Perhaps he thought a fourth condition is also necessary where (4)=there are no defeaters of his belief.

Someone I call Truenorth is an example of a person who meets all of conditions (1)-(4) but, intuitively, lacks warrant for his belief.[31] Truenorth has an internal compass that makes him reliable in his judgments about direction. You can blindfold Truenorth, spin him around, and with the blindfold still in place, ask him what direction is north (or south or east or west). His internal compass works properly if he has not drunk too much Irish whiskey, and all environments on Earth are appropriate except when he is standing near some powerful electronic magnets. When that compass is working properly in an appropriate environment, he will always give the correct answer to questions about which direction is north (south, east, and west). However, imagine that Truenorth has not yet confirmed the reliability of his internal compass. In this respect he is like Laurence BonJour's Norman, the clairvoyant whose first clairvoyant experience is of the president in New York.[32] However, unlike Norman there is no defeater for Truenorth. Norman should wonder whether his vision of the president in New York is a hallucination and why no one else has reported having such experiences. We can imagine that Truenorth has had many "directional experiences" but has had no other experiences that confirm them. He assumes that everyone else has similar experiences, though whether they have or have not has never come up. According to Plantinga's theory of warrant, Truenorth is warranted in believing that a certain direction is north when someone asks him for the first time whether the indicated direction is north. But intuitively he is not warranted and does not know that the indicated direction is north. He has no confirmed track record to go on, no *internal evidence* concerning the reliability of his sense of direction. He is neither warranted nor justified, nor does he know that the direction he points to is north even though it is. He has a reliably produced true belief but nothing more. According to Plantinga's theory he is warranted and knows that the direction to which he points is north. According to other reliabilists, he is also justified in believing that it is.

Because Plantinga's theory of warrant is false, it cannot be used in a G. E. Moore shift to show that there is not excessive, unnecessary suffering (appearances to the contrary). There are lots of other arguments for the existence of God. Except for the ontological argument, none conclude to the existence of a *wholly good* Being. In light of all the suffering of innocents in the world, I do not think that any of these arguments can be supplemented to reach such a conclusion even if they are sound in concluding that an all-knowing and all-powerful Being exists, or to the weaker conclusion that a *very* knowledgeable and *very* powerful being exists. I think that even arguments to these weaker conclusions are unsound, but that is not at issue here. The problem of evil is a sound argument against the existence of an *all*-knowing, *all*-powerful, *and wholly good* Being.

Notes

1. The suffering itself may not be needed to bring about a greater good, but allowing it may be needed since the good which consists in the exercise of a person's free will may be realized only if no one interferes with that exercise.

2. Peter van Inwagen, *The Problem of Evil* (Oxford: Oxford University Press, 2006), 4.

3. See van Inwagen's "Reflections on the Chapters by Draper, Russell, and Gale" in *The Evidential Argument from Evil*, ed. Daniel Howard-Snyder (Indiana University Press, 1996), 219–43. See, especially, pages 234–35, where van Inwagen discusses my essay, "Defenseless" (193–205). See also his essay, "The Problem of Evil, Air, and Silence," note 11, 172–73, reprinted in the same collection, and his "The Magnitude, Duration, and Distribution of Evil: A Theodicy," *Philosophical Topics* 16 (1988), 161–87, esp. 167–68. I respond in an essay referred to in note 5, below.

4. This case was first discussed by me in "The Persistent Problem of Evil," *Faith and Philosophy* 6 (1989): 121–39.

5. See Bruce Russell, "The Problem of Evil: Why Is There So Much Suffering?" in *Introduction to Philosophy: Classical and Contemporary Readings*, 3rd ed., ed. Louis P. Pojman (Oxford: Oxford University Press, 2004), 207–208 for a description of this example and a list of other types of horrendous suffering. The Swinsons also coached their other children to take the fall before calling police about Ariana's death.

6. Derek Parfit, *On What Matters*, vol. 1 (Oxford: Oxford University Press, 2011), 216, 228. Parfit states the "mere means" principle on page 221. Hereafter I refer to Parfit's book as *OWM* and indicate which volume by *OWM* I or *OWM* II.

7. *OWM* I, 361; see also 229, 361–62 and *OWM* II, 47 (n. 9), 55, 146–47. My brackets.

8. Philippa Foot gives this example, but with the people in the cave having the dynamite, in "The Problem of Abortion and the Doctrine of the Double Effect," which first appeared in the *Oxford Review* (1967). It is reprinted in Philippa Foot, *Virtues and Vices, and Other Essays on Moral Philosophy* (Berkley: University of California Press, 1978), 19–32. The example appears on page 21. I add the bit about the relative amounts of suffering and so on.

9. Alastair Norcross also makes this point: "No sane person, for example, would think it impermissible to give a light, slightly unpleasant, slap to the face of the innocent child of a terrorist, if that were both necessary and sufficient to distract him momentarily, and save the lives of ten million people." Norcross, "Using as a Means" (lecture presented on March 10, 2014 at *Russell X*, a mini-conference in philosophy, Healdsburg, California), 4. Jim Sterba noted that the exceptions I have offered involve human beings who lack the power to prevent great harm to some without using others as mere means. But lack of power could not be the basis of exceptions for God. However, it might be true that there are some evils that can be prevented, or goods realized, that would logically or metaphysically treat others as mere means, and it would be morally permissible for God to treat these others in this way. These examples also open that door.

10. Stephen Wykstra, "Seeing Through MIST: Abductive Worldviewing, Constructive Skeptical Theism, and Buchak's 'Way Forward'" (talk delivered at Notre Dame University, February 2014, work still in progress), 9. Hereafter referred to as MIST.

11. See Timothy Perrine and Stephen Wykstra, "Skeptical Theism, Abductive Atheology, and Theory Versioning," 15. http://philpapers.org/archive/WYKSTRA. Perrine and Wykstra argue that if (i) the likelihood of (L) on (T&k) is very high and (ii) the likelihood of O=what we know about the facts of good and evil, is more likely on (L&T&k) than on Naturalism (N)

and k, then naturalism is not a better explanation of O than (L&T&k). That would not be true if the likelihood of (L) on k were low, that is, if P(L/k) were low. P(N/O&k) might be higher than P(T&L/O&k) if the prior probability, P(N/k), were higher than the prior probability, P(L/k). Of course, if P(T&L/k) were low because P(L/k) was low, then insofar as L is likely on (T&k), P(T/k) has always been low. But we may not have realized that until we realized that L is likely on (T&k) but is itself unlikely.

12. Perrine and Wykstra, "Skeptical Theism," 10.

13. Van Inwagen says, in *The Problem of Evil* (3), that he will tell "various just-so stories about the coexistence of God and evil" as counterexamples to the validity of the argument from evil to God's nonexistence. He seems to be arguing against a premise that says if God exists, then such-and-such would not happen. His argument seems to be that we do not know for certain that this sort of premise is true.

14. Ibid., 86.

15. Ibid., 86–87.

16. Ibid., 85–90 for the complete story that van Inwagen calls "the expanded free will defense"; 87 for the quote.

17. Ibid., 89. See also, 88 and 103, where van Inwagen says "the existence of horrors was one of the natural and inevitable consequences of this separation." By "horror" van Inwagen means any particular very bad event, 95.

18. Ibid., 128–31. Van Inwagen considers an expanded free-will defense that assumes rationality evolved gradually and naturally. While he grants that such an expanded free-will defense has some advantages, he concludes that "all in all" the story he tells that involves the sudden and miraculous appearance of rationality and free will "raises the fewest problems" (130). The selective breeding experiments begun by Dimitry Belyaev in the Soviet Union in the 1950s to produce domesticated foxes from wild ones do not provide evidence that changes in nature can occur rapidly because the results (tamer foxes) are not due to *natural* selection.

19. Ibid., 90 for the first two quotes, 92 for the second.

20. See Perrine and Wykstra, "Skeptical Theism," 21–22. They complain about the thinness of the data of good and evil on which Paul Draper bases his abductive argument.

21. See MIST, 18, where Wykstra tells the story of Polly, who moves from naïve to deep theism after Wykstra's young alter ego, Artsky, makes her "aware of types of suffering she had never imagined."

22. Perrine and Wykstra, "Skeptical Theism," 27–28.

23. Flew, "Theology and Falsification," *New Essays in Philosophical Theology* (London: SCM Press, 1955), 96–108. Reprinted in Louis P. Pojman, ed., *Philosophy of Religion: An Anthology*, 2nd ed. (Belmont, CA: Wadsworth, 1994), 398–402.

24. Ibid., 69–70. Italics are van Inwagen's.

25. James Pryor argues in his essay on the film *The Matrix* that what people in the Matrix lack is real freedom. See "What's So Bad about Living in the Matrix," in *Philosophers Explore the Matrix*, ed. Chris Grau (New York: Oxford University Press, 2005), 40–61. Text also available at http://www.jimpryor.net/research/papers/matrix/plain.html.

26. Van Inwagen, *The Problem of Evil*, all quotes from 114–15. In "Skeptical Theism," Perrine and Wykstra write of God valuing "regular laws of nature" and continuity (30), and Wykstra alone writes of coming to recognize "the value of having a world that is governed by regular laws of nature" in MIST, 17.

27. Van Inwagen, *The Problem of Evil*, 121. In e-mail correspondence William Hasker wrote that God would not implant false memories in people that would make them believe that they had committed horrendous evils when they had not, for then some of those people would feel

guilty for the rest of their lives for acts they had not committed. I agree that this would be a bad thing, but it is not nearly as bad as allowing all the suffering of innocents that has occurred if the Earth is really as old as we think and we have a pretty accurate picture of the suffering of innocents across time.

28. Alvin Plantinga, preface to *Warrant and Proper Function* (New York: Oxford University Press, 1993), v.

29. Ibid., 19. Plantinga offers what he calls "a first approximation" to an account of warrant.

30. Ibid., 46. See also Plantinga's summary of his account of warrant, p. 237.

31. Plantinga argues that sometimes warrant requires that you know, or at least warrantedly believe, that something is a reliable indicator of what you believe, say, that the way some brush along a mountain path looks is a reliable indicator that a bear has been by (*Warrant and Proper Function*, 44). I think what is required for you to know, say, that a bear has recently passed by is that you be internalistically justified in believing that the crushed brush is a reliable indicator. Otherwise, you would be like Truenorth but about the reliability of the indicator, not about compass directions. You would have no reason to believe that the indicator is reliable and so would not know that the indicator is reliable even if it is. Plantinga's theory of warrant and knowledge is externalistic and so leaves out this essential element of internalistic evidence and justification that is required for knowledge.

32. For the case of Norman and the accompanying discussion, see Laurence BonJour, *The Structure of Empirical Knowledge* (Cambridge, MA: Harvard University Press, 1985), 41–45.

6 Beyond the Impasse

Contemporary Moral Theory and the Crisis of Skeptical Theism

Stephen J. Wykstra

DOES CONTEMPORARY MORAL theory have untapped relevance to the problem of evil?[1] As a novice to moral theory, my hypothesis is that it does. To test this, I shall here look to moral theory for help in addressing a worrisome objection to "skeptical theistic" defenses (including my own) against evidential arguments from evil. The objection is that such defenses of theism covertly entail a moral skepticism itself inimical to theism. Even friends of skeptical theism here sense a looming crisis.[2] If contemporary moral theory is relevant to the problem of evil anywhere, it should—whether for friend or foe—be relevant here.

But contemporary moral theory covers a vast terrain: to look for help in the right place, we must clarify where the problem really lies. Our ordinary moral sensibility—"moral commonsense," as Michael Bergmann calls it—has a broadly consequential aspect. This aspect becomes most evident in moral-choice situations where deontological considerations of intrinsic wrongness, while immediately ruling out many options, still leave two or more options open. In such situations, Bergmann says, moral commonsense will evaluate the remaining options by inquiring into the good and bad consequences of each.[3]

Such consequential inquiry, of course, never brings into view the full set of consequences: it discloses but a subset—a limited sample, as it were, of the total population of each action's morally relevant consequences. The conflict with skeptical theism emerges when we ask whether, in using this sample to determine "the right thing to do," moral commonsense is tacitly assuming that the sample is representative of the total population of consequences. It seems to many that it does—that moral commonsense in its consequential aspect relies on what I will call the Representativeness Presumption (for short, REP):

REP: Our sample of morally relevant action-consequences is representative of the total population of morally relevant action-consequences.

If this is so, then moral commonsense seems on collision course with skeptical theism. For one part of skeptical theism is, as I'll call it, the Deep Universe Hypothetical (for short, DUH):

> DUH: If the theistic God created and governs our universe, then it is not unlikely that this universe is morally deep—one in which many events we can see are allowed (or caused) by God because doing so essentially serves goods sufficiently deep—in themselves, or in their connection to these events—as to be beyond our ken.

And in affirming DUH, skeptical theists seem to be embracing—or at least showing willingness to live with—an "Unrepresentativeness Supposition" (for short, UNREP):

> UNREP: The range of goods/connections we see are not representative of the goods/connections that exist.

The antimony between REP and UNREP is the site of the potential conflict on which this paper focuses.

The site of conflict gives us a clue as to what region of contemporary moral theory may be of help. While the consequential aspect of moral commonsense does not presuppose any form of utilitarianism,[4] all forms of utilitarianism do champion some form of consequential reasoning. In recent secular moral theory we find a resurgent utilitarianism, with vigorous discussion of the nature and viability of consequential moral reasoning. If that arena of discussion can illuminate the role of "representativeness" in consequential moral reasoning, it promises also to illuminate the moral skepticism objection against skeptical theism.

Before turning to secular moral theory, however, Part One will discharge a more sacred mandate:[5] to consider how the Pauline principle of Catholic moral theory, taken in relation to so-called trolley cases, might bear on the problem of evil. Here one possibility is that St. Paul's dictum to the church in Rome—"Never do evil that good may come of it"—exposes the God of skeptical theism as a rank consequentialist. Drawing on some moral-theoretic distinctions by Derek Parfit as well as by Augustine and Calvin, Part One shows how we may affirm the revolutionary significance of St. Paul's dictum while also giving consequential moral justification—for humans and for God—the scope required by skeptical theism.

Turning to the perceived conflict between skeptical theism and moral commonsense, Part Two takes its cues from an exchange at the 2010 Plantinga Retirement Conference,[6] at which Michael Bergmann's important paper defended skeptical theism against the moral skepticism objection, and my own paper—given through the persona of my twisted doppelganger "Artsky W. Evets"—attacked Bergmann's defense. Part Two argues that the impasse between

Bergmann and Artsky arises from lack of clarity about the notion of "objective moral wrongness"—a notion that both Artsky and Bergmann invoke with little attention to its extensive treatment within contemporary moral theory.

To remedy this, Part Three seeks help from Derek Parfit's recent refinement of a notion of objective moral wrongness adumbrated by Richard Brandt a half-century earlier. By extending Parfit's distinctions between different senses of the objective notion, Part Three argues that for Parfit's most relevant sense of wrongness, we must delimit the set of "morally relevant consequences" to consequences that lie, in principle, within an "optimal moral horizon" of the moral agent, and that this delimitation reconciles the REP and UNREP presumptions of moral commonsense and skeptical theism.

A last important question is how to harmonize this Parfit-refined version of skeptical theism with views of God emerging within the Hebrew and Christian traditions. Part Four seeks the desired concinnity by reflection on Jesus' teaching that in God's new kingdom, all of humanity—Gentile as well as Jew—is empowered to grow into being "friends of God." This divine-human friendship, it is proposed, involves an increasing overlap of the divine and human moral horizons, through an increasingly shared domain of goods about which God cares passionately, and equips us to care about as well.

1. The Pauline Principle Versus Skeptical Theism?

In his letter to the church in Rome (Romans 3:8), St. Paul resists those who say (or who take Christians to say) "Let us do evil that good may come of it." Catholic moral theorists find here a "Pauline principle" to resist unduly consequentialist modes of moral thinking that give "overall best consequences" such weight as to justify actions that we might on deontic grounds deem as intrinsically wrong. This was also, we'll see, the point stressed by Philippa Foot and Judith Jarvis Thompson in their pioneering use of trolley cases to challenge consequentialist moral theories.

But their appeal to trolley cars seriously backfired. In some such cases, the acts described, though extreme, have become seen by many as not just morally permissible but morally required. The Pauline principle, Sterba thus writes, "has been rejected as an absolute principle," because "there clearly are exceptions to it." In some such extreme cases, he writes, "surely doing evil that good may come of it is justified."[7]

1.1. Paulinism à la Parfit: Morally Decisive Reasons

But should we really describe such extreme cases as exceptions to the Pauline principle? Do they really show that the principle "is not an absolute"? And in such cases, should we really say that the agent is "doing evil"? While the phrasings (or my reading of them) may be minor slips, they are also *felices culpae* in which lie insights that might otherwise elude us.

1.1.1. Are Trolley Cases "Exceptions"?

Philippa Foot and Judith Jarvis Thomson, in their early work pioneering the use of trolley cases to test moral theories, expected those cases to mobilize strong intuitions against consequentialist theories. The results were not what they had hoped for. As Thomson recounts in her 2012 Dewey lecture, her own earliest publication sought to identify what was lacking in current philosophy by calling attention to obvious truths oddly absent from G. E. Moore's famous commonsense list of the "things we know." Reflecting on the strategy of trying to use such truths to refute consequentialist moral theories, she writes:

> Let us go back to Moore's list. I mentioned that moral directives—among propositions of many other kinds—are missing. Here is an example that is familiar from the literature: we ought not to kill one person to save five. Or a bit more carefully: we ought not to kill one bystander even if we would thereby save the lives of five bystanders from being killed by someone else. I think it belongs on Moore's list because it is obviously true.
>
> I will call those of us who think it obviously true the Believers. There are philosophers who think the Believers mistaken. On their view, if we are so situated, then we ought to kill the one bystander. Those philosophers are of course the Consequentialists.[8]

One reason the strategy misfires is that we can always raise the stakes. Suppose killing one innocent bystander is the only way to save not just five bystanders but fifty . . . or five hundred, or five thousand, or (with nuclear terrorism) five million. In some region on this continuum, it seems, our commonsense moral intuitions—perhaps even Foot's and Thomson's intuitions—must surely start to tremble and then to yield. With this many lives saved, it seems increasingly permissible—perhaps even obligatory—to kill the one innocent bystander. Call such a region the "proper-yielding region." It is easy to think—even for nonconsequentialists—that such proper-yielding regions show the Pauline principle is not absolute—that it has exceptions.

But there is here is a crucial meta issue: what does it take, to have an exception that shows some proposed moral principle is not "absolute"? Consider a more specific principle: "let us not lie that good may come of it." To seek an exception showing this is not absolute, we would look for a situation where an envisioned action is a lie, and yet is to be done (for the sake of the good that comes from it). Here we at least know what we are looking for. But to seek an exception showing the Pauline principle is not an absolute, it then seems, we would look for a situation where an action is a "doing of evil" and yet is to be done (for the sake of the good coming from it). But to look for this sounds like looking for a circle that is a square—unless, in the phrase "doing of evil," the word "evil" is given some restricted sense.

1.1.2. Augustine on Evil-1 and Evil-2

One pertinent restricted sense is distinguished by Augustine, who pioneered linking the problem of evil with contemporary moral theory. In Book 1 of *On Free Choice of the Will*, written soon after his conversion, Augustine does this through a dialogue between two characters—Augie and Evo, let's call them, to keep them distinct from the actual author Augustine and his actual student Evodius. Evo opens: "Tell me, please, whether God is not author of evil!" To this, his teacher Augie replies:[9]

> I will tell you, if you will first make clear what you mean by "evil" in your question. For we often use the word "evil" in two senses. Sometimes we use it to refer to the "evil" a man has done; other times we use it to refer to the "evil" a man has undergone.

Augie does not explain what the two senses of the word "evil" are; with a gesture at two types of sentences, he takes them to be pretty obvious. On reflection, he is of course right. When we say Voldemort did evil, we mean he did something morally wrong or wicked. Call this Evil-1. When we say modern medicine has ameliorated the evils of polio, small pox, and anthrax, we refer not to morally wrong deeds but to events or conditions of a certain sort—the sort that bring pain, suffering, loss. Call this Evil-2.

Augie now, distinction in hand, can answer Evo's question about whether God causes evil. Yes and no, he says.

Yes, God does cause Evil-2: God does so whenever in justice God chastises a sinner through punishment: punishment involves pain, suffering, or loss; so causing punishment always causes evil in the Evil-2 sense. In the King James translation of Scripture this older sense is ubiquitous: time and time again the prophets use language as does Jer. 32:42: "For thus saith the LORD; Like as I have brought all this great evil upon this people, so will I bring upon them all the good that I have promised them."

But no, says Augie, God does not ever cause Evil-1, or cause others to do Evil-1, for God is good. When Jeremiah says that God brought "great evil upon his people," the evils are events like plagues or conquests by enemies, and calling them "evils" means only that they bring massive pain, suffering, loss, and destruction.[10]

We are thus no closer to having, in trolley cases, exceptions to the Pauline principle. To be exceptions, they would need to be situations where doing x is doing evil yet is also—due to the good that comes of it—what one ought to do. But to see them as such involves sophistic equivocation. So far forth, then, the Pauline principle remains an absolute: proper-yielding trolley cases are in no way exceptions to it.

1.1.3. OUT OF THE FRYING PAN

But this defense has a problem: it appears to have the Pauline principle jumping from the frying pan into the fire. The principle now seems to be saying that we cannot do evil by lying, stealing, or killing for the sake of the good that comes from it, because when the good is sufficiently good, it makes the lying, stealing, or killing no longer a case of doing evil (Evil-1). We seem to have preserved the principle's absoluteness at the price of reducing it to a tautology.

One way to avoid this problem is to understand the Pauline principle as resting on standard moral rules (do not steal, do not lie, and so on) taken themselves as absolutes. So understood, St. Paul's dictum "let us not do evil that good may come of it" is then saying "let us never violate one of these standard rules—no matter what good comes of so doing!" There is, in this response, an instinct to be honored. From a Biblical point of view, treating the standard rules as absolutes is far closer to moral reality than taking them as prudential rules like "don't drink coffee after 6 p.m."[11]

The problem is that even so, Scripture seems to recognize that standard rules such as "do not lie" do indeed, when the consequences are extraordinary, have genuine exceptions. To protect new-born infants, for example, the Hebrew midwives disobeyed the Pharaoh and then brazenly lied about it. And God, Scripture tells us (Exo. 1:20), approved of their actions: "Because the midwives feared God, he gave them families of their own." For these standard negative rules, Scripture seems illuminated by the well-known moral-theoretic distinction pioneered by W. D. Ross: each such rule identifies a wrong-making feature of acts imposing on us a *prima facie* duty that can be overridden if the act has other features that, by generating conflicting and more weighty prima facie duties, dictate a different *all-things-considered* moral duty.[12]

But now the threat of tautology resurfaces. Is St. Paul's dictum no more than the tautology "Violating our *all-things-considered* moral duty that good may come of it is something we morally ought never to do"?

Here Parfit can help us. Parfit, tackling the "why be moral" question that Socrates put to Glaucon and Adeimantus, distinguishes several senses of "what we morally ought to do." One of these is the "morally-decisive-reason" sense.[13] To ask whether *x* is "what we morally ought to do" in this latter sense is, Parfit says, to ask whether the net moral reasons for doing *x* trump any and all net nonmoral reasons we may have for not doing the action. The trumping dimension holds true to ordinary language. Just as we keep a question open by saying "that it is the *legal* thing to do does not make it the morally *right* thing to do," so also we close the question by saying "it is the *right* thing to do—so do it!"

We can, with Parfit's cue, see the Pauline principle as generalizing this. It says that whenever an action violates our all-things-considered moral duty, this trumps any and all *nonmoral* reasons favoring the action. So taken, the principle is not a trivial tautology. Neither the gods petitioned in first-century Rome nor the idols pursued in twenty-first-century America give decisive weight to moral considerations. Both they and we easily allow net considerations from "the moral point of view" to be trumped by considerations from other viewpoints—of personal advancement, of social etiquette, of national security, even of "religious correctness." Against this stands the Pauline principle, rudely proclaiming, with all of Israel's prophets, that the God of Heaven and Earth cares overridingly about justice, and means us to care overridingly about it too. What is right from the moral point of view overrides net considerations from any or all of these other points of view.

So understood, St. Paul's principle is no truism: it is as revolutionary now as then. It does not, however, offer us any deontology of "intrinsic moral wrongs" that are indefeasible by the consequential aspect of moral reasoning. It does not put us in a position to say that a good agent (human, angelic, or divine) could never, no matter what his or her consequential reasons may be, perform an action of some particular descriptively characterized sort.[14]

1.2. Probing the Pauline Principle

In the opening of *On Free Choice of the Will*, Evo is clearly perplexed about the source of moral evil, of deeds that are Evil-1. Augie argues that God is a cause (sometimes) of events that are Evil-2 (bringing pain, loss, etc.), but never of deeds that are Evil-1 (morally wrong, sinful, wicked). This seems almost self-evident: God is, after all, morally good through and through; surely God could never cause someone to sin.

Intuitively, this "never" seems compelling. Still, young Augustine feels the need to give an argument for it. This is always a bad idea. His argument will have a problem. The problem will lead a more mature Augustine—and, in his footsteps a millennium later, John Calvin—to theologically challenge the "never." His challenge, and Calvin's deployment of it, will cast an illuminating shadow over the problem of God's relation to Evil-1.

1.2.1. Augustine's No-No Argument

Augie begins from the claim that since God is good, God cannot do evil. From this he steps or perhaps slides—call it a slep—to the claim that God never causes another agent to do evil ("God is not the author of the evil a man does"). The slep relies on a tacit premise: if God does not do evil deeds, then God does not cause others to do them either. Call this the "no-do so no-cause premise" or the no-no premise for short. It is the fulcrum of the no-no argument:

NO-NO 1: God does not himself do Evil-1 deeds.

NO-NO 1.5: If God does not do Evil-1 deeds, then God does not cause others to do Evil-1 deeds, either.

NO-NO 2: Therefore, God does not cause others to do Evil-1 deeds.

Now Augie treats NO-NO 1.5 as so obvious as to need no defense—indeed, to need no articulation: it is wholly tacit. Why? What is its intuitive rationale, its epistemic prime mover? One might suggest this:

NO-NO 1.5 Version A: If it is morally wrong for agent Y to do a deed, then it is morally wrong for any other agent X to cause Y to do this deed.

But this version puts agent X under moral requirements, and some theists—perhaps including Augustine—would resist this, instead seeing God as the source of moral requirements.[15] What Augie stresses is God's goodness: this itself, we might think, precludes some things, such as God's taking pleasure in sin. With this in mind, a better rationale may be:

NO-NO 1.5 Version B1: If the goodness of any being Y precludes Y from doing Evil-1 deeds, then that goodness also precludes Y from causing any other agent, X, to do Evil-1 (morally wrong) deeds.

Call this the general preclusion thesis, as it applies to any good being—human, angelic, or divine. But what it entails—and what Augie needs—is a more modest special preclusion thesis:

NO-NO 1.5 Version B2: If the goodness of God precludes God from doing any morally wrong deeds, then it also precludes God from causing any other agent, X, to do morally wrong deeds.

Though B2 is more modest, its epistemic rationale arises from B1, so in considering it, we should also keep B1 in view.

1.2.2. CALVIN'S CORRECTION

John Calvin—following, he says, the mature Augustine—rejects the special preclusion thesis. It contradicts, he thinks, a Biblical view of God's sovereignty. Consider the story of Joseph and his brothers (Gen. 37: 18–36). Joseph's brothers, desiring to rid themselves of their much-favored brother, resolve to kill him and leave the corpse in a pit to be devoured by animals. At the pleading of Reuben and Judah, they eventually decide instead to sell him to passing Ishmaelites. What caused the brothers to act so wickedly? We—softies that we are—want to say it was not God: God merely allowed their action. Calvin rebukes us. Scripture, he urges, teaches God's intimate sovereignty over all events including the brothers' evil deeds: the distinction between allowing an event and causing the event has no easy application to divine agency over human actions.[16]

Does Calvin then think that God is the sole cause of all that happens—that human selves (or created things in general) lack causal powers altogether? While Calvin often sounds this way, recent scholarship suggests that once Calvin's varied polemical emphases are seen in historical context,[17] his considered view is a nuanced version of Thomistic "concurrentist" metaphysics on which divine causation is fully compossible with creaturely causation.[18] Since on this picture divine and creaturely causes have roles at different levels, they do not obey the additivity postulate: divine will and human voluntary agency can, each of them, be *full* causes of one and the same action.

Admittedly, giving so strong a causal role to God is, for cases of horrendous moral evil, a pill too bitter for most of us to swallow. Still, Calvin gives the pill a sugar coating that may allow its use in other cases. For the deplorable action of Joseph's brothers, Calvin stresses that God, in his strong causal role, had different motives and intentions than did the brothers in their causal role. In self-causing their action, the brothers acted from jealousy, intending nothing but ill for Joseph. But in God's causation of the same action, God acts from love, intending nothing but good—good for Joseph, for his family, for the people of the whole region. Here Calvin finds something of great pastoral importance when Joseph later, after disclosing his identity to his brothers, affirms God's sovereignty. "You meant it to me for evil," he says, "but God meant it to me for good." Calvin's concurrentist view, we shall next see, lays a new track for a Pauline trolley line.

1.2.3. JIHAD TROLLEY

According to Sterba, the doctrine of double effect refines the Pauline Principle, delimiting mapping its "range of application" by identifying conditions under which it may be morally permissible (and sometimes even morally obligatory) to perform actions that foreseeably bring about Evil-2 events—events involving pain, suffering, and loss—for the sake of greater goods. To this, Calvin's concurrentist theodicy adds that under some such conditions, a good God can and does also act so as to bring about Evil-1 actions—voluntary actions that are morally wrong—by others. To appreciate Calvin's point, it will help to consider a case in which, arguably, a good human agent might may act so as to intentionally bring it about a morally evil act by another human agent. To this end, I submit:

> JIHAD TROLLEY. You, an experienced clinical psychologist, are in the first car of a high-speed train hijacked by three terrorists. Three of the terrorists—two men and a woman—are guarding the passenger car, while a fourth terrorist is running the train. The train is now speeding toward Washington. By cell phone you learn that two similar hijackings have caused immense loss of life in New York.
>
> As it happens, being born of missionary parents, you speak the same language as the three. From your seat you have closely observed their interactions.

It has become obvious that the woman is married to one of the men, who has a pathologically possessive attitude toward her.

You then hatch and execute a devious plan. With a few remarks, you lead the husband to believe his wife has been disloyal, committing adultery with the other man. The husband, as you anticipated, erupts in a murderous rage, firing on both and killing them. He then turns his weapon on himself. Seizing the occasion, you and other passengers storm the control cabin, disarm the fourth terrorist, and gain control of the train.

Here the husband's actions—murdering his wife and comrade, and committing self-murder—are clearly Evil-1 actions. Based on your shrewd clinical understanding of the husband's pathology, let us suppose, you deliberately provoked him to erupt in a violent rage that—you believed—would lead him to commit just this double murder. His actions were morally wrong; were your triggering actions also thereby wrong?

I find little inclination to say so, for just the reasons Calvin stresses. The husband's action was wicked, in part, due to its dominant murderous intention. Your actions had a different dominant intention. This makes a moral world of difference. The jihad trolley story thus suggests that an adequate double effect principle will include conditions under which a good agent (with one dominant intention) may act so as to bring it about that another agent, with a different dominant intention, commits a moral evil.

1.3. Sterba on Mandates to Intervene

At the first Notre Dame Conference, Sterba's circulated comments on my presented paper opened an important line of inquiry. Sterba wrote:[19]

> Steve distinguishes between causing evil and doing evil, allowing that God could be implicated in the former but not the latter. But does Steve think that intentionally causing or allowing evil can never all by itself be immoral?

Our answer to this question will, Sterba suggested, have implications for how we answer a further question:

> Q2 Given the Pauline principle, is it ever the case that God could directly permit or cause horrendous evil?

For if we answer Q1 by saying some evils are so horrendous that any allowing of them is immoral, then we must answer Q2 by saying that for those evils, it will never be the case that God could never either cause them *or* permit them.

1.3.1. BEHIND THE SUBTLETIES

Sterba is surely right in saying that an "allowing" is an action—and is sometimes an evil action. His phrasing above contains two noteworthy subtleties. First, he is focusing on cases of "intentionally causing or allowing evil." Second, he focuses on whether an intentional allowing of evil may not, in some cases, be evil "all by itself." The subtleties reflect his sketch of the Pauline principle—when refined by the double effect principle—as pertaining only to acts that have an intentional character in relation to something that is evil in an "intrinsic" or "all by itself" way. His overall thrust, as I understand it, is that for certain human actions, the action is so intrinsically wrong that any intentional allowing of that action by another human or divine agent would also be so categorically wrong as to never be justifiable by consequential considerations.

To address these subtleties, two remarks must here suffice. To allow is of course more than merely to not prevent. That I did not prevent Hurricane Katrina's devastation of New Orleans does not mean that I allowed it. To allow something requires that one anticipate an event, that one possess the power to intervene so as to prevent it, and that one does not exercise that power. (Sometimes this may be to give others a chance to so intervene.) There is a sense in which humans may sometimes, by negligence, "unintentionally" allow things. But if God exists, none of his allowings are unintentional in this sense.

Sterba asks whether, on my view of the Pauline Principle, some allowing may be, due to the character of the allowed event or action, itself intrinsically wrong in a way that makes the character of the act so evil "all by itself" (or "intrinsically") that no consequential goods could suffice to make the allowing justifiable in the all-things-considered sense. So far as Pauline principle of Catholic moral theory goes, I defer to Sterba's account. But with respect to the epistle to the Romans, St. Paul is not addressing this question. Far from playing "intrinsic" moral considerations against "consequential" moral considerations, he is, against an antinomian distortion of the gospel of grace, simply insisting that all-things-considered moral considerations reflecting God's revealed will remain in force and have the last word.

This leaves open the further question of whether some possible actions or events have an intrinsically evil character that absolutely precludes a good God from any allowing of them based on consequences. I don't rule this out, but can think of only two cases that might fit the bill. One might be a divine allowing of a catastrophic choice by some created agent (Lucifer, say) that subjects all sentient life to such endless hellish suffering as to make every creature's life on the whole a bad thing. The other might be an allowing that itself has a certain quality of evil that could never be outweighed by consequences. At the human level, allowing oneself to truly hate God might be something one should never do, even if it would save the entire planet from nuclear catastrophe.

1.3.2. THE MINE BY THE ROAD

Nevertheless, Sterba's "Comment . . ." points at an important path of inquiry that we do well to now sweep for Claymores. Sterba wrote (p. 1):

> Suppose I [Jim] decided not to deflect a deadly missile that one of you inexplicably let fly hitting Steve's head when I could easily have done so. Surely it would seem that my intentionally causing or permitting such bad consequences, absent some further explanation, would have been morally wrong and morally evil. If that is right, then we are still faced with the question of when, if ever, directly permitting or causing horrendous evil is something God could not do in virtue of the Pauline principle (assuming we interpret the principle as provisionally applying to cases of intentionally causing or permitting horrendous evil).

It does indeed seem that by intentionally permitting my head to be impacted by a deadly missile, Jim would—"absent some further explanation"—have done something that is "morally wrong and morally evil."

But does this mean that in virtue of the Pauline principle, there are some horrendous evils God could neither directly permit nor cause? In the innocent-sounding phrase "absent further explanation," there is danger of conflating an ontic inference and an explanatory inference. If we have reason to think an agent is a good agent, we have reason to think that when that agent allows some horrific evil, this is on account of there being (past, present, or future) some perceived morally relevant, connected, outweighing good that motivates this allowing. So absent there *being* some such intended good (grasped by the agent), it follows that if the agent allowed the evil, the agent lacked something in moral goodness.

But this ontic inference must be distinguished from a quite different explanatory inference. Consider Sterba's phrasing: if Jim were to allow the projectile to split my skull, then this act of allowing would, absent further explanation, "surely . . . seem . . . morally wrong or morally evil." Here Sterba seems to have in mind some third party—let's call him Peter—who is watching and making an inferential judgment about Jim's action. It is one thing to say that there *being* no outweighing good (grasped by Jim) means that Jim's all-by-itself-evil allowing was morally wrong. It is another thing to say that, absent further explanation grasped by a third party, Jim's allowing should be judged (by Peter or us) as morally wrong. It is easy to conflate the two inferences because they often—when applied to human agents like Jim—stay together. But they do not always stay together.

To see why, consider three cases along a continuum. Case 1: You, a sixth-grade teacher overseeing the playground, see one of your students above a supine third grader, about to insert a knife blade into her throat. You will—"absent further explanation"—confidently judge that the imminent deed serves no outweighing good, and you will without hesitation intervene. Case 2: You, now in the school cafeteria, see a woman in a white coat above a supine third grader, about to do the same. You now—"absent further explanation"—will hesitate in judging that the imminent deed serves no outweighing good, and you will hesitate to intervene. Case 3: You, touring your daughter's med school, see a brain surgeon about to use a drill to bore into someone's skull. You, even "absent further explanation," will have virtually no tendency to think the imminent deed serves no outweighing good, and you will not dream of intervening.[20]

In each case, the ontic inference holds: absent the existence of a morally out-weighing reason (grasped by the doer of the action), it equally follows, in all three cases, that the action is morally wrong. But for the explanatory inference, the cases increasingly come apart: "absent further explanation" (absent some agent-intended good grasped by us as a third party), we do not, in all three cases, have equally good reason to judge the deed morally wrong. They come apart for sev-eral reasons, but one is this: as we move along the continuum, we have increasing reason to think that the deed-doer is much better placed than us to perceive in any detail the good—in itself or in connection to the action—that motivates the agent. Here God is of course the limiting case.

1.3.3. Into the Fire—Again

But if this answers Sterba's worries, it may also be jumping from the frying pan into the fire. If God is the limiting case on the continuum, must this not also undercut our confidence in an important class of our own moral judgments—judgments about when we should intervene? Seeing the sixth grader, you will con-fidently judge that you should immediately intervene; seeing the woman in the white coat, you are far less confident about this; seeing the brain surgeon, you have no confidence at all. The less we know, the more we should refrain from judging or intervening.

But what must a skeptical theist then say in the face of some imminent hor-rific event that—since it is clearly about to happen—God seems quite ready to al-low or even, as in the case of the jihad trolley, cause? Would not skeptical theism rob us of a major commonsense moral reason for acting so as to prevent that im-minent event? Using the above distinction between ontological and explanatory contexts, we can thus address Sterba's worries. But those worries immediately crystallize into a much more recalcitrant threat. For skeptical theism now threat-ens to slide, for at least one important class of moral judgments, into a paralyzing moral skepticism. To understand this threat more completely, we turn to the slide-resisting effort of Michael Bergmann. We will view it, as promised, through the twisted eyes of my half-brother and doppelganger Artsky W. Evets.

2. Skeptical Theism in Crisis: The Bergmann/Artsky Impasse

Two things are affirmed by Mike Bergmann and my brother Steve. They affirm, first, that God's allowing of every horrific evil in our world is motivated by some connected fabulous good, where getting that good is so connected to the evil as to require, even for omnipotence, allowing this (or some roughly comparable) evil as the price, and where the good is so fabulous as to make that price right. When we fail to see such goods, this failure, they insist, poses no evidential problem. This is because (their second affirmation) if God does exist, then—God being God and all—this failure is pretty much what we should expect.

Intelligent skeptical theists are here slowly waking up to a threat: skeptical theism, logically carried through, leads to a paralyzing moral skepticism. Bergmann gives an ingenious M-Defense against this threat, but his defense fails. To see why, we must first see how he fails to fully excavate the threat. When we complete the excavation, his defense will fall of its own weight.

2.1. Deepening Bergmann's Excavation

Skeptical theism, Bergmann notes, has two independent parts. The first part he calls "T": it—the "theistic lobe" of skeptical theism, if you will—is the belief that the theistic God exists. The second part, or "skeptical lobe," he calls "S": it holds that we are in no position to form any belief at all on four key propositions. (We shall confine attention to the first of these.) To focus on the skeptical lobe, Bergmann ("Commonsense Skeptical Theism," p. 12) imagines an ordinary person, Sally, who is a non-theist (an agnostic), who embraces moral commonsense, and who also embraces S. In embracing S, Sally thus affirms:[21]

> S: We have no good reason for thinking that (REP) the possible goods* we
> know of are *representative of* the possible goods there are.

Here the phrase "we have no good reason for thinking that" has a radical meaning: it means we are in complete darkness as to even the probability of REP. Using Bergmann's characteristic "for all we know" locution (p. 13 and passim), it is saying:

> for all we know it might be highly likely that the goods and evils we see bearing on this act are representative of all the goods and evils that do bear on it; then again, for all we know, this might be highly unlikely.

To explain why some people see this as undercutting moral commonsense so as to threaten moral skepticism, Bergmann now considers underdetermined choices—choices where direct deontic principles still leave open to us two or more significantly different live alternatives, the evaluation of which requires pivotal use of consequential considerations. Here, as an illustrative example, we might imagine Sally as school nurse. Nurse Sally is out of pain relievers and is considering whether to offer ten-year-old Tommy Tucker a placebo tablet. There are no deontological norms (or school rules) that make this a morally wrong thing to do. She takes a moment, then, to weigh the positive and negative consequences of this action and its alternatives.

Nurse Sally knows, of course, that a placebo pill may have some tendency to help Tommy. But she also recalls the Tucker mom telling her, confusedly, that one of the kids has a phobia of tablets. Weighing the benefit of reducing his pain against the risk of sending him into a panic attack, nurse Sally may judge—and come to believe—that it would be morally wrong for her to offer Tommy a tablet. Moreover, the moral commonsense on which Bergmann focuses presents itself as a form of knowing; so in some deontically underdetermined situations—ones that confer sufficient positive epistemic grounding on her judgment—Sally may be said to know that giving Tommy the tablet is the morally wrong thing to do.

Now, for such deontically underdetermined actions, what sort of grounding might such knowing have? For commonsense moral knowing, Bergmann suggests that such moral knowing will, in the main, often have roughly the following two-fold grounding:[22]

> TWO-FOLD: The main reason for judging that the act would be right is that (FOLD-1) she can see that the immediate result of the action would be enormously beneficial for the child, and (FOLD-2) she has no reason to think any significant harm will come from it.

Consider, now, how Bergmann goes on to excavate the alleged underlying conflict between skeptical theism and moral commonsense. As Bergmann sees it, the conflict is due to the skeptical lobe of skeptical theism. It is because Sally embraces this lobe, Bergmann thinks, that she will need to say:

> I have no idea how likely it is that the consequences of the act would, in the long run, be for the best. For all I know, it might be highly likely that the long-run consequences of the act would be much better than the long-run consequences of my refraining from it. Then again, for all I know, this might be highly unlikely. I really have no idea what the remote connections might be.[23]

And now, to lay bare the alleged conflict or tension, Bergmann juxtaposes two things. It will help to label these two things "KNOWS" and "NO IDEA." On one hand, there is the epistemic strength that Sally takes her moral judgment to have:

> [KNOWS] As a matter of moral common sense . . . Sally thinks she *knows* it's wrong to perform the act because of its harmful consequences (the immediate ones she can foresee).

On the other hand, there is Sally's awareness of what follows from the skeptical lobe of her skeptical theism. Nicely underscoring the contrast with an "and yet," Bergmann continues (p. 13):

[NO-IDEA] And yet because she accepts S [what is asserted by the skeptical lobe of skeptical theism], Sally thinks she has no idea whether or not its ultimate consequences are likely to be for the best overall.

In his own excavation of the alleged underlying conflict, Bergmann stops here. But keeping before us Bergmann's contrast of KNOWS and NO-IDEA, we must dig deeper to uncover *why* they conflict. For at the deepest level, the conflict stems from the precise relationship between two pairs of things. The first pair comprises the two "folds"—hereafter FOLD-1 and FOLD-2—in the two-fold grounding condition by which, we've seen, Bergmann grounds certain typical consequential of judgments of moral commonsense. The second pair comprises the two "for all we know" parts—hereafter, FAWK-1 and FAWK-2—in Bergmann's above statement of the skeptical lobe of Sally's skeptical theism.

To bring out these relationships, it will help to run the exposition for a case where Sally confidently judges an action is the morally *right* thing to do. When we do this for KNOWS, we get:

(KNOWS) As a matter of common sense, Sally takes her judgment that action A is morally right as a case of moral knowing because (FOLD-1) she can see one likely result of action *x* that would be of significant benefit to the child, and (FOLD-2) she has no reason for thinking action *x* would lead to any comparably significant harmful consequences for the child.

When we do the same for NO-IDEA, we get:

(NO-IDEA) And yet, because she accepts S [the skeptical lobe of skeptical theism] Sally realizes that we have no idea about the full consequences of her action, since (FAWK-1) for all we know it is very probable that her action will have dire harmful consequences for the child, and equally, (FAWK-2) for all we know this is very improbable.

To see the root of the conflict between KNOW and NO-IDEA, we must focus on the relationship between FOLD-1 and FAWK-1. Regarding FOLD-1, we must ask why it is so vital to the great epistemic strength registered by KNOW. One reason, clearly enough, is that the short-term positive reason provided by FOLD-1 is defeasible: it would not carry much weight if Sally did see that her action, in the longer term, would bring catastrophic harm to the child. But it also seems vital for a deeper reason. In the great epistemic strength registered by KNOW, is Sally not presuming that her *seeing* no catastrophic consequences in the short term is some evidence for their *being* none in the longer term she can't see?

I contend that she is. Exactly this inductive presumption is implicit in KNOW. For this reason, the root of the conflict between KNOW and NO-IDEA is a deeper conflict between FAWK-1 and FOLD-1. For FOLD-1 is vital because Sally—and moral commonsense—needs to take *seeing* no catastrophic consequences of an action as *some* probabilistic evidence for their *being* none. But FAWK-1 means that this need cannot be met, for FAWK-1 says we are completely in the dark about the probability or improbability of long-term catastrophic consequences.

The necessity of the above inductive presumption rests on the fact that moral commonsense purports to give us knowledge of the morally right thing to do. Consider a rank novice in chess who, playing a grandmaster, decides to make a given move based on her seeing a desirable short-term consequence, and seeing no undesirable long-term consequence. Without an inductive presumption, the novice might be pragmatically reasonable in making this move: she will at least stand a chance of learning what she has overlooked. But without it, she could not be epistemically reasonable in thinking she knows that it is "the (objectively) right move to make" in the position. To reasonably suppose that, she would need an inductive presumption that her seeing no catastrophic consequence is some decent evidence for there being none. The same holds for Sally's claim to know "the (objectively) right action to do" in a situation.

2.2. Pressing Bergmann's Defense: Hiker Sally's Agony

Bergmann, having somewhat superficially excavated the alleged conflict, seeks to show the conflict is not real. His defense strategy is to propose a moral principle that meets two conditions: first, it is plausible as an articulation of a principle of moral commonsense, and second, it fully coheres with FAWK-1 and FAWK-2 of skeptical theism. Paraphrased slightly, Bergmann proposes (pp. 13–14):

> (M) For any action A that is not intrinsically wrong, we morally ought to de-
> cide whether to do A by "considering . . . the consequences we can reasonably
> expect" of performing A and its alternatives. We should refrain from A if the
> reasonably expected consequences of performing A seem significantly worse
> than those of any live alternative, and should perform A if the reasonably ex-
> pected consequences of A seem significantly better than that of every live
> alternative.

Principle M serves Bergmann's purpose because by it, an action's moral rightness or wrongness depends solely on consequences the moral agent "can reasonably expect." Consequences about which the agent can form no reasonable expectations are—by principle M—irrelevant to judging an action's moral status. If we can show that such consequences are relevant, the M defense is in trouble.

To this end, then, consider hiker Sally. Sally is a former U.S. Army Ranger who, while hiking in a remote area of northern Canada, finds a young boy man-acled to a railroad track—each foot to one rail, each hand to the other. Cutting short a longer story (how Sally dispatches the responsible psychopath), Sally is left with three options. She can stay with the boy, hoping against hope that help will arrive. She can build a shelter around him and hike out for help—leaving him on the track for three days. Or she can use her battlefield medic skills to amputate his hands and feet, and carry him out. The key feature of the scenario is that on the evidence available to her, Sally is in radical probabilistic darkness about how often a train runs on the tracks. For all she knows, it is probable that it comes by twice a day; for all she knows, it is equally likely that it comes by twice a year.

Later, Sally recounts her mental state at the time this way:

> Legally speaking, I had no idea what the law would do if I freed the boy and carried him out. But my concern was with what I morally ought to do. On this, I just kept going in circles. I just could not tell what the right thing to do was—not without having some inkling about the probable train schedule. I do not believe in God, but I spent two hours praying for light on what I ought to do. No answer. I even tried to remember Sterba's ethics class. All I could recall was that nauseating Sartre essay he had us read. I had no idea what the right thing to do was. It was up to me, and I just had to make a damned existential choice. It was so bad I got the shakes.

As Sally sees it, there is surely a right answer. Sally was in a situation where consequential moral reasoning breaks down; her radical probabilistic ignorance of the train schedule leaves her in an existential/moral quandary. But if principle M is right, there can be no moral quandary. Principle M says that if one cannot form reasonable expectations about some consequences (e.g., those depending on the train schedule), then those consequences are irrelevant to what one morally ought to do. But that now seems wrong. What is clearest—clearer than abstract principle M—is that Sally's radical ignorance of the train schedule creates an agonizing moral quandary, shattering Sally's plain-ethics ability to judge what "the right thing to do" is. The scenario means we must stand Bergmann's defense on its head. If principle M entails that this agony of hiker Sally is silly, then it is principle M that must go.

Hiker Sally's epistemic agony also suggests what is involved when our moral judgments are epistemically confident. Such judgments rest on a presumption of representativeness. How exactly to formulate this presumption is important unfinished business in moral theory:

> M-REP: For any deontically underdetermined action about which we properly form an epistemically confident moral judgment, our underlying presumption is that (REP) the morally relevant consequences (of the action and its significant alternatives) whose likelihoods we can access are representative of the morally relevant consequences there are.

In summary, the agony of hiker Sally arises because, as she sees, the REP presumption does not hold in her particular situation. There are some morally relevant consequences she can form reasonable expectations about. She can be confident, for example, that if she were to use her athletic and battlefield surgical skills, it is very probable that she could successfully carry the child out (a very good thing), though with permanent bodily impairment (a very bad thing). But in her particular situation, she knows it is entirely up for grabs whether these foreseeable consequences are representative of the morally relevant consequences there are. Though she has no inkling of the train schedule, she knows train tracks when she sees them. She thus knows that in this situation, the relevant REP presumption is no longer a reasonable one.

2.3. How Theism Makes It Worse: Invisible Railways

So how is hiker Sally's situation like ours? Sally's radical skepticism is local: she is clueless about a crucial consequence-maker in her particular situation. Skeptical theism makes this cluelessness global. But how it does this is worse than Bergmann lets on. Bergmann sees the threat of moral skepticism as arising only from the skeptical lobe of skeptical theism. But how much S undercuts commonsense moral knowing is hugely magnified if one also accepts the theistic lobe T of skeptical theism.

The reason is simple. If theism is true, then if you could lift every horrific suffering in our world, you would find beneath each one some fabulous outweighing good for the sake of which it is allowed by God. Sometimes that good might be a future good related to specific instances of suffering: God chastises those he loves, and so God may allow—even cause—me to go through a period of intense suffering because this is the best way of trying to teach me some lesson that will allow me to live a God-honoring life, serving others better and enjoying God more deeply. Some goods may be more global: God may allow other suffering for less person-specific reasons: such allowing, as a general policy, may be essential to having a world that allows the evolution of morally and spiritually responsible creatures who grow into stewards of the earthly domain for which God intends them.

And, most crucially, skeptical theism affirms that if theism is true, then such goods as these—goods we think we can grasp—may be only a small fraction of the goods God has in mind. It affirms that if God exists, then each instance of actual suffering is related in a suitable way to some local or global good that provides a "rationale" by which a being supreme in goodness, wisdom, and power can allow it. This suffering is allowed, in short, because it lies on hidden railroad tracks on which run hidden railroad cars carrying hidden axiological freight traveling on hidden schedules—all the details of which are clearly visible to God, but—so often, so often—are vexingly inscrutable to us.

Not so for standard atheism. Standard atheism asserts that if God does not exist, then—to quote Forrest Gump—shit happens. Shit happens; it stinks; there is no silver lining; what you see is what you get. There is no such hidden railway system. This means that the standard atheist has far less reason to think that, by and large, REP is not satisfied. Bergmann's analysis thus fails to excavate this dimension of the entails-moral-skepticism threat to skeptical theism.

2.4. Bergmann's Reply and the Current Impasse

Thanks a lot, Artsky. With his hiker Sally case, my brother Artsky has defended two theses: that commonsense moral judgments rest on some version of a REP (a "representativeness presumption"), and that REP conflicts with the skeptical lobe—a conflict magnified by the theistic lobe—of skeptical theism.

In response to the criticism from Artsky W. (Wykstra), Bergmann finds reason to fine-tune his principle M, but sees Artsky as handicapped by a fundamental misconception. In his rejoinder (appended as "Postscript" to his published paper) he says (p. 30):

> . . . it looks like Wykstra thinks that in preserving common sense, skeptical theists need to equate *that which objectively ought to be done* with *that which in fact has the best overall consequences*. But . . . it strikes me as quite implausible to think that equating these two things is a dictate of common sense.

Bergmann thus takes Artsky to implausibly attribute to moral commonsense the following implausible end-of-time equation:

For the restricted class of deontically underdetermined actions	
The action that objectively ought to be done	The action that has, to the end of time, the best overall consequences

Bergmann himself, as a fan of moral commonsense, likely rejects this equation as well. And with good reason, for the restricted equation is simply a special case of the unrestricted equation embraced by so-called objective utilitarianism—widely seen as likely to have devastating drawbacks.[24] For who among us can ever, even remotely, estimate the full consequences of any action—consequences after all going, as Dan Howard-Snyder acidly puts it, "to the end of time."[25] Consider two twin brothers, each choosing where to sit in a college class. For each, that choice may lead to the brother's meeting that special someone, to eventual marriage, to children, and to children's children unto many generations—some of whom may, well before the end of time, turn out to be either a Gandhi or a Hitler. Can any action's objective moral rightness—in any sense that has a claim on us—really be a function of any such unfathomable future consequences? Some contemporary objective consequentialists, biting the bullet, nod yes. My intuitions coincide with Bergmann's: if Artsky's case rests on the idea that the restricted equation is part of moral commonsense, his case looks utterly implausible.

But does Artsky's case really rest on the end-of-time equation? A clue to pursue here lies in our earlier formulation of M-REP.

> REP: For actions about which moral common sense properly forms epistemically confident moral judgments about the right (or wrong) thing to do, the morally relevant consequences whose likelihoods we can access are representative of *the morally relevant consequences there are.*

Could it be that this class of "the morally relevant consequences there are," while falling far short of the full to-the-end-of-time consequences, nevertheless goes well beyond the set of consequences to which one may happen to have access at the time of an action?

3. Looking for Light: Brandt and Parfit on Moral Wrongness

By moral commonsense, Bergmann thinks, we regularly have knowledge of "the objectively right thing to do." We regularly make epistemically confident judgments about the moral status of actions, and we properly do so—including for the restricted class of deontically underdetermined actions. Now Artsky thinks that in so doing, moral commonsense relies on a REP presumption. In turning to contemporary moral theory, I have sought light on three issues. First, what light does moral theory shed on this "representativeness" relation? Second, what might be meant by speaking of all the "morally relevant" consequences? Third, does the very phrase "the right (or wrong) thing to do" conceal crucial ambiguities? Let's begin with this third question and work backward.

3.1. Brandt on Moral Wrongness: the "Objective" Concept

Fifty years ago, Richard Brandt opened his important "Toward a Credible Form of Utilitarianism" with the metaethical proposal that there is a sense of right and wrong that is "objective"—a rightness or wrongness depending, as Brandt puts it "on what the facts really are, and not merely on what one thinks they are."[26] Brandt, writing during the Cold War, considers Khrushchev's demand that Eisenhower publically apologize for the U2 spy flights. What, Brandt asked, might Ike have discovered, had he asked the moral question of whether he had moral duty to apologize?

In the complex Cold War situation, Brandt observed, this question might have put Ike in need of considerable time for inquiry, consultation, and reflection. In his busy presidential days, he might have had time to unearth and reflect on only some of the morally relevant facts. These may have led him to judge that his moral duty was to refuse to apologize; but he might, Brandt says, have held this judgment with considerable tentativeness. Later, in retirement years, Ike might have discovered new facts, leading him to change his mind—to think (my way of putting it) that his real moral duty, the really right thing for him to have done, was indeed to have apologized. And he might have been right. On this basis Brandt ventures—with his own considerable tentativeness—that there is such a thing as one's "objective duty" or such a thing as "the objectively right (or wrong) thing to do" in a situation.[27]

Brandt's takeaway claim here is that if there is a credible form of utilitarianism, it is this "objective" rightness and wrongness that will be its explicandum. My takeaway is more modest: that in mature moral reasoning about deontically underdetermined actions, the morally relevant consequences (and the principles that make them relevant) are not all obvious or easily discerned. Discerning them may require sustained and difficult inquiry into facts, as well as a delicate sense of relevance-determining principles that itself rests on growth into moral maturity. On both counts, our actual moral judgments as humans regularly miss the mark.

Going further than Brandt, I want to distinguish two families of contexts in which we seek to judge the "right thing to do" (or "to have done"). On one hand there are prospective contexts in which we seek to discern the right thing to do in some upcoming situation. On the other hand there are retrospective contexts, where we seek to discern whether, in some past situation, what we did was the right or wrong thing to have done. In retrospective contexts, the aim of moral reflection is not self-blame but self-improvement: to increase our ability to "get it right" (or at least "get it better") in the future. We are like a bomb-squad expert reflecting back on some effort where he did as well as he could—but failed—to disarm an ingenious bomb chained to an innocent victim. By our postmortem analysis, we hope to see clues to be noticed when, in the future, we face a bomb of this diabolically clever design.

3.2. Parfit on Moral Status: The Ordinary Sense of Wrong

Consider next Derek Parfit's work on varied senses in which an action might be said to be morally wrong. It is, says Parfit, "often assumed that the word 'wrong' has only one moral sense."[28] Against this, Parfit defines three primary senses of "wrong" (and correlated senses of "right"), urging that unless we have all of them in our conceptual repertoire (p. 151), "we shall fail to see many important truths." Each of Parfit's definitions relies on a more basic "ordinary sense" of "wrong," so we must begin with that.

Parfit treats the ordinary sense of wrong as a kind of theoretical primitive: it is to be located not so much by definition as by ostensive gesture, and its meaning is to be grasped through its relation to the other concepts. It is, he says (p. 150)

> ... the sense in which we call an action wrong when we have in view the acts
> of people who know all the morally relevant facts.

This is Delphic in density. His thought is that basic concept is the one in play when we—the ordinary concept users—have in view the act of a person who knows the full set of morally relevant facts. The person, one might put it, is without epistemic excuse: she cannot say "I just did not realize the rope was so frayed when I lowered my climbing buddy over the cliff." The concept thus, I take him to mean, has a connotation of blame-worthiness.

Parfit's thought here, I also take it, is that when ordinary concept users say that some agent's action is wrong in this ordinary sense, the concept users typically are right or reasonable in assuming that the agent knows the full set of morally relevant facts. That is, Parfit sees this full set of "morally relevant facts" as something that ordinary moral agents do regularly know, and that we, who ascribe ordinary moral rightness and wrongness to their actions, may regularly and rightly take them to know. (Were this not so, it could scarcely be an ordinary sense.) This tells us that Parfit, who understands this full set of "morally relevant considerations" to include consequences, cannot here have in mind the full "to-the-end of-time" set of consequences.

But neither can he have in mind the mere set—à la Bergmann—of "reasonably expected" consequences. To see why, we must turn to Parfit's three further main senses of "wrong."

3.3. Chisholming Parfit: Three Sorts of Moral Status

Parfit's explications of these three senses are not easy to grasp, for each piggybacks on the ordinary sense by way of a subjunctive conditional nested within a larger "just when" biconditional. "Some act of ours [mine[29]] would be," he writes (pp. 150–151):

> (I) wrong in the fact-relative sense just when [if and only if] this act would be wrong in the ordinary sense if [I] knew all the morally relevant facts;
>
> (II) wrong in the belief-relative sense just when this act would be wrong in the ordinary sense if [my] beliefs about these facts were true;
>
> (III) wrong in the evidence-relative sense just when this act would be wrong in the ordinary sense if [I] believed what the available evidence gives [me] decisive reason to believe, and those beliefs were true.

To unravel what these come to, it will help—as a ladder—to try to associate each sense of wrong with a corresponding sense of "duty." The association cannot go the full distance—the ladder will need to be kicked way—but this itself will be of some significance.

3.3.1. FACT-RELATIVE MORAL WRONGNESS

In Parfit's "fact-relative sense," we've seen, an action of mine is wrong just in case "it would have been [blame-worthily] wrong for me to do, were I to have known all the morally relevant facts."

This sense of "moral wrongness" is close to what some moral theorists regard as violation of "objective moral duty." To say an action was my objective duty in some situation is to say that it was the action that I ought to have taken (in some ordinary primitive sense) were I to have been cognizant of all the morally relevant facts in the situation. Perhaps I could not have known them all—in which case I can scarcely be faulted for not doing my objective duty. But when I am trying to determine what I ought to do, my aim—it is plausible to say—is to try to get a fix on what my objective duty is. Peter van Inwagen proposes[30] that the epistemic probability of some proposition for me is just my best rational estimate of what its objective probability is; similarly, perhaps our proper subjective moral duty in some situation is what is disclosed by our best effort to get a fix on what our objective moral duty is. Like Ike, we may have a hard time in estimating the latter—but it is what we are *trying* to get a fix on.

3.3.2. BELIEF-RELATIVE MORAL WRONGNESS

In Parfit's belief-relative sense, we've seen, an action of mine is wrong just in case it would be wrong in the ordinary blameworthy sense, were all my beliefs about the morally relevant facts/ consequences to be true beliefs.

This sense correlates with a weak kind of "subjective duty"—the duty (in a primitive sense) I would have in a situation if all my relevant beliefs about the situation are true. Suppose that I am paranoid—I have been doing too much crystal meth—and as a result believe that you, at my front door, intend to butcher me and my loved ones. Then my belief-relative moral duty is to act energetically to stop you. Similarly, to do otherwise is, in Parfit's belief-relative sense, to act wrongly.

3.3.3. EVIDENCE-RELATIVE MORAL WRONGNESS

Of most relevance to us, however, is Parfit's evidence-relative sense. An act of yours is wrong in this sense, we've seen, just in case this act would be wrong in the ordinary sense if you believed what the available evidence gives you decisive reason to believe, and these beliefs were true.

Let us consider both of Parfit's conditions. The first is that your act *would* have been wrong in the ordinary sense, had you considered all the evidence available (in some sense) to you, and believed whatever this evidence decisively supports. What does this mean? Imagine that you are Artsky's psychotherapist, and you break an appointment with him so you can watch the last game of the World Series. You know Artsky is struggling with depression, but your current evidence is that the depression is well controlled by his meds, and that he will be fine not seeing you this week. However, on the way out the door, you fail to heed your receptionist, who urges you to listen to a recent voicemail immediately. Had you done so, you would have heard Artsky's wife crying, telling you that the medication has stopped working and that Artsky has been having suicidal mood swings. You would have believed this (her testimony gives you decisive reason to do so), and realized you had a duty to be there for Artsky. Your act of watching the ballgame meets the first condition for being wrong in an evidence-relative sense.

It is, however, clearly not wrong in the belief-relative sense, and it may not be wrong in the fact-relative sense either, nor even in Parfit's evidence-relative sense. For imagine this special case: Artsky's wife is telling you the truth, but has already used his mood swings as a convenient cover for murdering him, and her voice mail is just part of making this look like a suicide. Then watching the ballgame would not be wrong for you in the fact-relative sense, because it would not have been wrong in the ordinary sense, had you known all the relevant facts. But would it, in the special case, still be wrong in Parfit's evidence-relative sense for you to watch the ballgame? I think that Parfit, for this situation, would want the answer to be "yes," and would hope that his two conditions would give this result. But do they?

This is a tricky question. One might think they do not. Transposed into the key of moral duties, the first condition defines your duties in terms of the evidence available to you, and while Parfit does not define "available," it is plausible to suppose that the voicemail information will count as "available" (for you have evidence of its existence), but that the wife's murderous activities does not. But what of the second condition? It seems to require that what your available evidence decisively supports is also true. In the scenario, one such belief—that Artsky has been having suicidal mood swings is—is true. But you also believe—implicitly but firmly—that Artsky is still alive, that his wife has not murdered him, and that her voicemail is a cry for help from a concerned spouse. All these things, although they meet Parfit's first condition (your overall background evidence amply supports them), do not meet his second condition (for they are in fact false).

But does this mean his definition gives the wrong result for the special case? I don't think so. For both conditions are embedded in the antecedent of a subjunctive that is itself nested within the larger conditional comprising the overall definition. By the overall definition, your action is wrong in the evidence-relative sense just in case, were you to believe what the available evidence gives you decisive reason to believe *and* the world is such as to make those beliefs true, your action would be wrong in the ordinary sense. By that definition, then, your action in the special case is wrong in the evidence-relative sense—which is, I surmised above, the result Parfit would here want.

4. Beyond the Impasse

Here, recall, was the impasse. Artsky's critique argued that if Bergmann's principle M is correct, then in the wilderness scenario, hiker Sally should deem considerations of the train contingencies as irrelevant to what she ought to do, and so should feel no epistemic agony on account of her ignorance of them. But, he argued, these considerations clearly are relevant, and her epistemic agony makes sense; hence, principle M is not correct. So underlying Artsky's critique is the idea, broached in the introduction of this essay, that for an important class of actions, moral reasoning rests on what I earlier dubbed the Representativeness Presumption:

> (REP) the morally relevant consequences (of the action and its significant alternatives) whose likelihoods we can access are representative of the morally relevant consequences there are.

Embedding REP within the larger claim, Artsky's critique rests on a moral-theoretic claim we may call M-REP:

> M-REP: For any deontically underdetermined action about which we properly form confident moral judgments that the action is wrong, we rely on the implicit presumption that (REP) the morally relevant consequences (of the action and is significant alternatives) whose likelihoods we can access are representative of the morally relevant consequences there are.

Now Bergmann, we saw earlier, saw Artsky's critique as resting on an implausible assumption—that for deontically underdetermined choices, the moral rightness of action is a function of whether, compared with its alternatives, it has the best (or about as good as any) overall consequences, and moral wrongness is a function of whether its overall consequences are far worse than those of alternative actions. (And here by "overall consequences" is meant the full "to-the-end-of-time" set of consequences of an action.) The key question, we saw, was whether Artsky's M-REP really needed to presuppose anything as implausible as this. With some relevant-looking moral theorizing by Brandt and Parfit now in hand, we must return to that key question.

4.1. Morally Relevant Facts and the Optimal Moral Horizon

Brandt's and Parfit's key ideas share a deep commonality and significant difference. Brandt's key "objective" notion of "moral duty" and Parfit's key evidence-relative sense of wrongness give this result: one may, through no culpable ignorance, miserably fail to discern what is or was the right thing to have done. Both thinkers would agree that Ike, even after doing his cognitive best in 1961, might fail to discern his objective duty with respect to Khrushchev's demand, and fail to see that a given action was the morally wrong thing to do. The range of considerations and consequences might be too complex, too elusive, too hard to get at, given his resources.

The deep difference is that for Brandt (preparing the way for his more credible rule utilitarianism), the "objectively right thing to do" is a function of the full "to the end of time" set of actual or probable consequences. Brandt thus needs to address the same threat of moral skepticism as critics perceive in skeptical theism. For Parfit, in contrast, what makes an action wrong, in the most relevant evidence-relative sense, is a function of the set of "morally relevant" consequences that are "available" to the agent. We might say that for evidence-relative moral wrongness, the facts that are morally relevant are those delimited precisely by their being in some sense available. But Parfit does not explain how this set is to be delimited.

This is an opportunity to have our own go at it. While taking cues from Parfit, we may begin with the axiom that my action is not your action, even if they are actions of the same type. The suggestion is that since morality comes to its sharpest focus in a person's actions while also keeping in view those virtuous or vicious dispositions that condition his/her actions), our delimitation of morally *relevant* facts will need to be indexed to the person in question, and to the kind of agent that person is. A fact that is morally relevant to a choice must be in principle accessible—in a broad sense available—within the moral praxis of the specific person whose action it is.

It helps to have a label for this sort of accessibility/availability. When some fact, consideration, or consequence has this sort of accessibility to a given agent, let us say that it is within that agent's "moral horizon."[31] Bergmann's principle M in effect says that, so far as consequence-type facts go, an agent's moral horizon is limited to the facts that this agent, at the time of deciding whether to do or avoid the act, can reasonably foresee as probable consequences of the decision. But by the lights of Brandt and Parfit, this makes the agent's moral horizon too narrow. It fits, to be sure, some senses of "right" and "wrong"—senses that are, indeed, crucial to one strand within our moral praxis: our moral deliberation when, in some time-constrained situation, we decide what to do next. In such prospective contexts, our judgments about "the right thing to do" should be made in a way that Bergmann suggests: when they are so made, the action is in that sense "morally right."

But there are other strands within commonsense moral praxis that are equally important. There is that diagnostic retrospective context in which we might ask whether what we did was, in some past situation, the right (or wrong) thing to do—asking this not in order not to berate ourselves, but in order to learn to do better next time. Such learning is an important strand in our moral praxis, and it is one reason why, without all four Parfitean senses of "wrong," Parfit thinks we will miss important truths.

In this context, then, we need to ask what wider concept of "moral horizon," what elasticizing of the "available" boundary, is needed. Here it helps to identify a few of the sorts of stumbling stones that, at times almost unavoidably, have tripped up our past moral decision making. Sometimes we stumbled because we were morally insensitive—our consciences were dull, whether from our own unrepentant patterns of behavior, or from similar patterns in the family and cultural systems in which we are embedded. Other times, we failed to grasp empirical regularities or character dispositions that would have allowed us to anticipate important consequences. We did not realize how offhand jokes can affect those who look up to us, or how sharing our own story might backfire when told to the wrong person or at the wrong time. Other times, there were unusual external factors that blocked from view facts that, had we known them, would have made a pivotal difference to our choices. Yet other times, like a chess master with the clock ticking, we simply lacked time to process that mass of relevant fact that was, as it were, our fingertips.

These and other similar limiting factors can be called "horizon blockers." Horizon blockers, in a given situation, are factors that block from our view morally relevant facts that, had we known them, could significantly affect the moral judgment in a situation. We can now define a person's optimal moral horizon in a given situation as including all those morally relevant facts that would be accessible were there no horizon blockers operative in the situation.

My proposal is now, first, that a key notion (or family of notions) of objective moral status needs to be defined by reference to the agent's optimal moral horizon. The class of morally relevant facts (including deontic truths, future consequences, and the like) will comprise all those within the agent's optimal moral horizon. Synthesizing elements from Brandt and Parfit, we can define an agent-specific notion of objective wrongness and rightness) as follows:

> An actions is wrong in the objective agent-specific sense if doing the action would have been wrong (or right) in the ordinary sense if the agent were to have known all the optimal morally relevant facts within his or her optimal moral horizon.

4.2. Toward a Plausible REP

We can now use the above to refine the REP presumption that creates the impasse between Artsky and Bergmann. Doing so will bring out strengths in what each has said.

Bergmann acknowledges that the hiker Sally story contains one small grain of irritating sand, leading him to add a layer of protection to his M principle. He tweaks M into M* by, for one thing, adding a second condition—a "reasonably connect" requirement (Cond 2). Paraphrasing a bit, here is what he gives (p. 29) as M*:

> Principle M*: We ought to morally do (or refrain from) an action A if
> (Cond 1) the reasonably expected value of performing (or refraining) from A seems significantly higher than that of any of the live alternatives, and
> (Cond 2) the judgment (in Condition 1) is made in the light of consideration of all the possible consequences we can, after an appropriate period of reflection, "reasonably connect" with doing A or its live alternatives.

And here is what he gives (p. 29–30) as sufficient-condition definition of "reasonably connect":

> Reasonably Connect: A possible consequence can be "reasonably connected" with action A if it is only "somewhat likely" (rather than "extremely unlikely"), or if we have "some grasp of what the event is like and some idea of how it could be a consequence."

Here a natural objection is that Bergmann's revision is an ad hoc epicycle made merely to save his theory. The notion of an optimal moral horizon addresses this by giving the revision a rationale. Consequences that, in Bergmann's very weak sense, are "connectable," are still within the agent's optimal moral horizon. And they are important because they play roles not only in the heuristic prospective context that Bergmann seems to have in mind, but also in the retrospective contexts within which fact-relative concepts of wrongness play such crucial roles.

The notion of optimal moral horizon also redeems Artsky's critique, showing that it need not rest on some implausible to-the-end-of-time view of morally relevant consequences. A more promising rationale is that when moral common-sense judgments are cases of knowing, or being properly confident about, what the right thing to do is, this is because they reflect a tacit confidence that REP* is satisfied: the morally relevant considerations and consequences we grasp are representative of all those that are within our optimal moral horizon. Here "representative" can be understood quite simply as follows: our judgment that action A is the right (or wrong) thing to do would remain intact and retain its integrity if horizon blockers were removed, and we remade the judgment based on the full set of morally relevant facts—that is, the full set of facts within our optimal moral horizon.

Further issues remain. While my proposal may provide a rationale for Bergmann's revision of M to M*, it remains unclear whether his added condition, Cond 2, adequately handles our intuition about hiker Sally's agonizing moral situation. Here it is worth noting three things. The first is that an "aprobable" event like a train arriving does not fall under the first disjunct in Cond 2, since it is not even "somewhat probable" for Sally. It falls only under the second disjunct: Sally has at least some idea of "what it is like" and "how it might be a consequence" of some actions she is considering. But, second, this second disjunct includes a huge class of possibilities, so by Cond 2 as part of a sufficient but not necessary condition, M* will yield moral judgments only in cases where Sally is able to bear in mind, as time allows, all members of this class. M* thus becomes far more demanding than might appear. Finally, Cond 2 still fails to address the real nerve of Artsky's argument. As long as Sally can form no reasonable probabilistic expectations about the catastrophic train event, M* leaves it irrelevant to what the right thing is for her to do—which, by M* as much as by M, depends solely on the "reasonably expected" (not merely "reasonable connected") consequences.[32] If we think Sally's situation does lead her to fail to know what the objectively right thing to do is, principle M* does not get us or Sally out of the woods.

4.3. Theistic Consequentialism: REP and Friendship with God

The notion of an optimal moral horizon may also indicate how a Judeo-Christian skeptical theism can see moral commonsense in its consequential aspect. The idea so far is that morally relevant consequences are a function of agent's optimal moral horizon. God's moral horizon is very different from ours; skeptical theists sometimes see the gulf as akin to that between the goods purposed by a wise mother and those accessible to her one-month-old infant. But what makes the infant special is her potential to mature into a person who, eventually, will become a partner in shared projects with her parents and other adults. Something analogous to this is a striking aspect of the Johannine invitation of Jesus which the Quakers—the Society of Friends—have so helped us appreciate:

> No longer do I call you servants, for the servant does not know what his master is doing; but I have called you friends, for all that I have heard from my Father I have made known to you. (John 15:15)

And what is this "all I have heard from my Father" that Jesus makes known to his disciples? Later so-called gnostic gospels tend to portray it as esoteric information about some hidden realm. But by the canonical gospels—arguably much closer to the source—it has to do with the goods about which the Father passionately cares and for which he mentored the Son to care with equal passion. Our own growth into being friends of God involves being baptized into these goods and being mentored to nurture them competently. The Hebrew Scriptures, the New Testament, and the history of the Church all give us a many-layered story of this *shared domain* of goods for which God, through the messy events of history and individual lives, is patiently but unwaveringly mentoring human hearts to passionately care.

Skeptical theists, with their Deep Universe Hypothetical, tend to emphasize that the shared goods occupy but a tiny fraction of God's total axiological space. But to see the fraction as tiny does not mean that God cares any less about the goods in it or about our learning to care about them. It means only that our role is not to be godlike masters at maximizing the total net good in the universe. That is God's job. Ours is to keep faith with the reality of the shared domain by growing in passion and wisdom for the goods in that shared domain.

A Jesus-friendly version of skeptical theism will, it thus seems to me, see this shared domain of goods as the grounding of our proper optimal moral horizon. And relative to this horizon, it is not implausible to say that for deontically under-determined deeds, our usual consequential moral judgments do satisfy an appropriate REP* presumption. It is, usually, entirely reasonable to presume that the morally relevant facts in our sample are representative of the "full set" of morally relevant facts within our proper optimal moral horizon. And seeing these shared goods as defining our proper moral horizon helps us understand hiker Sally's epistemic agony. Sally did not agonize because she could not see all the to-the-end-of-time consequences. What eluded her, as she knew, were specific consequences which, by the contingencies of her abnormal situation, were blocked from view. Such abnormal situations are exceptions that prove the rule; Sally's agony bears witness to a REP presumption that is normally in play. From a theistic view, her agony also bears witness to the grip of that shared domain of goods for which all humans, as a tiny but image-bearing part of God's vast and deep creation, are called to care.

Notes

1. For many kinds of support in this perilous undertaking, I thank Notre Dame's Center for the Philosophy of Religion, Jim Sterba and the Templeton Foundation, my colleagues in Calvin's Tuesday Philosophy Colloquium, the stimulating hospitality of Rutgers' Center for Philosophy of Religion (especially Dean Zimmerman, Marilyn Adams, Bob Adams, and their seminar students), former Calvin students Tim Perrine and Luis Oliveira, and Wes "Cisco Kid" Siscoe. Last and most, I thank copyeditor Carol Noble, whose extensive suggestions have hugely improved this paper.

2. See, for example, Hud Hudson, "The Father of Lies?" in *Oxford Studies in Philosophy of Religion*, vol. 5, ed. Jonathan L. Kvanvig (Oxford: Oxford University Press, 2012), 147–66.

3. Michael Bergmann, "Commonsense Skeptical Theism," in *Reason, Metaphysics, and Mind: New Essays on the Philosophy of Alvin Plantinga*, ed. Michel Rea and Kelly James Clark (Oxford: Oxford University Press, 2012), 9–30.

4. Moral commonsense has a strong deontological core, in that it assumes we have duties and obligations and "oughts" that cannot be given a utilitarian reduction. Even in its efforts to predict and weigh future consequences of an act, moral commonsense evaluations are clearly shot through with irreducibly deontological constraints. Here I was helped by comments from Jim Sterba, as well as from Calvin colleague David Billings.

5. This mandate, with background on the Pauline Principle, was given to invited speakers by James Sterba in a document entitled "A Conference on the Topic of Contemporary Moral Theory and the Problem of Evil: A Thesis with Respect to the Topic." The document has considerable overlap with Sterba's introduction to the present volume.

6. The two papers are Bergmann's "Commonsense Skeptical Theism" (see note 4) and my own "Does Skeptical Theism Force Moral Skepticism: Hesitations over Bergmann's Defense," in Rea and Clark, *Reason, Metaphysics, and Mind*, pp. 30–37. Bergmann's paper includes a "Postscript" (pp. 29–30) containing his conference rejoinder to my critique.

7. Sterba, "A Conference on the Topic of Contemporary Moral Theory and the Problem of Evil," p. 2.

8. Judith Jarvis Thomson, "How It Was," *Proceedings and Addresses of the American Philosophical Association* 87 (November, 2013): 118–19. Also available in *Portraits of American Philosophy*, ed. Steven M. Cahn (Lanham, MD: Rowman & Littlefield, 2013), 47–62, and online at: http://www.apaonline.org/page/dewey.

9. Latin lacks our definite and indefinite articles; to pose the question as "Is God *the* author of evil?" would presuppose that God is the sole author of evil, which Augustine means to deny. Here I work from a translation by Calvin Latin major Nick Monsma, with one eye on the Latin and another two others on standard translations by Thomas Williams, Anna Benjamin, and others.

10. I am applying the distinction to the English word "evil," but the parallel holds for Augustine's Latin *malum*—which thus yields both our "malefactor" (a moral concept) and "malady."

11. Here I was helped by Alan Donagan, "Moral Absolutism and the Double Effect Exception: Reflections on Joseph Boyle's 'Who is Entitled to Double Effect?' " in *Reflections on Philosophy and Religion*, ed. Anthony Perovich (Oxford: Oxford University Press, 1999), 127–39.

12. More promising as exceptionless absolutes are the fundamental commands affirmed by the Torah and reaffirmed by Jesus: "Love God with all your heart and all your soul and all your strength/mind" and "Love your neighbor as yourself" (Deut. 6:4–5; Lev. 6:18; Matt. 22:37–40).

13. Derek Parfit, *On What Matters*, vol. 1 (Oxford: Oxford University Press, 2011), 167. Parfit distinguishes his "morally decisive reasons" sense of "what we morally ought to do" from a less consequent "decisive-moral reason" sense. To say that an action is what we morally ought to do in the former sense is to say the moral reasons for doing the action outweigh any reasons we may have for not doing the action. To say it is what we morally ought to do in the latter, less consequent sense is to say that the moral reasons for doing the action outweigh any moral reasons for not doing the action.

14. One sometimes hears glib examples like "it is never right, no matter what, to torture a cat just for the fun of it"; but here "just for the fun of it" is already stipulating a situation where the agent has no other consequential rationale that is of prima facie moral significance.

15. Important considerations are raised by Marilyn Adams. See, for example, Marilyn Adams, "Ignorance, Instrumentality, Compensation, and the Problem of Evil," *Sophia* 52, no. 1 (2013): 7–26.

16. See especially chapter 18 of Book I of Jean Calvin, *Institutes of the Christian Religion* (In Two Volumes), ed. John T. McNeill, trans. Ford Lewis Battles (Philadelphia: Westminster, 1960).

17. On reading Calvin's polemics within their historical contexts, see pp. 19 ff. of Susan Schreiner's *The Theater of His Glory: Nature and the Natural Order in the Thought of John Calvin* (Grand Rapids, MI: Baker, 1991).

18. For a sympathetic account of Thomistic concurrentism, see Alfred J. Freddoso's "God's General Concurrence with Secondary Causes: Why Conservation is not Enough," *Philosophical Perspectives* 5 (1991): 553–585. On the deployment of this view within Reformed theology,

see Luke Van Horn's "On Incorporating Middle Knowledge into Calvinism: A Theological/ Metaphysical Muddle," in *Journal of the Evangelical Theological Society*, 55/4 (2012): 807–27.

19. James Sterba, "Comments on Steve Wykstra's Paper," p. 1. This document was part of the bound volume of papers and responses circulated prior to the first conference.

20. That is not to say, of course, that there is nothing the surgeon could do that would rightly lead you to believe he is deranged and should be stopped.

21. In this and other quotations, I've added italics, bracketed elements, and punctuation devices to highlight features of Bergmann's account.

22. My phrasing here closely follows that of Bergmann on p. 13.

23. Bergmann's recurrent phrasing—consequences are said to be long-term or short-term, remote or immediate—may suggest that on skeptical theism, it is only goods realized in the remote future that are beyond our ken. This temptation must be resisted. As Plantinga observes, in allowing the evils that befall Job, God's aims have to do with his current transactions with Lucifer, which are entirely unknown to Job, and remain rather baffling to us.

24. This is, of course, because end-of-time consequences will typically be beyond our ken. No help is provided, or so Fred Feldman persuasively argues against Francis Howard-Snyder, by reformulating the equation in terms of expected utility. See Fred Feldman, "Actual Utility, the Objection from Impracticality, and the Move to Expected Utility," *Philosophical Studies* 129, no. 1 (2006): 49–79. Cf. Francis Howard-Snyder, "The Rejection of Objective Consequentialism," *Utilitas* 9, no. 2 (1997): 241–48.

25. Daniel Howard-Snyder treats this in "Epistemic Humility, Arguments from Evil, and Moral Skepticism," in *Oxford Studies in the Philosophy of Religion*, vol. 2, ed. Jonathan L. Kvanvig (Oxford: Oxford University Press, 2009), 17–57, and in "Agnosticism, the Moral Skepticism Objection, and Commonsense Morality," in *Skeptical Theism: New Essays*, eds. Justin McBrayer and Trent Dougherty (Oxford: Oxford University Press, 2014), 293–306.

26. Richard B. Brandt, in *Contemporary Utilitarianism*, ed. Michael D. Bayles (Garden City, NY: Anchor Books: 1968), 150.

27. Brandt seems to take these as interchangeable expressions.

28. Parfit, *On What Matters*, 150 ff. The quotations that follow are all from this section.

29. Parfit puts these in first-person plural; I have in brackets substituted first-person singular variant with a view to agent-specific application of them.

30. Peter van Inwagen, "Reflections on the Chapters by Draper, Russell, and Gale," in Daniel Howard-Snyder, *The Evidential Problem of Evil* (Bloomington: Indiana University Press: 1996), 219–243. See especially pp. 220–228.

31. See Jonathan Bennett, *The Act Itself* (Oxford: Oxford University Press: 1995), especially 4–52.

32. Thanks to Wes Siscoe for raising a good question here.

7 Perfection, Evil, and Morality

Stephen Maitzen

God and the Problem of Evil

Many people believe in the existence of God as described by classical monotheism, a personal agent whose essence includes perfection—that is, unsurpassable greatness—in knowledge, power, and goodness.[1] Or, to put the point more cautiously, many people *say* they believe in the existence of such a being. A number of recent writers have warned against taking people's say-so on this topic as reliable evidence of what they genuinely believe.[2] Nevertheless, I will ignore those warnings and take people at their word who say they believe in God.

These believers have no real choice but to set the bar high in regard to the attributes that God must possess. If you believe in God at all, then it only makes sense to believe in an essentially perfect God: there is insufficient motivation to believe in a God of any other kind. First, and perhaps least importantly, if you reject the idea that God must be unsurpassably great, then you sacrifice the most plausible *a priori* basis for believing in God's existence, namely the Ontological Argument in any of its various versions. As far as I know, every version of the Ontological Argument relies on the assumption that any being deserving the title "God" must be as great as anything could possibly be. From this assumption, the most plausible form of the argument infers that any such being actually exists if it so much as possibly exists.[3] From the premise that such a being possibly exists, the argument then concludes that the being actually exists. Now, even the most plausible form of the argument certainly deserves to be challenged, but the argument does not even get started without the assumption that God is unsurpassably great.

Second, and more importantly, imagining an imperfect God produces results that are theologically awkward or worse. Unlike a perfect God, an imperfect God need not be eternal or everlasting: such a God might be only finitely old, perishable, and might go out of existence just when we need him most! If God is imperfect, why think that God has the power to make the universe out of nothing, or even the power to make the universe out of preexisting stuff? If God is imperfect, why trust that God has the power to achieve justice in the end, to vindicate all wrongs, or even to compensate for all wrongs?[4] The affirmation "with God, all things are possible"[5] is supposed to comfort believers, but if God is imperfect, what assurance do they have that all things *are* possible with God? Furthermore, the more limited and imperfect one imagines God to be, the more one makes God resemble the deities that polytheistic religions invoke to explain various aspects of the natural world: one god for the sun, a second for the moon, a third for fertility, and so on. But surely deities of that sort have been outmoded by science's ability to explain those aspects of the universe in purely naturalistic terms.

Now, one might worry about some of the attributes that an unsurpassably great God must possess. For example, some argue that omniscience—the property of knowing all the truths there are—falls prey to paradoxes such as the Knower Paradox or Cantorian paradoxes from set theory.[6] If they are right, then omniscience is impossible. In that case, believers in God should construe God's perfect knowledge as God's knowing every proposition it is *possible* to know and, therefore, as God's having propositional knowledge that is perfect in the sense of being impossible to improve or increase. Similarly, if believers think that the "openness" of the future makes it impossible for any being to foreknow every truth about the future,[7] then they should hold that perfect knowledge does not require foreknowing every truth about the future, the latter knowledge being impossible. I hasten to add, however, that the impossibility of such foreknowledge does not imply the impossibility of having *extremely well-justified beliefs* about the future, beliefs so well-justified that it would be immoral not to act on them merely because they do not count as knowledge.[8] Finally, if believers think that the openness of the future implies that no future-contingent propositions are even true in the first place, then they can allow that perfect knowledge *does* require foreknowing every truth about the future, but the range of such truths will be much narrower than we might otherwise have thought.

If omnipotence, construed as the power to do anything at all, falls prey to this or that paradox, then omnipotence construed that way is impossible: no being could have the power to φ on just any way of replacing "φ." In that case, believers should hold that perfect power—power that is impossible to improve or increase—amounts to something different from omnipotence in the loose sense just described.

Finally, one might suppose that God exists in every possible world without possessing essential moral perfection—that is, without being morally perfect in every possible world—on the grounds that God could encounter a moral dilemma: a disjunction of alternatives that forces God to do something wrong no matter what he does. But this supposition is implausible for three reasons. First, because moral dilemmas would seem to violate the widely accepted principle that "ought" implies "can," it is controversial that even finite agents like us could ever encounter them.[9] But if we could encounter moral dilemmas, then it would be on account of physical, technological, or epistemic limitations that there is no reason to think could possibly constrain the God described by classical monotheism.[10] Second, if God could face a moral dilemma, then there is no reason he could not face many of them, and therefore we would have no guarantee that God could achieve even a slim balance of justice over injustice in the end. Why bother believing in or worshipping a God who cannot provide even the latter guarantee?

Third, it is theologically perilous to suppose that God might fall short of moral perfection in particular. For whatever reason, we tend to judge those who are morally deficient much more harshly than we judge those who are deficient merely in power or knowledge. Imagine three men none of whom saves a toddler from drowning in a lake: one only because he cannot swim, a second only because he is too oblivious to notice the toddler's noisy flailing, and a third only because he likes to watch toddlers drown. Only the third agent merits the description "truly despicable." Any God who could come at all close to meriting that description is, again, not worth believing in or worshipping.

For the aforementioned reasons, the only well-motivated options seem to be these: either a perfect God exists or no God at all exists. Therefore let us assume that God, if God exists, must be perfect in at least knowledge, power, and goodness. The following question, then, looms large: why does a God answering to that description ever allow evil that he could prevent? The problem of evil, as I see it, arises as a philosophical challenge to theism because of the allegation that humans and other animals experience suffering that a perfect God, if one exists, morally ought to have prevented and therefore would have prevented. Descriptions of suffering allegedly of that type abound in the philosophical literature. In order to have a specific example before us, consider the case of Dominick Calhoun, a four-year-old boy from Michigan who died after days of being beaten and burned by his mother's boyfriend.[11] "I've been doing this a long time, and this is the worst case of child abuse I've ever seen," said the local police chief about Dominick's case; "in all respects, he was tortured." Dominick's body was found covered with bruises and with all of his teeth knocked out. His grandmother reported that "burns covered his body" and that his brain was "bashed out of his skull." A neighbor told police he heard Dominick screaming, over and over again, "Mommy, make him stop."[12] The allegation is that God, being perfect, would have prevented Dominick's torture. Yet the torture occurred. So God does not exist.

Might God Lack Moral Obligations?

Defenders of theism might respond to the allegation by insisting that God has no moral obligations at all, or perhaps no moral obligations to humans or other animals, or perhaps no moral obligation to prevent suffering on the part of humans or other animals. Some contemporary theistic philosophers do indeed respond that way. For example, Marilyn McCord Adams follows various medieval theologians in concluding that "God has no obligations to anything else and so . . . does not stand in need of *moral* justification."[13] She offers two main reasons for this conclusion. First, "agents have obligations [only] to those on whom they depend for their existence," and God depends on no one else for his existence. Second, on the medieval view that she accepts, God operates according to

> patron-client (or ruler-subject) relations that are structured by the Honor Code. . . . Patrons have no obligation to take on or service clients. Rather it would be a shame not to [take on clients] and a shame not to see to the well-being of clients after they have been taken on: a shame in the sense that it would send the message that there is less to the patron (s/he was not really so well resourced and powerful) than had been supposed.[14]

According to this second reason, God's allowing Dominick to be tortured to death cannot possibly violate a moral obligation that God owes to Dominick. At worst, it threatens to undermine God's nonmoral reputation.

Adams admits that her view "startles and confuses contemporary philosophers of religion."[15] In oral remarks defending the view, she emphasized two points: (1) "Right reason" requires God to love *himself* "above all," on the grounds that God alone possesses infinite metaphysical goodness. But—evidently—right reason does not require God to love a finitely good creature such as Dominick, not even enough to prevent Dominick's death by torture. (2) God owns the universe and everything in it, so God can do, or not do, as he pleases with any human inhabitant, a point that, admittedly, Adams offered more diffidently than the previous one.[16]

I see nothing attractive in the view Adams defends. It really does sound medieval, in the pejorative sense of the term. Nor do I see anything persuasive about her points (1) and (2). First, it seems totally alien to our ordinary moral outlook to hold that we have moral obligations only to those on whom we depend for our existence. If anything, the reverse is true: we regard our strongest moral obligations as owed to those who most depend on *us* for *their* existence, including infants, young children, and dependent adults. Second, I cannot see how it counts as anything but a huge step backward to abandon a model of divine justice in favor of a model in which God instead adheres to a feudal honor code. Indeed, many girls and women in countries around the world today desire nothing more than to escape the influence of honor codes that, for example, regard violent death as appropriate treatment for a *victim* of rape. Substituting an honor code for an ethic of justice is atavistic and regressive in at least two ways: (a) It regards the suffering inflicted on a victim as first and foremost an injury to the victim's patron rather than to the victim himself or, far more often, herself. (b) It values the patron's reputation over securing justice for the victim and regards the latter as strictly speaking irrelevant to the former; indeed, "restoring" the patron's honor is often used as an excuse for subjecting the victim to even more injustice. Third, we routinely believe that we can have moral obligations even to those whom we do not love "above all" else. Even if we dislike the neighbor's dog, we have a moral obligation (to the dog, primarily) not to torture it for our own gratification. Fourth, ownership of a sentient being simply does not imply that the owner can do no wrong regardless of what he or she does to such a being. On the contrary, we commonly think that dog owners, for instance, have positive obligations to feed and care for their dogs, above and beyond the negative obligation not to torture their dogs for entertainment: all else equal, it is wrong, and not merely bad, to let one's dog die of starvation. Hence Adams's argument that God owns the universe and hence can do what he pleases with it gains no support from enlightened moral practice.

A second way in which theists might deny that God has moral obligations is by embracing theological voluntarism, more popularly known as "divine-command theory." In the standard contemporary versions of theological voluntarism, all moral obligations depend on God's will or God's commands. As Mark C. Murphy puts it in explicating Robert Merrihew Adams's highly influential version of the view, "the morally obligatory and the divinely commanded are *identified*, in the way that water is to be identified with H_2O. . . . [T]he complete immediate explanation of [any] moral obligation is in terms of God's commands."[17] On such a view, it becomes clear that God cannot have any moral obligations. With regard to willing, an agent's willingness to do something cannot be a necessary condition for the agent's being morally obligated to do it: it is a conceptual truth that no moral obligation depends for its existence on the obligated agent's wanting to fulfill it. But if God's obligation depended on his own will, then God's obligation *would* depend on God's wanting (i.e., willing) to fulfill it. With regard to commanding, it simply makes no sense to imagine that God could "command himself" to do something: the concept of commanding is essentially second-person, or at least other-directed. If any agent has moral obligations only because of God's will or God's commands, and if God cannot have moral obligations in either or those ways, then God cannot have any moral obligations, including a moral obligation to prevent Dominick's torture.

However, theological voluntarism turns out to be a doubtful basis for trying to eliminate God's moral obligations. Indeed, in my view it is an untenable basis, for reasons I have offered elsewhere[18] and for reasons offered by other critics.[19] In addition, theological voluntarism faces a problem arising from this question: Do we have a moral obligation not only (for example) to refrain from stealing because God has commanded us to refrain, but also a moral obligation to obey God's commands as such, which is to say a moral obligation to obey God's commands simply because they are God's commands?

Presumably theological voluntarism says that we do: it would be odd for theological voluntarism to say that we have no such obligation or that the obligation in question is nonmoral (e.g., merely prudential). But if all moral obligations depend on God's commands, then we have a moral obligation to obey God's commands, *qua* God's commands, only if God has commanded us to do so by issuing a command to this effect: (C) "Obey all of my commands!" But notice that the message of C is unavoidably self-referential: "Obey all of my commands, including *this* command!" Therein lies the problem. The self-referential string of words "Obey this command!" is unintelligible: obey *which* command? Any command, such as C, containing an unintelligible element is itself unintelligible. In order to avoid this problem, God's overarching command needs to be, not C, but instead C*: "Obey all of my *other* commands!" In that case, however, our moral obligation to obey C* requires a further divine command, C**: "Obey all of my other commands (including C*)!" And so on without end. Our moral obligation to obey God's commands, as such, therefore requires God to issue infinitely many prior commands; even if God has the power to issue that many commands, we surely do not have the power to grasp them all. We avoid this vicious regress only if we reject the claim that all moral obligations (assuming any exist) depend on God's commands.

If the command-based version of theological subjectivism fails, then the will-based version also fails. If God's willing that we φ were enough by itself for our being morally obligated to φ, then we could be morally obligated to φ even though we have no clue that we are and even if we could not possibly discover this element of God's will on our own.[20] But under such circumstances surely we could not be morally obligated to φ. In order, then, for us to become morally obligated to φ *whenever* God wills that we φ, God must *communicate* to us that element of his will by way of an assertion: we are morally obligated to φ only if God says to us that he wants us to φ. But then the following problems arise.

Unlike commands, assertions are truth-valued. There is no conceptual gap between commanding and truly commanding: it makes no sense to think that God or anyone else might command us to φ without truly commanding us to φ. (We might mistake something else *for* a command, or we might misunderstand or ignore a command, but if it is a command then it is truly a command.) By contrast, there is a conceptual gap between asserting and asserting the truth: it does make sense to suppose that God might say to us that he wants us to φ without truly wanting us to φ. One might try to close the gap by presuming that God could not possibly deceive us, at least not concerning what he wants us to do. But that presumption is highly questionable: it requires presuming that God could not ever have a morally sufficient reason for deception.[21] If one tries to close the conceptual gap by ruling out divine deception despite the implausibility of the aforesaid presumption, then one gives God's assertions the *performative* quality of commands: just as there is no conceptual gap between commanding and truly commanding, there would be no conceptual gap between God's saying to us that he wants us to φ and his wanting us to φ. In that case, the will-based version collapses into the command-based version, already criticized.

Here is a related problem. Let D be the generic action-type "do whatever God tells us he wants us to do." Are we morally obligated to D? Presumably the will-based version says that we are: it would be odd for the will-based version to say that we have no such obligation or that the obligation in question is nonmoral. In that case, as argued above, God must *tell* us that he wants us to D, which amounts to the self-referential assertion (E) "I want you to do whatever I tell you I want you to do, including *this*." Therein lies the problem. The self-referential string of words "I want you to do *this*" is unintelligible—do *what*?—making E itself unintelligible. God's assertion must instead be E*: "I want you to do everything *else* I tell you I want you to do." We then have a moral obligation to do what God tells us via E* to only if God tells us he wants us to do that, which requires a further assertion, E**, and so on without end.

One might object that God need not tell us that he wants us to D, because it is obvious that he wants us to D, and God can expect us to infer what is obvious. But if it is obvious that God wants us to D, then it is obvious that (F) God cannot possibly tell us a falsehood about what he wants us to do. But, again, F is *not* obvious; on the contrary, F is at least questionable. So we cannot simply infer that God wants us to D on the grounds that it is obvious. Instead, God must tell us that he wants us to D, which launches an infinite regress analogous to the regress faced by the command-based version. One might reply that wholesale skepticism about God's assertions follows if we do not regard F as obvious: if F is not obvious, then why believe anything that God says just because he says it? Such skepticism may in fact be the correct attitude toward the assertions of a being as extraordinary, mysterious, and inscrutable as God.[22] The will-based version, however, must reject it: if, for all we know, God wants us to φ when he tells us he wants us *not* to φ, then his wanting us to φ cannot be relevant to our moral obligations. The will-based version therefore faces pressure to close the conceptual gap between God's assertions and their truth, that is, to make God's telling us (sincerely or not) that he wants us to φ sufficient by itself for our being morally obligated to φ. In that case, it again collapses into the command-based version. Neither the command-based nor the will-based version, therefore, is plausible.

Kant's metaethical theory offers a third, and for my purposes final, way of denying that God has moral obligations. According to Kant, moral obligation essentially involves constraint, and God's will, already being perfect, is not, strictly speaking, constrained by morality; rather, God's will necessarily and of its own accord conforms, or corresponds, to the requirements of morality. Because God cannot possibly fail to fulfill the requirements of morality, God has no obligation to fulfill them.[23]

I do not find Kant's argument at all compelling. I do not see how the concept of moral obligation implies that the agent whose obligation it is might fail to fulfill it. Again, the principle that "ought" implies "can" is widely accepted in metaethics, although some philosophers do dispute it. But Kant insists on a rather less plausible principle: "ought" implies "might not." Presumably Kant agrees that part of the concept of an agent's being morally obligated to φ is that, at least presumptively, the agent's failing to φ would be morally wrong (rather than simply bad). Call that the "core concept" of moral obligation. The core concept takes no stand on whether the agent might fail to fulfill the obligation. To the core concept, Kant proposes to add the principle that "ought" implies "might not." The burden rests with whoever claims that the concept implies that further principle. Kant's argument, as far as I can tell, does not meet that burden.

From here on, therefore, let us presume that God—like agents in general—*can* have moral obligations, because we have seen no good reason to think otherwise. Nevertheless, those who remain unconvinced and who continue to hold that God has no moral obligations can treat the remainder of this analysis hypothetically: suppose that God could have moral obligations; then what?

Can God Pass the Buck?

To return to the question at the heart of the problem of evil: How is it that God never violates any of his moral obligations when he permits suffering that he could prevent? In answer to that question, one often encounters an apologetic proposal that I take to be captured by these representative quotations:

> (WH) God . . . withholds His intervention in order to give us the opportunity to do the right thing. . . . [I]n very many cases . . . God refrains from preventing an evil in order to give humans the opportunity to do so.[24]
> (DHS) [Theists may reasonably believe] that God permits a lot of [suffering] precisely because he intends for us to try to prevent it.[25]

Apparently this proposal strikes some people as so obviously unproblematic as to need no further elaboration or defense: in making the proposal, neither of the two quoted authors pauses to consider what might be said against it.

Leave aside the fact that the proposal does not cover the enormous amount of suffering that no human being is (or was) realistically in a position to prevent, such as the suffering experienced by nonhuman animals in the wild and the suffering endured by humans for the 99 percent (at least) of human history prior to the discovery of effective medical treatments. Leave aside also the fact that God, if he exists, allows many an instance of horrific suffering, such as Dominick Calhoun's, to continue long after he must have realized that no human being will intervene on behalf of the sufferer. I argue that the proposal fails no matter how narrowly it ranges.

The proposal fairly clearly implies that we human beings end up with a moral obligation to try to prevent the suffering in question. The William Hasker quotation, WH, explicitly refers to our doing "the right thing" by intervening: in other words, our failing to intervene would be wrong of us. I presume that the Daniel Howard-Snyder quotation, DHS, implicitly refers to God's intending that we do the morally required thing in trying to prevent the suffering in question, not that we perform some merely neutral action in those circumstances. Without that presumption, WH and DHS become weak even as *attempted* justifications of God's nonintervention. That is, I interpret both quotations as assuming that intervention on our part is at least sometimes morally obligatory rather than merely permissible, which might explain why God intends that we intervene.

But if God exists, how could *we* acquire the moral obligation to intervene? Consider the following scenario. You are at the lake on a sunny summer day, intending to swim. You are alone there except for an unsupervised toddler whom you see fall into one-meter-deep water near the shore and start to drown. You are a reigning world-champion swimmer and dressed for swimming: you know you could wade in and save the child at essentially no cost to yourself. Just then, you see me arrive at the lake. You know I am a novice swimmer who bears no special responsibility for the child, and you see that I am not dressed for swimming. I take it that the following fact is obvious: you have no moral permission to stand by *in order to* give me the chance to intervene. That is, if you would otherwise be obligated to intervene, you do not escape that obligation by intending that I intervene instead. By analogy, God is the champion swimmer dressed for swimming, compared to whom any human agent is the novice swimmer not dressed for swimming. Therefore, God likewise has no moral permission to stand by in order to give less capable agents the chance to intervene. Furthermore, according to standard theism, God stands in a parent-like relation to each human being, while not every human being stands in that relation to every other human being. So the analogy is even closer if we suppose that you are also the toddler's parent and I am not. But if you are the toddler's parent and I am not, then it is even clearer that you lack moral permission to stand by so that I can intervene: the proposal under examination fails even more obviously.

One might reply that God lacks a moral obligation to intervene because God lacks any moral obligations at all, but we have already considered and rejected that reply. Or one might reply that God lacks a moral obligation to intervene if intervening would interfere with human free will, but that reply also fails, despite its rampant popularity. If a taboo against interfering with human free will sufficed to defeat the moral obligation to intervene, then none of us would have been obligated to intervene on behalf of Dominick Calhoun, no matter how easy and risk-free intervention might have been, if it meant interfering with the free will of his torturer. No morally sane person accepts that result.[26]

Or one might reply, as Hasker has, that if God intervened to prevent all behavior that was "significantly harmful," then "morality, assuming it existed at all, would lack much of the significance we ordinarily assume it to have."[27] But Hasker's reply simply begs the question, because the moral obligation to prevent significant harm is a *consequence of* the existence (or threat) of significant harm, and no perfect God is forced to allow significant harm in the first place: the theistic notion of heaven, an exalted state of existence in which agents experience joy but never significant harm, is at least logically coherent. Yes, without the threat of significant harm we would not have significant morality, but the point is that we would not need it. The moral obligation to prevent significant harm is not an end that is valuable for its own sake, let alone an end valuable enough for its own sake to justify God's permission of suffering.

Similarly, one might claim that if God prevented all human suffering, humans would have no room for soul-making of the kind extolled by such writers as John Hick.[28] But I would reply to this claim just as I did to Hasker's: the claim is true but question-begging. Soul-making is supposed to be positive when it instills or strengthens such qualities as compassion, forbearance, and courage, rather than their opposites. But compassion, forbearance, and courage have positive value—they are virtues—only because of the existence or threat of suffering that God (if he exists) has himself *chosen to allow*. In a world without the threat of suffering (as theists routinely imagine heaven to be), compassion, forbearance, and courage are no more valuable than physical strength is in a world without the threat of something heavy.

If I may be permitted a psychological conjecture: the sheer abundance of suffering throughout our history has conditioned many of us to "make a virtue of necessity," that is, to mistake significant morality for an end in itself rather than to recognize it as merely necessitated by our contingent circumstances. We have come to regard significant morality as something intrinsically worth preserving, rather than as a consequence of living in our dangerous world. I conjecture that something similar explains many people's attitudes toward (positive) soul-making: they mistake it for an end in itself, and hence they view suffering as a prerequisite for achieving an intrinsically valuable end. Because that view of suffering is mistaken, the value of (positive) soul-making fails to justify God's permission of suffering in the first place.

To return, then, to the question under discussion: How can we human beings have a moral obligation to prevent suffering, at least if we easily can and at little or no personal risk, when God—for whom it is always easier and less personally risky—has no such moral obligation himself? How can the far weaker bystander be morally obligated to intervene when the far stronger bystander is not? Perhaps the proposal under examination means to say that God *would* be morally obligated to intervene except for the fact that, having seen that we are in a position to intervene successfully, he has unilaterally transferred that obligation to us. In such cases the moral obligation to intervene that God would otherwise have had becomes our obligation instead. But the proposal fares no better on this interpretation. Again, leave aside the fact that it does not cover the suffering that we humans are (or were) in no realistic position to prevent, and leave aside the obvious fact that we do not prevent a tremendous amount of suffering that we *are* in a realistic position to prevent. The proposal fails because it presumes that one bystander can unilaterally transfer his or her moral obligation to another bystander whenever the latter has a realistic chance of successfully intervening.

Nothing in our moral theory or practice lends any credence to that presumption. Not even legal obligations work that way—despite the fact that legal obligations, unlike moral obligations, are things we routinely exchange, for example, by way of contracts. Jill cannot offload her legal obligation onto Jack simply because Jack becomes able to do what the law already requires Jill to do. The commonplace practice of delegating responsibilities may make it appear that one bystander can unilaterally transfer a moral obligation to another bystander, but the appearance is illusory. Those with special responsibilities arising from their office or their role can delegate some of those responsibilities to subordinates: the general can delegate to the colonel his or her responsibility to capture an enemy stronghold; the fire captain can delegate to the lieutenant the responsibility to rescue someone trapped in a burning building. But these scenarios differ from the case of the drowning toddler in at least two relevant ways. First, in the case of the drowning toddler, at least one of the agents—the novice swimmer—has no special responsibility to the toddler, whereas in the delegation scenarios all the agents have special responsibilities arising from their roles: none of them are mere bystanders. Second, in the case of the drowning toddler, the agent intending to delegate the responsibility is vastly more capable than the other agent of fulfilling it, which is not true in the delegation scenarios.

In addition, it is not clear that the responsibilities in the delegation scenarios are *moral* obligations to begin with. The fire lieutenant who refuses to enter the burning building after being ordered to by his or her superior is guilty of professional misconduct and dereliction of professional duty. But it is not clear that he or she is guilty of immoral conduct. To see why, stipulate that you, a mere bystander, are (for whatever reason) exactly as capable and exactly as equipped as the lieutenant to rescue the victim in the burning building. You do nothing immoral by refusing to enter the building. Your entering the building would be morally supererogatory, not obligatory: entering a burning building is a far cry from a champion swimmer's wading into one-meter-deep water! By stipulation, the only relevant difference between the fire lieutenant and you is the lieutenant's professional role, which suggests that the lieutenant's refusal is wrong—perhaps even reprehensible—professionally rather than morally. If so, then a crucial difference emerges between the delegation scenarios and the case of the drowning toddler: in the former scenarios, the relevant obligations are nonmoral.

In sum, we have seen no good reason to think that God can unilaterally transfer his moral obligation to another bystander, contrary to what the apologetic proposal reflected in the WH and DHS quotations apparently presumes. No plausible moral theory allows the unilateral transfer of moral obligations. Not even God—indeed, *especially* not God—can pass the buck that way. Furthermore, let us not lose sight of the morally outrageous character of the apologetic proposal itself. If God exists, he did not intervene to prevent Dominick Calhoun's torture. According to the proposal, God refrained from intervening in order to give one or more human beings the chance to do "the right thing." Well, the plan backfired, and Dominick bore the cost. The mother's boyfriend did not refrain from torturing Dominick, and neither the mother nor the neighbors phoned the police.[29] But the attitude that the proposal ascribes to God is morally reprehensible even if some human being *had* rescued Dominick. No being who merits the label "perfect" could permit, or even risk, a child's horrible suffering precisely *so that someone else* can try to prevent it from occurring or from continuing. No being who deserves to be called even "decent" could do that. Any human agent who acted that way would have to be depraved or deranged. Such treatment of a child can only be regarded as morally intolerable exploitation, even if it is exploitation on the part of the child's creator. Any being who exploits innocent children falls short of perfection in at least one of power, knowledge, or goodness—and hence cannot be God.[30]

I will close by briefly addressing a reaction that I sometimes get when I put such claims as bluntly as I just did. Living in a society still dominated by an inherited theistic outlook, atheists like me are not infrequently accused of being "angry at God" and venting our anger in the form of arguments such as those I have offered here. The accusation is patronizing, question-begging, and false. Any atheist who can think straight knows that anger at God makes no sense. I am no more "angry at God" than I am angry at Santa Claus for failing to relieve me of the burden of Christmas shopping. If I am angry at anyone, it is at those of my fellow human beings who (to extend the metaphor) would say morally outrageous things in order to defend the Santa Claus story as true and to excuse Santa Claus for repeatedly failing to do what the story makes it clear he ought to do.[31]

Notes

1. For a characterization of classical monotheism in these terms, see Alvin Plantinga, "Reason and Belief in God," in *Faith and Rationality: Reason and Belief in God*, ed. Alvin Plantinga and Nicholas Wolterstorff (Notre Dame, IN: University of Notre Dame Press, 1983), 20.

2. See, for example, Daniel C. Dennett, *Breaking the Spell: Religion as a Natural Phenome-non* (New York: Viking, 2006); Georges Rey, "Meta-Atheism: Religious Avowal as Self-Deception," in *Philosophers without Gods*, ed. Louise M. Antony (New York: Oxford University Press, 2007), 243–65; and Adèle Mercier, "Religious Belief and Self-Deception," in *50 Voices of Disbelief: Why We Are Atheists*, ed. Russell Blackford and Udo Schüklenk (Oxford: Wiley-Blackwell, 2009), 41–47.

3. The classic discussion is Alvin Plantinga, *The Nature of Necessity* (Oxford: Clarendon Press, 1974), chap. 10. Plantinga's version of the argument requires the controversial modal principle "If possibly necessarily *p*, then *p*."

4. On the difference between vindication (i.e., justification) and mere compensation, see Stephen Maitzen, "Ordinary Morality Implies Atheism," *European Journal for Philosophy of Religion* 1 (2009): 110; and Stephen Maitzen, "On Gellman's Attempted Rescue," *European Journal for Philosophy of Religion* 2 (2010): 194–96.

5. Matt. 19:26 (AV); for similar biblical affirmations, see also Job 42:2, Jer. 32:17, and Luke 1:37, all cited in Brian Leftow, "Why Perfect Being Theology?" *International Journal for Philosophy of Religion* 69 (2011): 106.

6. See Patrick Grim, "The Being that Knew Too Much," *International Journal for Philosophy of Religion* 47 (2000): 141–54.

7. See, for example, William Hasker, *Providence, Evil and the Openness of God* (New York: Routledge, 2004).

8. William Hasker, himself a defender of the openness of the future, emphasizes this point in William Hasker, "Defining 'Gratuitous Evil': A Response to Alan R. Rhoda," *Religious Studies* 46 (2010): 308. The point becomes crucial when we consider how God ought to respond if, for example, God believes that an innocent child is about to be tortured.

9. See Terrance McConnell, "Moral Dilemmas," *The Stanford Encyclopedia of Philosophy* (Fall 2014), ed. Edward N. Zalta. http://plato.stanford.edu/entries/moral-dilemmas.

10. See Maitzen, "On Gellman's Attempted Rescue," 196–98.

11. See Stephen Maitzen, "Atheism and the Basis of Morality," in *What Makes Us Moral?* ed. A. W. Musschenga and Anton van Harskamp (Dordrecht: Springer, 2013), 257–69; and Stephen Maitzen, "The Moral Skepticism Objection to Skeptical Theism," in *The Blackwell Companion to the Problem of Evil*, ed. Justin P. McBrayer and Daniel Howard-Snyder (Malden, MA: Wiley-Blackwell, 2013), 444–57.

12. As reported at http://www.cnn.com/2010/CRIME/04/15/michigan.child.torture, at http://www.mlive.com/news/flint/index.ssf/2010/04/dominick_calhoun_argentine_tow.html, and at http://abclocal.go.com/story?section=news/local&id=7441716 (accessed 6 August 2014).

13. Marilyn McCord Adams, "Ignorance, Instrumentality, Compensation, and the Problem of Evil," *Sophia* 52 (2013): 16, emphasis in original.

14. Adams, "Ignorance, Instrumentality, Compensation," 17.

15. Adams, "Ignorance, Instrumentality, Compensation," 16.

16. Marilyn McCord Adams, "*Caveat Emptor!* Moral Theory and Problems of Evil" (presentation, Center for Philosophy of Religion, University of Notre Dame, IN, November 15, 2013). http://www.youtube.com/watch?v=K4rsQmM1cx4, at 1:07:47.

17. Mark C. Murphy, "Restricted Theological Voluntarism," *Philosophy Compass* 7 (2012): 681, emphasis in original.

18. Stephen Maitzen, "A Semantic Attack on Divine-Command Metaethics," *Sophia* 43 (2004): 15–28; and Stephen Maitzen, "Skeptical Theism and God's Commands," *Sophia* 46 (2007): 235–41.

19. See, for example, Wes Morriston, "God and the Ontological Foundation of Morality," *Religious Studies* 48 (2012): 15–34; and Murphy, "Restricted Theological Voluntarism."

20. A further worry arises: If God's willing that we φ were by itself enough to obligate us to φ, then God could obligate us to φ even though we cannot in fact φ, in violation of the principle that "ought" implies "can." Interestingly, the Bible may in fact portray God (in the person of Jesus) as wanting us to achieve something that we cannot achieve: "Be ye therefore perfect, even as your Father which is in heaven is perfect." Matt. 5:48 (AV).

21. For detailed discussion of this presumption and its implausibility, see Erik J. Wielenberg, "Sceptical Theism and Divine Lies," *Religious Studies* 46 (2010): 516–18; and Maitzen, "The Moral Skepticism Objection," 446–47.

22. See also Wielenberg, "Sceptical Theism and Divine Lies."

23. See Immanuel Kant, *Groundwork for the Metaphysics of Morals* (Ak 4:414). I thank Paul Abela for the citation.

24. Hasker, "Defining 'Gratuitous Evil,'" 307–08.

25. Daniel Howard-Snyder, "Epistemic Humility, Arguments from Evil, and Moral Skepticism," *Oxford Studies in Philosophy of Religion*, vol. 2 (2009): 43–44. This point is apparently endorsed by Graham Oppy, "Rowe's Evidential Arguments from Evil," in *The Blackwell Companion to the Problem of Evil*, 63. Importantly, the central example in Howard-Snyder's essay is a case of child suffering comparable to Dominick Calhoun's in its brutality (Howard-Snyder, "Epistemic Humility," 18).

26. For further criticism of the unaccountably popular "free will" reply to the problem of evil, see Maitzen, "Ordinary Morality Implies Atheism," 120–22; and Stephen Maitzen, "Agnosticism, Skeptical Theism, and Moral Obligation," in *Skeptical Theism: New Essays*, ed. Trent Dougherty and Justin P. McBrayer (Oxford: Oxford University Press, 2014), 277–79.

27. William Hasker, "The Necessity of Gratuitous Evil," *Faith and Philosophy* 9, no. 1 (1992): 29.

28. John Hick, *Evil and the God of Love*, 2d. ed. (New York: Palgrave Macmillan, 2007).

29. "Mom, Boyfriend Sentenced in Dominick Calhoun's Fatal Beating," *WMEN.COM*, last modified 2012, accessed August 6, 2014, http://www.wnem.com/story/17026690/hayes-baker-to-learn-fates-in-dominick-calhouns-torture-death. See also note 12, above.

30. For defense of these claims, see Maitzen, "Ordinary Morality Implies Atheism," and Stephen Maitzen, "Does God Destroy Our Duty of Compassion?" *Free Inquiry* 30 (2010): 52–53.

31. I thank James Sterba for his generous invitation to contribute to this volume and for his insightful written comments. I thank Colton Heiberg, John Danaher, and Felipe Leon for helpful remarks about some of the issues discussed here.

Conclusion

So what has been achieved by this attempt to bring the untapped resources of ethical theory to bear on the problem of evil? I think we can see that a great deal has been achieved once we reflect back on the contributions to this volume.

Marilyn McCord Adams

In her contribution to this volume, Marilyn Adams cautions us to focus on how horrendous moral evils can be. She also cautions us to attend to the fragility and gross imperfections in human agency. She then takes from theology the idea that our relationship with God should be one of a developing friendship, in order to frame the problem of evil as how a trustworthy friend could allow the inflicting of horrendous evil on us for our own good. In this way, Adams focuses on what God has to do to compensate those who have suffered from horrendous evils in this world.

However, what Adams does not take up is the question of how an all-good God could have allowed the horrendously evil consequences of serious wrong-doing to be inflicted on innocent victims in the first place. This is especially problematic in light of the Pauline principle's requirement never to do evil that good may come of it.

Now Adams could attempt to neutralize the Pauline principle by interpreting it as claiming that that we never do an action if none of its attendant goods could turn it into one that is morally justified. But this cannot be what the Pauline principle is claiming since the principle clearly states that attendant goods are irrelevant to what should be done once it has been determined that the means to be used for getting to those goods is evil, or evil in itself, that is, evil independent of its consequences. So the Pauline principle, correctly interpreted, is opposed to such a consequentialist reformulation.

Alternatively, Adams could try to use the distinction between *doing* and *allowing* to help us with respect to the problem of evil. Thus, in the strictest sense, she might claim, God does not do evil but only allows it. Now there clearly is a moral distinction between doing evil and allowing it, and doing evil is usually worse then allowing it. Still, allowing evil can be a pretty bad thing to "do," as in allowing someone to be raped when you could have easily prevented it. So it is not clear how this distinction can help us with respect to the problem of evil since it still allows that God is "doing" some pretty bad things.

Another possibility is that Adams could appeal to the doctrine of double effect, claiming that God does not intend horrors but only brings them about as an unintended, foreseen side-effect of what he does intend to do. However, for the theist, everything that happens in the world happens either because God directly brings it about or because God allows it to happen. So really nothing that God does is just merely foreseen.

Finally, Adams might try using the following counterexample against the Pauline principle. Suppose a couple accept a posting in an undeveloped country, thereby subjecting their children to all sorts of hardships. The question is: Could these parents still be justified in undertaking such a posting provided that they appropriately compensate their children for the hardships they endure? If so, Adams could argue that God can be similarly justified for permitting evils, even horrendous evils.

As it turns out, my partner and I once inflicted hardships on our own daughter during a Fulbright assignment abroad comparable to those in the posting example. However, our claimed justification was one of double-effect, where we foresaw, but did not intend, the hardships of our assignment, while at the same time attempting to mitigate those hardships with other benefits for our daughter. Nevertheless, as I argued above, such double-effect justifications are not available to God, who never merely foresees anything he does.

So Adams, in pursuing her compensation strategy, is still lacking a justification for God's permitting horrendous evils in the first place, particularly in light of the Pauline principle's prohibition of doing evil (which morally must include permitting evil) that good may come of it.

John Hare

John Hare considers and endorses Kant's claim to have undermined every previous attempt to support the existence of God in the face of the evil that exists in the world. For Kant, there is no theoretical argument that can establish the existence of an all-good, all-powerful God. Rather, Kant holds that God and an afterlife are just reasonable postulates of the morality that is binding on us.

Unfortunately, the very morality to which Kant appeals to support his postulates appears to condemn God for intentionally doing evil. This is because for Kant morality imposes an absolute, or near-absolute, prohibition on intentionally doing evil. Yet the evil that exists in the world is possible only if God intentionally permits it, where permitting evil is almost as morally problematic as intentionally doing evil. Thus, this constitutes a significant problem of evil grounded in a Kantian understanding of morality that surely must be given a theistic solution before it could make sense to entertain Kant's two postulates that are purportedly based on that same conception of morality.

Now Hare might think that the distinction between God's antecedent and consequent will, which he mentions in his essay, could help us out with respect to the problem of evil. Yet while this distinction does have relevance to debates about predestination, it really has no relevance to the problem of evil. In a traditional reading of the distinction, God, according to his antecedent will, is said to will us all to be saved, but then, in light of our actions, God is said to will, according to his consequent will, that just some of us be saved while others be damned. Nevertheless, the horrendously evil actions for which their perpetrators may be damned in the next life, according to God's consequent will, are still permitted by God in this life, with their horrible consequences for their victims. So we still have the question how could God permit such horrendous evils in violation of the Pauline principle.

Of course, Hare, like Adams, might try to defend his Kantian view here by appealing to the distinction between what we intend and what we merely permit, where the distinction is hedged in various ways. Accordingly, Hare might claim that the evil we permit must not be intended as a means and must not be disproportionate to the intended good. Hare might also claim that that permitting and intending have different implications for the assessment of human character and that roughly the same should hold true for divine character as well.

However, intending is contrasted, not with permitting, which is itself an intentional act, but with foreseeing. Moreover, the evil that God would be permitting has to be intended as a means to something good, even though the Pauline principle forbids doing just that. Lastly, while doing and permitting do have different moral implications for both human and divine character, it remains true that permitting wrongdoers to inflict horrendously evil consequences on their victims when it can easily be prevented would, in human contexts, still imply a defective moral character. So we still need a good reason to think a similar assessment would not be true in the case of God.

Linda Zagzebski

Linda Zagzebski thinks that the goodness of an agent is primary and that the goodness of the agent's actions and the consequences of the agent's actions are secondary. Metaphysically, this seems to be true, but, epistemologically, we seem to learn about the goodness of agents from the goodness of their actions and from the consequences of their actions.

Zagzebski could grant that we can come to know about God through God's actions and their consequences, but then maintain that we can also come to know about God independently through religious experience, Scripture, and the teachings of the Church. She might think that we would then have to weigh the one source of knowledge against the other. Yet these do not look like two sources of knowledge in the relevant sense because they both seem to rely on the purported actions of God and their consequences. For example, the Bible is thought to be God communicating to us through human authors. Of course, some actions, like transubstantiation, are only recognized as actions of God in certain faith traditions, whereas others, like permitting horrendous evils and their consequences are, so to speak, out there for all to see, and need to be accounted for. Moreover, the actions of God in permitting horrendous evils and their consequences do have a certain primacy, given that unless we can somehow account for them, thus rendering them morally justified, nothing else would suffice to secure God's moral goodness.

Laura Garcia

In her essay, Laura Garcia distinguishes cooperating with evil from just permitting it. For Garcia, to cooperate in the evil act of another is "to endorse, assist, or further that act either formally or materially." By contrast, permitting evil can just involve failing to prevent an evil when one is in a position to do so. Using these definitions, Garcia reaches her desired conclusion that God does not cooperate with evil.

As it turns out, most atheists have not been concerned to show that God cooperates with evil in Garcia's sense. For them, it suffices to show that God's would-be failure is simply that of intentionally permitting evil. They see no reason to go further and show that God also fails by cooperating with evil, particularly horrendous evils.

Garcia could defend God's intentionally permitting evil by claiming that God simply intends to create finite persons who by their very nature are free to choose well or badly. On this interpretation, God intentionally permits evil whether or not any evil act is committed. Now it is true that atheists would have little reason to object to God's permitting evil in cases when the evil is not actually done. The main problem, as atheists see it, is with God's permitting evil, when evil is done, particularly horrendous evil, and God could prevent it. It is this second kind of permitting that does seem to present the main challenge for theists.

Garcia points out that very few contend it is never permissible to do evil that good may come of it. In the introduction, I contend that doing evil is permissible when the evil in question is trivial (e.g., as in the case of stepping on someone's foot to get out of a crowded subway), or easily reparable (e.g., as in the case of lying to a temporarily depressed friend to keep her from committing suicide). The problem only arises when the evil that is permitted is horrendously evil and there are innocent victims. It is only the permitting of such evils that raises a challenge to the existence of God.

Yet even granting that doing or permitting significant evil that good may come of it may be only rarely justified for us, Garcia still contends that an all-knowing, all-powerful God, for all we know, may have many justified ways of permitting evil, even horrendous evil. The problem is that just the reverse seems to be true. Thus, suppose that only way we could stop soldiers from torturing one child would be to expose other children to torture who are hiding nearby. Imagine that we could either rescue the one child from being tortured or we could prevent other children from being tortured. Here, due to our limited causal powers, we should permit the lesser moral evil in order to prevent the far greater moral evil. In comparable situations, however, God would always be able to prevent both moral evils. In the case we are considering, God could, for instance, arrange to have the soldiers spotted by opposing forces and then come under attack, and in this way enable all the children to get away safely. More generally, God could always prevent the significantly evil consequences of any action that is actually being performed without permitting the significantly evil consequences of any other immoral action that is actually being performed. God could do this by simply restricting people's freedom just enough to prevent the significant evil consequences of both actions. So with respect to the narrow range of significant cases where we are justified in violating the Pauline principle, God would not be similarly justified. So Garcia's skeptical theistic approach to the problem of evil comes into conflict with what we know about the moral requirements of the Pauline principle.

Bruce Russell

Bruce Russell has a quite different take on the relevance of ethical theory to the problem of evil. While he previously held that ethical theory, particular when it appeals to concrete cases, has an important role to play, he now thinks that it is epistemology that does all the important work, especially with regard to undercutting the skeptical theist's solution to the problem of evil.

Russell's main target is Stephen Wykstra and Timothy Perrine's version of skeptical theism with its expanded theism hypothesis, which Russell claims is no different in form from that of Young Earthism, the view that holds that the world is just a hundred years old. However, Wykstra and Perrine's skeptical theism does have an advantage over Young Earthism in that it can accept virtually all the findings of modern science, whereas Young Earthers would have to reject the sciences of geology and paleontology and other related scientific fields. Since Russell thinks that Peter Van Inwagen's version of skeptical theism is falsified on just that account, he should draw the same conclusion about Young Earthism. So all that remains of Russell's critique is his claim that Wykstra and Perine's skeptical theism is unfalsifiable, and thus is explanatory deficient on that account.

Russell claims that Wykstra and Perrine's view is unfalsifiable because it appeals for support to reasons beyond our ken. Yet what Russell fails to take into account is that Wykstra and Perrine limit their discussion to consequential reasons. It is only consequential reasons that they claim are beyond our ken. Wykstra and Perrine, following Michael Bergmann, set aside nonconsequential reasons for action, like the Pauline principle, which are often taken, when significant evil is at stake, to be absolute or at least near absolute. These reasons are clearly not beyond our ken, and the question arises as to whether Wykstra and Perrine's skeptical theism is falsifiable in terms of them.

In his chapter, Russell does consider the possibility of using a nonconsequential ethical theory to support his argument from evil, but he thinks that such a theory could only do so if it were shown to be exceptionless. He then conjures up Philippa Foot's case of a big guy stuck in the mouth of a cave where flood waters are rising that would drown at least all the spelunkers in the cave and maybe the big guy himself depending on whether his head in inside or outside the mouth of the cave. We are then to imagine that his fellow spelunkers were to use a stick of dynamite to blow the big guy out of the mouth of the cave. Russell thinks that this action would have to be regarded as a justifiable exception to the Pauline principle, and that once we have found one such exception, we can then see how it may be possible for God to have comparable reasons for permitting all the evil in the world.

The problem with this line of argument is that Foot's example is not an exception to the Pauline principle. The spelunkers in the cave using a stick of dynamite to blow the big guy out of the mouth of the cave would not being doing evil that good may come of it. Rather, they would be justifiably defending themselves against an innocent but lethal threat to their lives, and so not doing something morally wrong or evil at all. Of course, there are justified exceptions to the Pauline principle, but Foot's example is not one of them. In the introduction, I give the example of a person facing the choice of whether to shoot one of twenty innocent hostages as the only way of saving the remaining nineteen. Now this is a case of doing evil that good may come of it. Yet while this case does constitute a justified exception to the Pauline principle for us, such an exception would never apply to God because God could always prevent the evil consequences of both actions. Accordingly, Russell has failed to show that the nonconsequential part of morality, particularly the Pauline principle, might not be able to raise a viable challenge to Wykstra and Perrine's skeptical theism.

Stephen Wykstra

In his contribution, Stephen Wykstra seeks to transform the Pauline principle, which has long been the central principle of nonconsequentialist ethics into a compliant tool of a consequentialist ethics. Wykstra effects this transformation in two steps. First, he artificially limits the Pauline principle's prohibition of never doing evil that good may come of it to exclude justification in terms of "nonmoral" goods alone. This contradicts the traditional interpretation of the principle, which had always been understood to also exclude justification in terms of moral goods. Second, Wykstra interprets the evil that is prohibited by the principle to be what he calls an all-things-considered evil. To get to this all-things-considered evil, Wykstra starts out with actions that he claims are prima facie wrong or evil in themselves and then weighs those actions against the moral consequences of doing them. As Wykstra sees it, sometimes when actions that are wrong or evil in themselves are thus weighed against the moral consequences of doing them, they turn out to be right, all-things-considered, and hence, not to be prohibited by the Pauline principle after all.

Unfortunately, for Wykstra's account, it is just this purported justifying of actions that are wrong or evil in themselves by taking into account their moral and nonmoral good consequences that the traditional Pauline principle had sought to prohibit. According to the traditional principle, once something has been determined to be wrong or evil in itself (and hence not wrong or evil in terms of its consequences) then the moral or nonmoral consequences of the action can never justify doing it.

Of course, Wykstra thinks that actions that are wrong or evil in themselves can be justified by the moral consequences of doing them. And in a few cases, this is probably right, but the traditional Pauline principle does not recognize such cases. For the traditional Pauline principle, if something is wrong or evil in itself, and hence not in terms of its consequences, then its consequences can never serve to justify it. So if its consequences do serve to justify an action, it has to be understood to be one of the rare exceptions to the Pauline principle as traditionally interpreted.

By contrast, for Wykstra whatever is initially seen as wrong or evil in itself, like committing or allowing murder or committing or allowing rape, must always be weighed against the good consequences of doing such actions, and at least for God, the consequences will have to frequently justify God's allowing such wrongdoing or evil. Moreover, for Wykstra, when actions that are initially seen as wrong or evil in themselves, like allowing murder or rape, are regarded as justified for God in terms of their consequences, they are no longer prohibited by his version of the Pauline principle. This is because Wykstra's principle only prohibits what is still judged immoral after a weighing of their consequences has taken place. The upshot is that actions of God that turn out to be regular and frequent violations of the traditional Pauline principle are never violations of Wykstra's version of that principle.

In fact, in his chapter, Wykstra strains to find something which he thinks is initially judged as wrong or evil in itself that could not ultimately be justified in terms of its good consequences. "I can think of only two sorts of cases," he says. And further, as he puts it in the longer, penultimate version of his essay: "For all other cases, I can think of, I judge that any intentionally allowing (on God's part) could be morally permissible if it were really necessary—and seen as such—to some outweighing good."[1]

His first case is allowing all sentient life in all possible worlds to be subject to endless hellish suffering, so as to make each sentient life on the whole a bad thing. Wykstra thinks this case oversteps the limit of what God could allow. This implies that there are possible worlds short of that limit with tens, hundreds, even thousands of holocausts but also with just a few contented sentient creatures (maybe just a few happy rats) that God could justifiably permit for the sake of good consequences. Yet this cannot be right.

Stephen Maitzen

Stephen Maitzen maintains that if God exists there would be no need for soul-making. This is because, according to Maitzen, not only would God prevent the horrible suffering and death of Dominick Calhoun, but God would also eliminate all evil and suffering from the world. Hence, there would be no opportunities at all for us to engage in soul-making. Thus, suppose a friend of ours, Slim, is in need of help, maybe because he lost his balance and is about to fall and hurt himself. Maitzen thinks that God would necessarily intervene and stop Slim's fall. Moreover, if you or I were in a position to help Slim in Maitzen's ideal world, we would never get a chance to do so. This is because God, by virtue of always being in the best possible position to prevent any evil in the world, would be always be there first preventing the evil from happening.

Yet would being in such a world be morally ideal for us? Wouldn't it be morally preferable for us to have the opportunity to choose whether or not to do or prevent a wide range of actions and for God to be helper or intervener of last resort, and then only when significant evils are at stake? In support of this view, consider the analogy of a political state that is aiming to secure a significant degree of justice for its members. Such a state would not try to prevent all the moral evil that occurs in its domain, even if it were within its power to do so. Instead, a just state would focus on preventing the significant moral evils that impact people's lives. It would not seek to prevent lesser evils because any general attempt to prevent such evils would tend to interfere with people's significant freedoms.[2] Rather, a just state would leave such evils to be used by individuals for soul-making as far as possible. So why shouldn't God, like a just state, be focused on preventing (not permitting) simply the consequences of significant moral evils that impact us, leaving wrongdoers the freedom to imagine, intend, and even to take initial steps toward carrying out such wrongdoing?

Maitzen seems to be taken in by the account of the heavenly afterlife, defended by some theists, as a world where any wrongdoing is impossible and we are no longer free to engage in soul-making. But both here and in an afterlife, it seems morally preferable to be in a world where we have some freedom to do the good or evil necessary for soul-making, but where God always intervenes just to prevent the significantly evil consequences of our immoral actions. Such a world corresponds to what a just political state would secure for its citizens if it only had the power to do so. Accordingly, a heavenly afterlife where any wrongdoing is impossible and we are no longer free to engage in soul-making seems not a morally preferable world for us to live in either in this life or in any hereafter.

A Conclusion to a Conclusion

So the contributors to this volume have explored various ways to bring medieval ethics, Kantian ethics, and contemporary analytical ethics, as well as the ethics surrounding skeptical theism to bear on the problem of evil. Some progress was also made to bring the Pauline principle to bear on the problem of evil. Here, what emerged is that we are facing a new logical problem of evil quite different from the one dispatched by Alvin Plantinga decades ago in his debate with John Mackie. What Plantinga showed is that the existence of an all-good, all-powerful God is logically compatible with the existence of some evil in the world. What Plantinga did not show is that that such a God is logically compatible with the existence with all the horrendous evils in our world. So one of the interesting conclusions of this volume is that relating the Pauline principle to the horrendous evils in our world gives rise to a new logical problem of evil, one that theists have tended not even to address, let alone solve. This is surely as important a contribution as any other that this volume makes to the contemporary discussion of the problem of evil. Of course, an even more important contribution would be an actual solution to this new logical problem of evil. Given that work in this volume has clearly demonstrated the need for such a solution, we have good reason to hope that one will soon be forthcoming.

Notes

1. Penultimate version on file with the editor.
2. I am defining significant freedoms to be those freedoms a just political state would want to protect.

Contributors

MARILYN MCCORD ADAMS has taught medieval and philosophical theology at a number of schools including UCLA, Yale, and Oxford where she was Regius Professor of Divinity. Her books include *William Ockham, Some Late Medieval Theories of the Eucharist, Horrendous Evils and the Goodness of God*, and *Christ and Horrors: The Coherence of Christology*.

LAURA L. GARCIA is Scholar in Residence in the Philosophy Department at Boston College. She has published widely in philosophical theology, metaphysical anthropology, and the nature and vocation of women. Recent essays include "Edith Stein on the Primacy of the Individual" and "A Feminist Defense of Male/Female Complementarity." She is currently editing and writing the introduction for *Truth, Life and Solidarity: The Impact of John Paul II on Philosophy* (Spring Valley, NY: Crossroad Publishing, forthcoming).

JOHN HARE is Noah Porter Professor of Philosophical Theology at Yale University. He has published seven books, of which the most relevant to the present essay are *The Moral Gap* and *God's Command*.

STEPHEN MAITZEN is W. G. Clark Professor of Philosophy at Acadia University, Nova Scotia, Canada. His current research interests include vagueness and ontology; external-world skepticism; the concept of ultimacy in regard to being, value, and purpose; and the perennial pseudo-question "why is there something rather than nothing?" In 2006 he received Acadia's highest award for excellence in teaching.

BRUCE RUSSELL is Professor of Philosophy at Wayne State University. His areas of specialization are epistemology, ethics, philosophy of religion, and philosophy of film. In his work he defends the evidential weight of philosophical intuitions and the role of inference to the best explanation in the support of philosophical theories.

JAMES P. STERBA, Professor of Philosophy at the University of Notre Dame, has published thirty-two books, including the award-winning *Justice for Here and Now* (1998), *Three Challenges to Ethics* (2001), *The Triumph of Practice over Theory in Ethics* (2005), *Does Feminism Discriminate against Men?* with Warren

Farrell (2008), *Affirmative Action for the Future* (2009), *Are Liberty and Equality Compatible?* with Jan Narveson (2010), *Morality: The Why and the What of It* (2012), *The Pursuit of Justice: A Personal Philosophical History* (2014), and *From Rationality to Equality* (2015). He is past President of the American Section of International Society for Social and Legal Philosophy, Concerned Philosophers for Peace, the North American Society for Social Philosophy, and the Central Division of the American Philosophical Association.

STEPHEN J. WYKSTRA has taught for many years at Calvin College. He was 2014–15 Alvin Plantinga Research Fellow at Notre Dame's Center for Philosophy of Religion, and his current research seeks to synthesize his earlier work on skeptical theism and Christian evidentialism with a formal-epistemology foundation for a methodology of "worldview" research programs.

LINDA ZAGZEBSKI is George Lynn Cross Research Professor and Kingfisher College Chair of the Philosophy of Religion and Ethics at the University of Oklahoma. She is President of the Central Division of the American Philosophical Association (2015–16). Her current book project, *Exemplarist Virtue Theory*, was the topic of her 2015 Gifford Lectures at the University of St. Andrews. She publishes widely in philosophy of religion, virtue epistemology, and virtue ethics.

Index